D0595256

Conversion

PERSPECTIVES ON PERSONAL AND SOCIAL TRANSFORMATION

1

Conversion

PERSPECTIVES ON PERSONAL AND SOCIAL TRANSFORMATION

EDITED BY

Walter E. Conn, Ph. D.

ALBA · HOUSE   NEW · YORK

SOCIETY OF ST. PAUL, 2187 VICTORY BLVD., STATEN ISLAND, NEW YORK 10314

Library of Congress Cataloging in Publication Data

Main entry under title:

Conversion, perspectives on personal and social
transformation.

    Bibliography: p.
    1. ConversionAddresses, essays, lectures.
I. Conn, Walter E.
BT780.C58   248'.24   78-19079
ISBN 0-8189-0368-6

Produced in the United States of
America by the Fathers and Brothers of the
Society of St. Paul, 2187 Victory Boulevard,
Staten Island, New York, 10314, as part of their
communications apostolate.

2 3 4 5 6 7 8 9 (Current Printing: first digit).

© *Copyright 1978 by the Society of St. Paul*

For
MY MOTHER
and
AUNT MARY

ACKNOWLEDGMENTS

Minor and/or major deletions have been made in many of the essays as they appear in this volume. The reader is referred to the original sources for complete versions of the essays.

Grateful acknowledgment is made to the following authors and publishers for permission to use material under their copyright:

"Theology in Its New Context" by Bernard Lonergan. Reprinted from *Theology of Renewal* (New York: Herder and Herder, 1968), Vol. I, pp. 34-46. © Pontifical Institute of Mediaeval Studies, Toronto.

"Dimensions of Conversion" by Bernard Lonergan. Reprinted from *Method in Theology* (New York: Herder and Herder, 1972), pp. 237-243. © 1972 Bernard J. F. Lonergan. Used by permission of the Seabury Press, Inc.

"Formation and Transformation" by Rosemary Haughton. Reprinted from *The Transformation of Man* (Springfield, Ill: Templegate Publishing Co., 1967, Introduction and ch. 1. © 1967 Rosemary Haughton.

"Grace as Power In, and as Mercy Towards, Man" by Reinhold Niebuhr. Reprinted from *The Nature and Destiny of Man* (New York: Charles Scribner's Sons, 1943), Vol. II, pp. 107-115.

"The Awakening to Conversion" by Karl Barth. Reprinted from *Church Dogmatics,* trans. G. W. Bromily (Edinburgh: T. & T. Clark, 1958), Vol. IV/2, pp. 553-584.

"The Concept of Conversion" by John E. Smith. Reprinted from *Mid-Stream* 8 (an ecumenical journal of the Christian Church), Spring, 1969, pp. 12-23.

"The Idea of Conversion" by A. D. Nock. Reprinted from *Conversion* (Oxford: Oxford University Press, 1933), pp. 1-16.

"Conversion and Grace in the Old Testament" by Dom Marc-François Lacan. Reprinted from *Lumiere et Vie* 9 (1960), pp. 5-24. Excerpts from *The Jerusalem Bible,* © 1966 Darton, Longman & Todd, Ltd. and Doubleday & Company, Inc.

"Conversion and Kingdom in the Synoptic Gospels" by Dom Marc-François Lacan. Reprinted from *Lumiere et Vie* 9 (1960), pp. 25-47. Excerpts from the Jerusalem Bible © 1966 Darton, Longman & Todd, Ltd. and Doubleday & Company, Inc.

"The Divided Self and Conversion" by William James. Reprinted from *The Varieties of Religious Experience* (New York, 1902), chs. 8, 9, and 10.

"The Psychology of Conversion" by Robert H. Thouless. Reprinted from *An Introduction to the Psychology of Religion* (Cambridge: Cambridge University Press, 3rd ed., 1971), ch. 14.

"Conversion: Sacred and Secular" by Wayne E. Oates. Reprinted from *The Psychology of Religion* (Waco, Texas: Word Books, 1973), pp. 92-109. © 1973 Wayne E. Oates.

"Conversion" by Paul E. Johnson. Reprinted from *Psychology of Religion* (Nashville, TN: Abingdon Press, 1959).

"Toward a Theology of Conversion in the Light of Psychology" by Seward Hiltner. Reprinted from *Pastoral Psychology* 17 (Sept., 1966), pp. 35-42.

"Experience and Conversion" by Jacques Pasquier. Reprinted from *The Way* 17 (April, 1977), pp. 114-122.

"Conversion" by Karl Rahner. Reprinted from *Encyclopedia of Theology: The Concise Sacramentum Mundi* (New York: The Seabury Press, 1975). © 1975 Herder KG. Used by permission of the Seabury Press, Inc.

"The Characteristics of Conversion" by Bernard Häring. Reprinted from *This Time of Salvation* (New York: Herder and Herder, 1966), pp. 217-228.

"Conversion: The Central Moral Message of Jesus" by Charles E. Curran. Reprinted from *A New Look at Christian Morality* (Notre Dame, IN: Fides, 1968), ch. 2. © 1968 Charles E. Curran.

"Sin and Conversion" by Joseph Fuchs. Reprinted from *Theology Digest* 14 (Winter, 1966), pp. 292-301.

"Final Integration" by Thomas Merton. Reprinted from *Contemplation in a World of Action* (Garden City, NY: Doubleday Image books, 1973), ch. 13; and *Faith and Violence* (Notre Dame, IN: University of Notre Dame Press, 1968), pp. 111-118.

"Christian Conversion" by Hans Küng. Reprinted from *On Being A Christian*, trans. by Edwin Quinn (Garden City, NY: Doubleday, 1976), pp. 249-252.

"Critical Theology" by Gregory Baum. Reprinted from *Religion and Alienation* (New York: Paulist Press, 1975), ch. 9.

"Conscientisation" by Paolo Freire. Reprinted from *The Month* 7 (1974), pp. 575-578.

"A Spirituality of Liberation" by Gustavo Gutierrez. Reprinted from *A Theology of Liberation*, trans. and ed. by Sr. Caridad Inda and John Eagleson (Maryknoll, NY: Orbis Books, 1973), pp. 203-208.

"Social Sin and Conversion: A Theology of the Church's Social Involvement" by Peter J. Henriot. Reprinted from *Chicago Studies* 11 (Summer, 1972), pp. 115-130.

CONTENTS

Introduction

"Conversion" refers to an enormously wide range of realities—from the rather routine joining of a church to the emotionally charged sense of being "born again"; from the awareness of philosophical enlightenment to the profound religious experience of a Paul or an Augustine. Accounts and interpretations of each of these realities abound. This collection of interpretations is an aid to inquiring as fully and precisely as possible into the nature of religious conversion, especially as this radical personal transformation is central to theological reflection in an empirical mode.

Theology, according to many contemporary theologians, is based on conversion (see, e.g. Lonergan and Baum). Thus, reflection on conversion can provide the appropriate foundation for a renewed theology. But reflection on what kind of conversion? What, exactly, is conversion? What is this personal reality which would ground the experiential foundation of a contemporary theology? And what are the criteria for discerning authentic conversion?

The essays in Part One have various functions. The article by Bernard Lonergan clarifies the present theological context by locating it in terms of its classicist past, and by specifying the shift in theological method demanded by contemporary culture. Rosemary Haughton's fundamental question—what is the relationship between formation and transformation?—is key to any theological reflection on conversion.

The essays by Niebuhr and Barth are examples of how the reality of conversion has been interpreted in different ways (e.g., faith, justification, regeneration) by major theologians of the twentieth century. John Smith indicates some of the philosophical pre-suppositions for the possibility of conversion.

The Lonergan article can serve well as a framework for organizing and systematically questioning the other essays in the collection. After suggesting that reflection on conversion can provide the required foundation for a contemporary empirical theology, Lonergan states that conversion may be intellectual, moral or religious.[1] Since what Lonergan means by moral and religious conversion is central to all the present essays, as a general strategy the reader might find it helpful to compare and contrast Lonergan's understanding of moral and religious conversion with the various meanings of conversion presented throughout the collection.[2] This strategy should (1) provide a tentative schema for organizing and questioning the different perspectives represented in the volume, as well as (2) facilitate an evaluation of the adequacy and appropriateness of Lonergan's influential understanding of conversion in the light of significant psychological, biblical, and theological perspectives.

From a biblical perspective, for example (Part Two), is it possible to distinguish between moral and religious conversion? If so, how? What, precisely, is the essence of a religious conversion? What constitutes it as "religious?" If the "unjust man" is converted from sin, from what is the "just man" converted? (see Job in Lacan). Is there a distinctive Christian conversion? If so, what is it? How is it related to moral and religious conversion? Is a Christian conversion always a moral conversion? Is it always a religious conversion?

More generally, is every religious person religiously converted? Has every Christian experienced a Christian conversion? A religious conversion? A moral conversion? Should every Christian experience these conversions? These questions and others like them should help the reader to give specific content to some common terms whose meanings are all too often taken for granted.

Many questions arise from a psychological perspective also (Part Three). Taking a clue from the classic interpretation of William James, one might ask whether conversions are sudden events or gradual processes; or some combination of the two. Or are there other possibilities? Are conversions primarily adolescent phenomena, as James, Starbuck and other early investigators would have them (see Thouless)?[3] Or, as Hiltner more recently suggests with Jung, is mid-life a more more probable time for a radical conversion? Are these suggestions mutually exclusive? Is it necessary to choose between them?

Is conversion a single, once-and-for-all event in a person's life? Or may a person experience two or three or many conversions at different points in life? On these questions, Wayne Oates' reference to the crises associated with the developmental stages of Erikson's life-cycle may be helpful.[4]

Are all conversions positive experiences contributing to personal growth and maturity, or are some conversions regressive (see Oates)? Is it necessary or desirable to distinguish between a neutral, descriptive meaning of conversion and a positive, normative meaning? If so, what would conversion in a descriptive sense be? What would constitute a normative definition?

A crucial question to ask from the psychological perspective is whether there is any difference between a genuinely religious conversion on the one hand and a religiously colored "psychological" conversion which brings some unity and harmony to a troubled person's life on the other? If so, how are they to be distinguished? Again, what constitutes an essentially religious conversion? Will every religious conversion be associated, as Johnson and Hiltner suggest, with some particular psychological problem or life crisis? What kind of dynamics are involved in the relationship between the need for self-acceptance and the call to conversion (Pasquier)?

What kinds of questions and reflections emerge from a theological perspective that takes the personal experience of conversion seriously? (Part Four)

The essay by Rahner presents a systematic survey of various aspects of conversion from the perspective of a major contemporary Roman Catholic theologian.

The essays by Bernard Häring, Charles E. Curran, and Joseph Fuchs exemplify the way moral theology itself has been transformed its recognition of personal conversion as the central reality of the Christian life. No one has been more responsible for this radical transformation of the overall perspective of moral theology than Bernard Häring.[5] Both Häring and Curran ask how the Christian moral life is to be understood when the reality of conversion is given primacy of place, and when conversion is seen as a continuous process. Does such an interpretation of conversion as continuous process exclude the notion of conversion as a dramatic event which may occur at one or more critical points in life?

The notion of "fundamental option," stressing the whole orientation of one's life rather than individual acts by themselves, has been one of the most important—and difficult—contributions to the contemporary renewal of moral theology (see Rahner). Does Fuchs' interpretation of conversion as "fundamental option" suggest a way of understanding conversion as a radical personal transformation that both occurs in and through the event of a major decision and also demands to be lived out continuously within the routine decisions of our everyday moral life? If so, how is the implicit, non-reflexive character of this fundamental decision to be understood in relation to the ordinary emphasis on conversion as an explicitly experienced, sometimes even dramatic, event in one's life? Does conversion by its very nature involve a deliberate decision to transform one's life, and thus imply that one be in explicit possession of this reorientation? Does the very idea of conversion require that one be reflexively aware of it? Or can a radical conversion occur in an implicit, non-reflexive way in and through some particular decision? In other words, how significant is self-awareness in the reality of conversion?

Any adequate understanding of the spiritual conversions of

the moral and religious life requires an accurate and full appreciation of the human person, of his or her social and cultural existence, and of the possibilities for self-transcendence. Here Thomas Merton discusses the meaning of person and self-transcendence in terms of the possibilities of personal transformation as a "final integration" of the "spiritual unconscious" which lies beyond the empirical ego.[6]

In his attempt to identify the character of a specifically Christian conversion, Hans Küng forces us to consider a question that is both fundamental and intensely personal when he argues that God's will, the universal and final criterion of Christian conversion, is man's well being.

Indeed, if all the questions suggested in this Introduction are not to result in a semantic game of hollow definitions, one must always be asking what conversion in general or in any particular form means in one's own life. Am I reading about something I have experienced myself, or is what I am reading like a report about life on another planet? Beyond comparing and contrasting various meanings of conversion, do I have any experiential basis for personal verification of one or another of these meanings?

The question of personal verification implies personal involvement, and involvement quickly raises the issue of authenticity. How can one assess the authenticity or genuineness of a conversion? Ultimately, from the Scriptures to William James to contemporary moral theologians, is there any criterion other than the empirical test of a conversion's effect on the moral character of one's life? An authentic conversion will be known by its fruits in the love of one's neighbor. And few tests of neighborly love place heavier demands on the authenticity of a conversion than that of social justice.[7] Thus the essays in Part Five focus on the relationship between personal conversion and the transformation of unjust social structures.

This final section on the social dimension of conversion presents a critical theology of sin and conversion from Gregory Baum, intellectual conversion as the raising of social consciousness by Paolo Freire, spiritual conversion to neighbor with Gustavo Gutierrez, and the general question of social sin, conversion, and the church with Peter Henriot. As the reader critically reflects on these issues, he or she will want to relate this social dimension of neighborly love and structural justice not only to the theoretical question of authentic conversion from the biblical, psychological and theological perspectives, but also and most importantly to the existential issue of the presence or absence of genuine conversion in his or her own personal experience and social living.

One cannot bring together a collection like this without more than a little help from one's friends. Thus many thanks are in order, and I offer them with pleasant memories of enthusiastic cooperation. To Charles E. Curran, John Egenolf, Marilyn King, Stephen Kuder, Elaine Mullaly, Sandra Schneiders, and William M. Thompson for advice on the selections. To Mary Costello and Joyce Durosco for suggestions on the Introduction; to Lynn Scott for cheerfully typing long sections of the manuscript; and to Maurice Duchaine, for generous bibliographical advice, and especially for the support and encouragement of a friend.

One is doubly blessed when his wife is not only a loving companion but also a professional colleague. So I owe very special thanks to Joann, who offered both constantly joyful support and invaluable critical advice at every point along the way. And finally I dedicate this collection to my mother, Ethel Conn, and my aunt, Mary V. Keough, who have given me more than they or I know.

1. For constructive criticism of this threefold distinction, see Charles E. Curran on "existential conversion" in "Christian Conversion in the Writings of Bernard Lonergan," *Foundations of Theology: Papers from the International Lonergan Congress, 1970,* ed. P. McShane (Notre Dame, Indiana: University of Notre Dame Press, 1972), pp. 41-59, and reprinted in Curran, *Catholic Moral Theology in Dialogue* (Notre Dame, Ind.: Fides, 1972 and University of Notre Dame Press, 1976), pp. 220-244; Robert Doran on "Psychic Conversion," *The Thomist* 41 (April, 1977), pp. 200-236; and my reflections on "affective conversion" in "Bernard Lonergan's Analysis of

Conversion," *Angelicum* 53/3 (1976), pp. 362-404. For Lonergan's own most recent views on conversion see his reference to "affective conversion" in his paper on "Natural Right and Historical Mindedness" (in the 1977 Proceedings of the American Catholic Philosophical Association) and his allusion to Plato's allegory of the Cave in "Theology and Praxis" (in the 1977 Proceedings of the Catholic Theological Society of America),

2. A principle of selection dictated by the limits of space has required this collection to pass over the important and difficult question of intellectual conversion with little more than Lonergan's statement; an exception to this general rule is the consideration of the concrete social aspect of intellectual conversion in the essay by Paolo Freire. For Lonergan's full treatment of the topic, see his *Insight: A Study of Human Understanding* (New York: Philosophical Library, 1957).

3. For a consideration of the character of the contribution to Psychology of Religion made by such early investigators as William James, E. D. Starbuck, and G. S. Hall, as well as for a survey of the discipline's career through the twentieth century, see Peter Homans, "Toward a Psychology of Religion: By Way of Freud and Tillich" in *The Dialogue Between Theology and Psychology*, ed. Peter Homans (Chicago: University of Chicago Press, 1968), pp. 53-81.

4. For a systematic integration of the developmental theories of Erik Erikson, Jean Piaget, and Lawrence Kohlberg, see my "Moral Development as Self-Transcendence," *Horizons* 4 (Fall, 1977), pp. 189-205. *Horizons* 4 (Fall, 1977). The basic work of these authors on the affective/psychosocial, cognitive, and moral dimensions of personal development, as well as that of James Fowler on faith development, is essential to an adequate understanding of conversion. Also see Carl Jung, "The Stages of Life" in *The Portable Jung*, ed. Joseph Campbell (New York: The Viking Press, 1971), pp. 3-22. For an explicit treatment of the relationship between personal development and conversion, see my *Conscience and Conversion*, due from Trinity University Press early in 1979.

5. See especially Bernard Häring, *The Law of Christ*, trans. Edwin G. Kaiser (Westminster, Maryland: The Newman Press, 1961; original German edition, 1954), Vol. I, Part V, on "Conversion."

6. Compare Merton's view of the human person's spiritual dimension with Roberto Assagioli's understanding of the "superconscious" and the "Higher Self" in *Psychosynthesis* (New York: The Viking Press, 1971), chapters I and II.

7. The difficulty of achieving a proper understanding of the gospel's demand of charity in the social dimension is made evident in Stanley Hauerwas' critique of liberation theologies in "The Politics of Charity," *Interpretation* 31 (July, 1977), pp. 251-262.

About the Authors

BERNARD LONERGAN

Father Lonergan is Professor of Theology at Boston College. His writings include *Verbum: Word and Idea in Aquinas, Grace and Freedom, Insight: A Study of Human Understanding*, and *Method In Theology*.

ROSEMARY HAUGHTON

Mrs. Haughton is the author of many widely read books, including *Love, The Theology of Marriage, The Liberated Heart* and *The Transformation of Man*. She lives with her large family in Scotland.

REINHOLD NIEBUHR

Reinhold Niebuhr (1892-1971) was Professor of Christian Ethics at Union Theological Seminary, New York. His many books include *Moral Man and Immoral Society, Man's Nature and His Communities,* and *The Nature and the Destiny of Man.*

KARL BARTH

Karl Barth (1886-1968), a Swiss Protestant theologian, taught at the University of Basel. His writings include *The Epistle to the Romans, Protestant Thought: from Rousseau to Ritschl*, and *Church Dogmatics.*

JOHN E. SMITH

Professor Smith teaches philosophy of religion at Yale University. He is the author of *Experience and God* and *The Analogy of Experience.*

A. D. NOCK

A. D. Nock (1902-1963) was Professor of the history of religion at Harvard University. He is the author of *Sallustius, St. Paul* and *Conversion*.

MARC-FRANCOIS LACAN

Dom Lacan is a Benedictine at the Abbaye d'Hautecombe, Saint Pierre de Curtille, Chindrieux, France.

WILLIAM JAMES

William James (1842-1910) was a prominent American psychologist and philosopher. Among his many writings are *The Principles of Psychology, Pragmatism, The Will to Believe* and *The Varieties of Religious Experience*.

ROBERT H. THOULESS

Professor Thouless is Reader Emeritus in Educational Psychology, University of Cambridge. His writings include *The Control of the Mind, Straight and Crooked Thinking* and *An Introduction to the Psychology of Religion*.

WAYNE E. OATES

Professor Oates teaches psychology of religion at the Southern Baptist Theological Seminary. He is the author of *The Psychology of Religion*.

PAUL E. JOHNSON

Paul E. Johnson (1898-1974) taught Psychology of Religion at Boston University School of Theology. He is the author of *Psychology of Religion* and *Healers of the Mind*.

SEWARD HILTNER

Professor Hiltner teaches Theology and Personality at Princeton Theological Seminary. He has written *Pastoral Counseling, Preface to Pastoral Theology* and *Theological Dynamics*.

JACQUES PASQUIER

Father Pasquier teaches Pastoral Counseling at the Gregorian University, Rome.

KARL RAHNER

Father Rahner has been Professor of Theology at the Universities of Innsbruck, Munich and Münster. He is the author of such foundational works as *Spirit In the World, Hearers of the Word*, as well as the many volumes of *Theological Investigations*, and most recently, *Foundations of Christian Faith*.

BERNARD HÄRING

Father Häring is Professor of Moral Theology at the Academia Alfonsiana, Rome. In addition to his landmark volumes on *The Law of Christ*, his writings include the recent *Medical Ethics* and *Ethics of Manipulation*.

CHARLES E. CURRAN

Father Curran is Professor of Moral Theology at The Catholic University of America. His most recent works include *Ongoing Revision in Moral Theology, Themes in Fundamental Moral Theology* and *Issues in Sexual and Medical Ethics*.

JOSEPH FUCHS

Father Fuchs is professor of Moral Theology at the Gregorian University, Rome. He is the author of *Natural Law: A Theological Investigation* and *Human Values and Christian Morality*.

THOMAS MERTON

Thomas Merton (1915-1968) was a Trappist monk of Gethsemani, Kentucky. He is the author of many books, including *Contemplative Prayer* and *Mystics and Zen Masters*.

HANS KÜNG

Father Küng is Professor of Dogmatic and Ecumenical Studies on the Catholic Theological Faculty of the University of Tübingen, Germany. He is the author of *The Council, Reform and Reunion, Justification: The Doctrine of Karl Barth and a Catholic Reflection, The Church* and *On Being a Christian*.

GREGORY BAUM

Professor Baum teaches theology and religious studies at St.

Michael's College in the University of Toronto. His books include *Faith and Doctrine, Man Becoming* and *Religion and Alienation.*

PAOLO FREIRE

Dr. Freire is a Consultant in Education for the World Council of Churches, Geneva. He is the author of *Pedagogy of the Oppressed* and *Education for Critical Consciousness.*

GUSTAVO GUTIERREZ

Professor Gutierrez is a member of the theological faculty at the Catholic University of Peru. He edited and contributed to the Concilum volume, *The Mystical and Political Dimensions of the Christian Faith* and is the author of *A Theology of Liberation.*

PETER J. HENRIOT

Father Henriot is a staff member of The Center of Concern, Washington, D. C.

Part One

SETTING THE THEOLOGICAL QUESTION

Theology in Its New Context

BERNARD LONERGAN

Any theology of renewal goes hand in hand with a renewal of theology. For "renewal" is being used in a novel sense. Usually in Catholic circles "renewal" has meant a return to the olden times of pristine virtue and deep wisdom. But good Pope John has made "renewal" mean "*aggiornamento*," "bringing things up to date."

Obviously, if theology is to be brought up to date, it must have fallen behind the times. Again, if we are to know what is to be done to bring theology up to date, we must ascertain when it began to fall behind the times, in what respects it got out of touch, in what ways it failed to meet the issues and effect the developments that long ago were due and now are long overdue.

The answer I wish to suggest takes us back almost three centuries to the end of the seventeenth century and, more precisely, to the year 1680. For that, it seems, was the time of the great beginning. Then it was that Herbert Butterfield placed the origins of modern science, then that Paul Hazard placed the beginning of the Enlightenment, then that Yves Congar placed the beginning of dogmatic theology. When modern science began, when the Enlightenment began, then the theologians began to reassure one another about their certainties. Let me comment briefly on this coincidence.

When Professor Butterfield placed the origins of modern science at the end of the seventeenth century, he by no means meant to deny that from the year 1300 on numerous discoveries

were made that since have been included within modern science
and integrated with it. But he did make the point that, at the time
of their first appearance, these discoveries could not be expressed
adequately. For, the dominant cultural context was Aristotelian,
and the discoverers themselves had Aristotelian backgrounds.
Thus there existed a conflict between the new ideas and the old
doctrines, and this conflict existed not merely between an old
guard of Aristotelians and a new breed of scientists but, far more
gravely, within the very minds of the new scientists. For new
ideas are far less than a whole mentality, a whole climate of
thought and opinion, a whole mode of approach, and procedure,
and judgment. Before these new ideas could be formulated accu-
rately, coherently, cogently, they had to multiply, cumulate,
coalesce to bring forth a new system of concepts and a new body
of doctrine that was somehow comparable in extent to the Aristotelian and so capable of replacing it.

In brief, Professor Butterfield distinguished between new ideas
and the context or horizon within which they were expressed,
developed, related. From about the beginning of the fourteenth
century the new ideas multiplied. But only towards the close of
the seventeenth century did there emerge the context appropriate
to these ideas. The origin of this context is for Professor Butterfield the origin of modern science and, in his judgment, "it out-
shines everything since the rise of Christianity and reduces the
Renaissance and the Reformation to the rank of mere episodes,
mere internal displacements, within the system of medieval Chris-
tendom."[1]

Coincident with the origins of modern science was the beginning of the Enlightenment, of the movement Peter Gay recently
named the rise of modern paganism.[2] Moreover, while this movement commonly is located in the eighteenth century, the French
academician Paul Hazard has exhibited already in full swing
between the years 1680 and 1715 a far-flung attack on Christianity
from almost every quarter and in almost every style.[3] It was a
movement revolted by the spectacle of religious persecution and

religious war. It was to replace the God of the Christians by the God of the *philosophes* and eventually, the God of the *philosophes* by agnosticism and theism. It gloried in the achievements of Newton, criticized social structures, promoted political change, and moved towards a materialist, mechanist, determinist interpretation no less of man than of nature.[4]

It would be unfair to expect the theologians of the end of the seventeenth century to have discerned the good and the evil in the great movements of their time. But at least we may record what in fact they did do. They introduced "dogmatic" theology. It is true that the word "dogmatic" had been previously applied to theology. But then it was used to denote a distinction from moral, or ethical, or historical theology. Now it was employed in a new sense, in opposition to scholastic theology. It replaced the inquiry of the *quaestio* by the pedagogy of the thesis. It demoted the quest of faith for understanding to a desirable, but secondary, and indeed, optional goal. It gave basic and central significance to the certitudes of faith, their presuppositions, and their consequences. It owed its mode of proof to Melchior Cano and, as that theologian was also a bishop and an inquisitor, so the new dogmatic theology not only proved its theses, but also was supported by the teaching authority and the sanctions of the Church.[5]

Such a conception of theology survived right into the twentieth century, and even today in some circles it is the only conception that is understood. Still, among theologians its limitations and defects have been becoming more and more apparent, especially since the 1890's. During the last seventy years, efforts to find remedies and to implement them have been going forward steadily, if unobtrusively. The measure of their success is the radically new situation brought to light by the Second Vatican Council.

There is, perhaps, no need for me here to insist that the novelty resides not in a new revelation or a new faith, but in a new cultural context. For a theology is a product not only of the religion it investigates and expounds, but also of the cultural ideals and norms that set its problems and direct its solutions. Just as theology in the thirteenth century followed its age by assimilating Aristotle, just as theology in the seventeenth century resisted its age by retiring into a dogmatic corner, so theology today is locked in an encounter with its age. Whether it will grow and triumph, or whether it will wither to insignificance, in no small measure depends on the clarity and the accuracy of its grasp of the external cultural factors that undermine its past achievements and challenge it to new endeavors.

The topics, then, that I am to raise are not directly theological. For that very reason they are all the more apt to be overlooked in an age characterized by specialization. For the same reason it is all the more important to draw attention to them on such an occasion as the present, for the cultural context sets up an undertow that accounts for tendencies and exigencies that must be met, yet, if not understood, are too easily neglected or thwarted because they seem superfluous, arbitrary, perplexing, disquieting, or dangerous.

First, then, theology was a deductive, and it has become largely an empirical science. It was a deductive science in the sense that its theses were conclusions to be proven from the premises provided by Scripture and Tradition. It has become an empirical science in the sense that Scripture and Tradition now supply not premises, but data. The data has to be viewed in its historical perspective. It has to be interpreted in the light of contemporary techniques and procedures. Where before the step from premises to conclusions was brief, simple, and certain, today the steps from data to interpretation are long, arduous, and, at best, probable. An empirical science does not demonstrate. It accumulates information, develops understanding, masters ever more of its materials, but it does not preclude the uncovering of further relevant data, the emergence of new insights, the attainment of a more comprehensive view.

Secondly, this shift from a deductivist to an empirical approach has come to stay. One has only to glance at the bibliographies in *Biblica*, in Altaner's *Patrologie*, in the *Bulletin de théologie ancienne et médiévale*, and in *Ephemerides theologicae Lovanienses* to become aware of the massive commitment of contemporary Catholic thought to an empirical approach. But to understand this movement, to grasp the reasons for it, one must do more than glance at bibliographies; one has to get down to reading the books. Then one gradually discovers that the old dogmatic theology had misconceived history on a classicist model, that it thought not in terms of evolution and development, but of universality and permanence. Vincent of Lerins had proclaimed God's truth to be *quod semper, quod ubique, quod ab omnibus*,[6] and such a view was still quite congenial in the *grand siècle* of French literature.[7] On such assumptions it was quite legitimate to expect the theologian, if only he knew the faith of today, to be equally at home in the Old and New Testaments, in the Greek and Latin Fathers, in the writings of medieval, Renaissance, and more recent theologians. But today such an assumption appears fantastic and preposterous. In almost endless studies the writings of age after age have been examined minutely, and all along the line the notion of fixity has had to give way to the fact of development. Moreover, development is complex, intricate, manifold. Its precise character at any time can be ascertained only through detailed studies of the resources, the problems, the tendencies, and the accidents of the time. Where once the dogmatic theologian was supposed to range over centuries, now Scripture, patristics, medieval, and modern studies are divided and subdivided among classes of specialists. Where once the dogmatic theologian could lay down an overall view that echoed the conciliar *semper tenuit atque tenet sancta mater Ecclesia*, now an overall view tends to be either a tentative summary of the present state of research, or a popular simplification of issues that are really not simple at all.

Thirdly, while theology has become largely empirical in its method, it has invoked a new vocabulary, new imagery, new concepts to express its thoughts. The Aristotelian analyses, concepts, words, that in the Middle Ages became part of the Catholic

patrimony to resist both Renaissance scoffing and Protestant condemnation, almost suddenly in the twentieth century have gone
out of fashion. With equal rapidity the vacuum is being refilled
with biblical words and images, and with ideas worked out by
historicist, personalist, phenomenological, and existential reflection. There is so much new in Catholic speculative theology that
Karl Rahner felt the need to issue a *Theological Dictionary*[8] and
Heinrich Fries organized over one hundred experts to collaborate
and produce a two volume *Handbuch theologischer Grundbe-
griffe*.[9]

As the empirical approach, so too I believe, the new conceptual apparatus has come to stay. Religion is concerned with man's
relations to God and to his fellow man, so that any deepening
or enriching of our apprehension of man possesses religious significance and relevance. But the new conceptual apparatus does
make available such a deepening and enriching. Without denying
human nature, it adds the quite distinctive categories of man as
an historical being. Without repudiating the analysis of man into
body and soul, it adds the richer and more concrete apprehension
of man as incarnate subject.

It is not possible to briefly communicate what precisely is
meant by the contrast between nature and history or what is
added to the couple, body and soul, by the phrase "incarnate
subject." Summarily, I may say that such terms refer to a dimension of human reality that has always existed, that has always
been lived and experienced, that classicist thought standardized
yet tended to overlook, that modern studies have brought to light,
thematized, elaborated, illustrated, documented. That dimension is
the constitutive role of meaning in human living. It is the fact that
acts of meaning inform human living, that such acts proceed from
a free and responsible subject incarnate, that meanings differ from
nation to nation, from culture to culture, and that, over time,
they develop and go astray. Besides the meanings by which man
apprehends nature and the meanings by which he transforms it,
there are the meanings by which man thinks out the possibilities

of his own living and makes his choice among them. In this realm of freedom and creativity, of solidarity and responsibility, of dazzling achievement and pitiable madness, there ever occurs man's making of man.

The wealth, the complexity, the profundity of this modern apprehension of man might be illustrated by pointing to its implications for philosophy, for human science, for art and literature, for education and psychiatry. But what must be mentioned is its significance for the notion of divine revelation. God becomes known to us in two ways: as the ground and end of the material universe; and as the one who speaks to us through Scripture and Tradition. The first manner might found a natural religion. The second adds revealed religion. For the first, one might say that the heavens show forth the glory of God; what can mere words add? But for the second, one must answer that, however trifling the uses to which words may be put, still they are the vehicles of meaning, and meaning is the stuff of man's making of man. So it is that a divine revelation is God's entry and his taking part in man's making of man. It is God's claim to have a say in the aims and purposes, the direction and development of human lives, human societies, human cultures, human history.

From this significance for revealed religion there follows a significance for theology. In the medieval period theology became the queen of the sciences. But in the practice of Aquinas it was also the principle for the moulding and transforming of a culture. He was not content to write his systematic works, his commentaries on Scripture and on such Christian writers as the Pseudo-Dionysius and Boethius. At a time when Arabic and Greek thought were penetrating the whole of Western culture, he wrote extensive commentaries on numerous works of Aristotle to fit a pagan's science within a Christian context and to construct a world view that underpinned Dante's *Divine Comedy*. To this paradigm theology today must look if it is to achieve its *aggiornamento*. Its task is not limited to investigating, ordering, expounding, communicating divine revelation. All that is needed, but more must be done. For revelation is God's entry into man's making of man, and so theology not only has to reflect on revelation, but also it has somehow to mediate God's meaning into the whole of human affairs. It is not a small task, but because it is not—in a culture in which God is ignored and there are even theologians to proclaim that God is dead—it is all the more urgent.

My reflections have come full circle. Not only does the cultural context influence theology to undo its past achievements, but theology is also called upon to influence the cultural context, to translate the word of God and so project it into new mentalities and new situations. So a contemporary Catholic theology has to be not only Catholic but also ecumenist. Its concern must reach not only Christians but also non-Christians and atheists. It has to learn to draw not only on the modern philosophies but also on the relatively new sciences of religion, psychology, sociology, and the new techniques of the communication arts.

I have been speaking of our renewed theology and now I must add that a renewed theology needs a renewed foundation. The old foundation will no longer do. But we cannot get along with no foundation at all. So a new foundation and, I should say, a new type of foundation is needed to replace the old.

First, some foundation is needed. If change is to be improvement, if new tasks are to be accomplished fruitfully, discernment is needed and discrimination. If we are to draw on contemporary psychology and sociology, if we are to profit from the modern science of religions, if we are to revise scholastic categories and make our own the concepts worked out in historicist, personalist, phenomenological, or existentialist circles, then we must be able to distinguish tinsel and silver, gilt and gold. No less important than a critique of notions and conclusions is a critique of methods. The new largely empirical approach to theology can too easily be made into a device for reducing doctrines to probable opinions. A hermeneutics can pretend to philosophic neutrality yet force the conclusion that the content of revelation is mostly myth. Scientific history can be so conceived that a study of the narrative of salvation will strip it of matters of fact. If our renewed theology is not to be the dupe of every fashion, it needs a firm basis and a critical stance.

Secondly, the old foundations will no longer do. In saying this I do not mean that they are no longer true, for they are as true now as they ever were. I mean that they are no longer appropriate. I am simply recalling that one must not patch an old cloak with new cloth or put new wine in old wineskins. One type of foundation suits a theology that aims at being deductivist, static, abstract, universal, equally applicable to all places and to all times. A quite different foundation is needed when theology turns from deductivism to an empirical approach, from the static to the dynamic, from the abstract to the concrete, from the universal to the historical totality of particulars, from invariable rules to intelligent adjustment and adaptation.

Thirdly, I shall no doubt be asked to give some indication of the nature or character of the new foundation. To this topic I have elsewhere given considerable attention, first, to assure historical continuity, in a study of cognitional theory in the writings of St. Thomas,[10] then in a contemporary development entitled *Insight*,[11] to take into account the fact of modern science and the problems of modern philosophy. On the present occasion I offer a few brief approximations.

As a first approximation, let us consider the foundation of a modern science. It does not consist in any part of the science itself, in any of its conclusions, in any of its laws, in any of its principles. All of these are open to revision, and it is in the light of the foundation that the revision would take place. What, then, is the foundation? It is the method of the science. It is the method that generates the conclusions, laws, principles that are accepted today. It is the method that will generate the revision of conclusions, laws, principles tomorrow. The scientist ultimately relies on his method.

Now one might be inclined to think of method as a set of verbal propositions enouncing rules to be followed in a scientific investigation and, of course, it is true that there are the hodmen of science who carry out the routines prescribed to them by those who understand the purpose of an investigation and the manner in which it might advance scientific knowledge. I use the word method to denote not the prescriptions given the hodmen, but the grounds that governed the prescribing. Such grounds, though perfectly familiar to the director, usually are not objectified or verbalized by him. Indeed, he cannot achieve such objectification with any accuracy, unless he is ready to devote as much time and effort to cognitional theory as he has already devoted to his physics, or chemistry, or biology. This does not happen. But, were it to happen, there would result the account of a normative pattern that related to one another the cognitional operations that recur in scientific investigations. There would be listed, described, illustrated, compared such operations as inquiring, observing, describing, problem defining, discovering, forming hypotheses, working out presuppositions and implications, devising series of experiments, performing them, and verifying. The greatest stress would be placed on the importance of personal experience of the operations, of identifying them within one's experience, and of finding within that experience not only the operations, but also the dynamic and normative relations that bind them to one another. In this fashion, you will agree, the subject as scientist would come to know himself as scientist. But the subject as scientist is the reality that is principle and foundation of science, of science as it has been, of science as it is, of science as it will be.

Our first approximation illustrates by an example what might be meant by a foundation that lies not in a set of verbal propositions named first principles, but in a particular, concrete, dynamic reality generating knowledge of particular, concrete, dynamic realities. It remains that we have to effect the transition from natural science to theology, and so we turn to our second approximation.

Fundamental to religious living is conversion. It is a topic little studied in traditional theology since there remains very little of it when one reaches the universal, the abstract, the static. For conversion occurs in the lives of individuals. It is not merely a change or even a development; rather, it is a radical transformation on which follows, on all levels of living, an interlocked series of changes and developments. What hitherto was unnoticed becomes vivid and present. What had been of no concern becomes a matter of high import. So great a change in one's apprehensions and one's values accompanies no less a change in oneself, in one's relations to other persons, and in one's relations to God.

Not all conversion is as total as the one I have so summarily described. Conversion has many dimensions. A changed relation to God brings or follows changes that are personal, social, moral, and intellectual. But there is no fixed rule of antecedence and consequence, no necessity of simultaneity, no prescribed magnitudes of change. Conversion may be compacted into the moment of a blinded Saul falling from his horse on the way to Damascus. It may be extended over the slow maturing process of a lifetime. It may satisfy any intermediate measure.

In a current expression, conversion is ontic. The convert apprehends differently, values differently, relates differently because he has become different. The new apprehension is not so much a new statement or a new set of statements, but rather new meanings that attach to almost any statement. It is not new values so much as a transvaluation of values. In Pauline language, "When anyone is united to Christ, there is a new world; the old order has gone, and a new order has begun" (2 Cor 5:17).

Though conversion is intensely personal, utterly intimate, still it is not so private as to be solitary. It can happen to many and they can form a community to sustain one another in their self-transformation, and to help one another in working out the implications, and in fulfilling the promise of their new life. Finally, what can become communal can become historical. It can pass from generation to generation. It can spread from one cultural milieu to another. It can adapt to changing circumstance, confront new situations, survive into a different age; flourish in another period or epoch.

When conversion is viewed as an ongoing process, at once personal, communal, and historical, it coincides with living religion. For religion is conversion in its preparation, in its occurrence, in its development, in its consequents, and also alas in its incompleteness, its failures, its breakdowns, its disintegration.

Now theology, and especially the empirical theology of today, is reflection on religion. It follows that theology will be reflection on conversion. But conversion is fundamental to religion. It follows that reflection on conversion can supply theology with its foundation and, indeed, with a foundation that is concrete, dynamic, personal, communal, and historical. Just as reflection on the operations of the scientist brings to light the real foundation of science, so too reflection on the ongoing process of conversion may bring to light the real foundation of a renewed theology.

I met the question of theological renewal, of its *aggiornamento*, by asking how far we are behind the times. I went back three centuries, for it was then that dogmatic theology had its beginnings, and it has been towards a total transformation of dogmatic theology that the developments of this century have worked. A normative structure that was deductivist has become empirical. A conceptual apparatus that at times clung pathetically to the past is yielding place to historicist, personalist, phenomenological, and existentialist notions.

I have urged that so great a transformation needs a renewed foundation, and that the needed renewal is the introduction of a new type of foundation. It is to consist not in objective statement, but in subjective reality. The objective statements of a *de vera religione, de Christo legato, de ecclesia, de inspiratione scripturae, de locis theologicis,* are as much in need of a foundation as are those of other tracts. But behind all statements is the stating subject. What is normative and foundational for subjects stating theology is to be found, I have suggested, in reflection on conversion, where conversion is taken as an ongoing process, concrete and dynamic, personal, communal, and historical.

Dimensions of Conversion

Joseph de Finance has drawn a distinction between a horizontal and vertical exercise of freedom. A horizontal exercise is a decision or choice that occurs within an established horizon. A vertical exercise is the set of judgments and decisions by which we move from one horizon to another. Now there may be a sequence of such vertical exercises of freedom, and in each case the new horizon, though notably deeper and broader and richer, none the less is consonant with the old and a development out of its potentialities. But it is also possible that the movement into a new horizon involves an about-face; it comes out of the old by repudiating characteristic features; it begins a new sequence that can keep revealing ever greater depth and breadth and wealth. Such an about-face and new beginning is what is meant by a conversion.

Conversion may be intellectual or moral or religious. While each of the three is connected with the other two, still each is a different type of event and has to be considered in itself before being related to the others.

Intellectual conversion is a radical clarification and, consequently, the elimination of an exceedingly stubborn and misleading myth concerning reality, objectivity, and human knowledge. The myth is that knowing is like looking, that objectivity is seeing what is there to be seen and not seeing what is not there, and that the real is what is out there now to be looked at. Now this myth overlooks the distinction between the world of immediacy, say, the world of the infant and, on the other hand, the world mediated by meaning. The world of immediacy is the sum of what is seen, heard, touched, tasted, smelt, felt. It conforms well enough to the myth's view of reality, objectivity, knowledge. But it is but a tiny fragment of the world mediated by meaning.

For the world mediated by meaning is a world known not by the sense experience of an individual but by the external and internal experience of a cultural community, and by the continuously checked and rechecked judgments of the community. Knowing, accordingly, is not just seeing; it is experiencing, understanding, judging, and believing. The criteria of objectivity are not just the criteria of ocular vision; they are the compounded criteria of experiencing, of understanding, of judging, and of believing. The reality known is not just looked at; it is given in experience, organized and extrapolated by understanding, posited by judgment and belief.

The consequences of the myth are various. The naive realist knows the world mediated by meaning but thinks he knows it by looking. The empiricist restricts objective knowledge to sense experience; for him, understanding and conceiving, judging and believing are merely subjective activities. The idealist insists that human knowing always includes understanding as well as sense; but he retains the empiricist's notion of reality, and so he thinks of the world mediated by meaning as not real but ideal. Only the critical realist can acknowledge the facts of human knowing and pronounce the world mediated by meaning to be the real world; and he can do so only inasmuch as he shows that the process of experiencing, understanding, and judging is a process of self-transcendence.

Now we are not discussing a merely technical point in philosophy. Empiricism, idealism, and realism name three totally different horizons with no common identical objects. An idealist never means what an empiricist means, and a realist never means what either of them means. An empiricist may argue that quantum theory cannot be about physical reality; it cannot because it deals only with relations between phenomena. An idealist would concur and add that, of course, the same is true of all science and, indeed, of the whole of human knowing. The critical realist will disagree with both: a verified hypothesis is probably true; and what probably is true refers to what in reality probably is so. To change the illustration, what are historical facts? For the empiricist they are what was out there and was capable of being looked at. For the idealist they are mental constructions carefully based on data recorded in documents. For the critical realist they are events in the world mediated by true acts of meaning. To take a third illustration, What is a myth? There are psychological, anthropological, historical, and philosophic answers to the question. But there also are reductionist answers: myth is a narrative about entities not to be found within an empiricist, an idealist, a historicist, an existentialist horizon.

Enough of illustrations. They can be multiplied indefinitely, for philosophic issues are universal in scope, and some form of naive realism seems to appear utterly unquestionable to very many. As soon as they begin to speak of knowing, of objectivity, of reality, there crops up the assumption that all knowing must be something like looking. To be liberated from that blunder, to discover the self-transcendence proper to the human process of coming to know, is to break often long-ingrained habits of thought and speech. It is to acquire the mastery in one's own house that is to be had only when one knows precisely what one is doing when one is knowing. It is a conversion, a new beginning, a fresh start. It opens the way to ever further clarifications and developments.

Moral conversion changes the criterion of one's decisions and choices from satisfactions to values. As children or minors we are persuaded, cajoled, ordered, compelled to do what is right. As our knowledge of human reality increases, as our responses to human values are strengthened and refined, our mentors more and more leave us to ourselves so that our freedom may exercise its ever advancing thrust toward authenticity. So we move to the existential moment when we discover for ourselves that our choosing affects ourselves no less than the chosen or rejected objects, and that it is up to each of us to decide for himself what he is to make of himself. Then is the time for the exercise of vertical freedom and then moral conversion consists in opting for the truly good, even for value against satisfaction when value and satisfaction conflict. Such conversion, of course, falls far short of moral perfection. Deciding is one thing, doing is another. One has yet to uncover and root out one's individual group, and general bias.[12] One has to keep developing one's knowledge of human reality and potentiality as they are in the existing situation. One has to keep distinct its elements of progress and its elements of decline. One has to keep scrutinizing one's intentional responses to values and their implicit scales of preference. One has to listen to criticism and to protest. One has to remain ready to learn from others. For moral knowledge is the proper possession only of morally good men and, until one has merited that title, one has still to advance and to learn.

Religious conversion is being grasped by ultimate concern. It is other-worldly falling in love. It is total and permanent self-surrender without conditions, qualifications, reservations. But it is such a surrender, not as an act, but as a dynamic state that is prior to and principle of subsequent acts. It is revealed in retrospect as an undertow of existential consciousness, as a fated acceptance of a vocation to holiness, as perhaps an increasing simplicity and passivity in prayer. It is interpreted differently in the context of different religious traditions. For Christians it is God's love flooding our hearts through the Holy Spirit given to us. It is the gift of grace, and since the days of Augustine, a distinction has been drawn between operative and cooperative grace. Operative grace is the replacement of the heart of stone by a heart of flesh, a replacement beyond the horizon of the heart of stone. Cooperative grace is the heart of flesh becoming effective in good works through human freedom. Operative grace is religious conversion. Cooperative grace is the effectiveness of conversion, the gradual movement towards a full and complete transformation of the whole of one's living and feeling, one's thoughts, words, deeds, and omissions.[13]

As intellectual and moral conversion, so also religious conversion is a modality of self-transcendence. Intellectual conversion is to truth attained by cognitional self-transcendence. Moral conversion is to values apprehended, affirmed, and realized by a real self- transcendence. Religious conversion is to a total being-in-love as the efficacious ground of all self-transcendence, whether in the pursuit of truth, or in the realization of human values, or in the orientation man adopts to the universe, its ground, and its goal.

Because intellectual, moral, and religious conversions all have to do with self-transcendence, it is possible, when all three occur within a single consciousness, to conceive their relations in terms of sublation. I would use this notion in Karl Rahner's sense[14] rather than Hegel's to mean that what sublates goes beyond what is sublated, introduces something new and distinct, puts everything on a new basis, yet so far from interfering with the sublated or destroying it, on the contrary needs it, includes it, preserves all its proper features and properties, and carries them forward to a fuller realization within a richer context.

So moral conversion goes beyond the value, truth, to values generally. It promotes the subject from cognitional to moral self-transcendence. It sets him on a new, existential level of consciousness and establishes him as an originating value. But this in no way interferes with or weakens his devotion to truth. He still needs truth, for he must apprehend reality and real potentiality before he can deliberately respond to value. The truth he needs is still the truth attained in accord with the exigences of rational consciousness. But now his pursuit of it is all the more secure because he has been armed against bias, and it is all the more meaningful and significant because it occurs within, and plays an essential role in, the far richer context of the pursuit of all values.

Similarly, religious conversion goes beyond moral. Questions for intelligence, for reflection, for deliberation reveal the eros of the human spirit, its capacity and its desire for self-transcendence. But that capacity meets fulfillment, that desire turns to joy, when religious conversion transforms the existential subject into a subject in love, a subject held, grasped, possessed, owned through a total and so an other-worldly love. Then there is a new basis for all valuing and all doing good. In no way are fruits of intellectual or moral conversion negated or diminished. On the contrary, all human pursuit of the true and the good is included within and furthered by a cosmic context and purpose and, as well, there now accrues to man the power of love to enable him to accept the suffering involved in undoing the effects of decline.

It is not to be thought, however, that religious conversion means no more than a new and more efficacious ground for the pursuit of intellectual and moral ends. Religious loving is without conditions, qualifications, reservations; it is with all one's heart and all one's soul and all one's mind and all one's strength. This lack of limitation, though it corresponds to the unrestricted character of human questioning, does not pertain to this world. Holiness abounds in truth and moral goodness, but it has a distinct dimension of its own. It is other-worldly fulfillment, joy, peace, bliss. In Christian experience these are the fruits of being in love with a mysterious, uncomprehended God. Sinfulness similarly is distinct from moral evil; it is the privation of total loving; it is a radical dimension of lovelessness. That dimension can be hidden by sustained superficiality, by evading ultimate questions, by absorption in all that the world offers to challenge our resourcefulness, to relax our bodies, to distract our minds. But escape may not be permanent and then the absence of fulfillment reveals itself in unrest, the absence of joy in the pursuit of fun, the absence of peace in disgust—a depressive disgust with oneself or a manic, hostile, even violent disgust with mankind.

Though religious conversion sublates moral, and moral conversion sublates intellectual, one must not infer that intellectual comes first, then moral and finally religious. On the contrary, from a causal viewpoint, one would say that first there is God's gift of his love. Next, the eye of this love reveals values in their splendor, while the strength of this love brings about their realization, and that is moral conversion. Finally, among the values discerned by the eye of love is the value of believing the truths taught by the religious tradition, and in such tradition and belief are the seeds of intellectual conversion. For the word, spoken and heard, proceeds from and penetrates to all four levels of intentional consciousness. Its content is not just a content of experience but a content of experience and understanding and judging and deciding. The analogy of sight yields the cognitional myth. But fidelity to the word engages the whole man.

1. Herbert Butterfield, *The Origins of Modern Science, 1300-1800*, New York, 1966, p. 7.

2. *The Enlightenment, An Interpretation*, New York, 1966.

3. *The European Mind*, London, 1953.

4. The lasting influence of such enlightenment right up to the present has been illustrated rather fully by F. W. Matson, *The Broken Image*, New York, 1964.

5. See Yves Congar, "Théologie," DTC 29, 432 f.

6. *Commonitorium*, II, Cambridge, 1915, p. 10.

7. See Owen Chadwick, *The Idea of Doctrinal Development, From Bossuet to Newman*, Cambridge, 1957, pp. 17 ff.

8. New York, 1965.

9. Munich, 1962 and 1963.

10. Originally published in *Theological Studies* (1946-1949), and recently revised and reissued by David Burrell, C.S.C., under the title *Verbum, Word and Idea in Aquinas*, Notre Dame, 1967.

11. *Insight. A Study of Human Understanding*, London and New York, 1957.

12. See *Insight*, pp. 218-242.

13. On grace as operative and cooperative in St. Thomas, see *Theological Studies* 2(1941), 289-324; 3(1942), 69-88; 375-402; 533-578. In book form, B. Lonergan, *Grace and Freedom in Aquinas*, London: Darton, Longman & Todd, and New York: Herder & Herder, 1971.

14. K. Rahner, *Hörer des Wortes*, München: Kösel, 1963, p. 40.

Formation and Transformation

ROSEMARY HAUGHTON

The ideal of the formation of man is the process of using all the influences of culture—family affection, humane, educational and political and social structures, and all the scientific know-how available—to help people to understand themselves and each other and the world they share, to adjust themselves to both without either undue aggressiveness or frightened conformity, and so to form satisfying and stable emotional and social relationships. This is to be done through a well-ordered community setting in which mutual responsibility and the care of the weak are taken for granted. All this, ideally, should produce the whole human being, the perfection of man. Nobody expects perfection in practice, but it is an imaginable ideal all the same, and one that seems worth striving for because even its imperfect attainment produces a verifiable amount of human happiness.

But there is another notion of the purpose or perfection of man—the idea of transformation. It is not imaginable at all, which is why we tend to place transformed man in a separate "place" called heaven. Transformation is a total personal revolution. It begins with repentance—the rejection along with actual sins of the whole apparatus of natural virtue as irrelevant and misleading —and proceeds eventually to the desired dissolution of all that ordinary people ordinarily value in themselves or others. The result of this dissolution, this death of the natural man, is the birth of the whole human being, the perfection of man, meaning both man as an individual and man as a race, because the process is at once personal and communal. And it takes place in Christ and nowhere else. It is what Christians call the resurrection, or eternal life.

Only a Christian can write about this, because only a Christian can seriously entertain the notion of transformation as a human fact, without meaning by it any kind of gnostic or Buddhist separation of the eternal soul from the perishable body.

Until recently, the Catholic tradition of Christianity appeared, at least to those outside it, to be mainly concerned with the *formation* of man, as an ethical, social, political and even aesthetical creature, rather than with his *transformation*. From the point of view of the outside world, the Catholic Church is an educational system that should produce civilized, high-principled, unselfish, generous people, therefore its success or failure can be judged accordingly. When the Catholic Church is condemned, it is for manifest failure to produce the goods advertised, and Catholics are compared to their detriment with non-Catholics in matters of practical charity. When it is praised it is because it does turn out people who are up to this standard—Pope John for instance, or St. Vincent de Paul, or St. Francis.

The Reformed tradition, on the other hand, has tended to play down the formation aspect. It is faith that saves, blind trust in Christ's redeeming act that makes a Christian, and no human ethical achievements are relevant—they are even a distraction. Formation is there, but it is let in by a theological back door and kept in the kitchen. In the writing of Bonhoeffer, for instance, the "formation" type of values are simply non-existent, there is no foothold for anyone trained to make ethical value judgments in the tradition of western humanist culture. Writers of the Catholic stream of European classical culture, however— Francis de Sales, Newman, Claudel, Maritain, Belloc, Waugh— move in a recognizable world, and their specifically Christian oddness is acceptable because it adds precisely the element of mystery and strangeness which is missing from the Fabian-humanist tradition, and which people want. The strangeness is strange and exciting precisely because it occurs in a recognizable though richly obscure and complex cultural setting. It gives a feeling of safety and opportunity combined. But the strangeness of the Reformed tradition, when it is encountered "pure" (that is, unmixed with humanist-Catholic accommodation as it is apt to be in the Anglican version) is the strangeness of nightmare, where nothing means what it seems to mean, solid ordinary things melt into vapor, and harmless ones take on terrifying significance.

This is how the situation does *still* appear to the majority of ordinary humanists—whether they are Christian-flavored or not. But the appeal of Catholicism for reasons of this kind is fading. A generation has grown up that is suspicious of a rich tradition, scared by massive continuity, unwilling to acknowledge permanent ethical values, revolted by togetherness and the bland assurance that springs from the feeling of being part of a great whole. It is not only students and young intellectuals who reject the notion of human life implied in the concept of formation as I have described it. Middle-aged workmen in pubs, smart secretaries, adolescents in coffee bars and elderly women with dogs—all kinds and sorts of people betray an obscure awareness of life as uncertain, cut-off, undirected, and depending for its value (if any) on moments of purely individual heroism, insight, or love. The daily round, the rigid framework may be all the more essential to prevent the collapse of human life, but it is not authentic, it is not relevant to the real life which is always now but never present or graspable.

The "flashpoint" of decision is the moment when formation gives way to transformation. But the two have nothing in common at all, they do not even meet. Without the long process of formation there could be no transformation, yet no amount of careful formation can transform. Transformation is a timeless point of decision, yet it can only operate in the personality formed through time-conditioned stages of development, and its effects can only be worked out in terms of that formation.

This is the dilemma. A good formation, according to a sound customary and moral Law, is necessary if a person is to be able to respond to the demand for the decision to love. Yet if this formation is really good and really thorough it may, just because it is good, prevent the person from being aware of the need for repentance and decision. No need for repentance will appear, therefore no change of heart, no transformation, will be possible.

Here are the two related but contradictory facts about the relation between formation and transformation. Formation, according to a law which is holy and just and good, is necessary if man is to live. Yet, in practice, if its influence is unbroken, it leads not to life but to death of love by asphyxiation. Transformation therefore can only occur when formation breaks down, and this often happens because people break the law, because they sin. Yet nobody could say that love is the result of sin, for sin is disorder and separation and nonsense, and love shows itself as peace and unity and lucid sense.

This is the paradox that St. Paul wrestled with, and it is one whose elements we can observe any time we take the trouble to look at ourselves or other people, or read any kind of novel that is about real people.

[Major deletions have been made in this edited version.]

Grace as Power in, and as Mercy Towards, Man

REINHOLD NIEBUHR

An analysis of the relation of grace as power and grace as pardon in Biblical thought, though it may prove Biblical doctrine to be essentially consistent, will hardly convince modern man of the relevance of the doctrine. All modern theories of human nature whether Christian, semi-Christian or non-Christian, have arrived at simpler solutions for the moral problem. These simpler solutions are, broadly speaking, comprehended in the one strategy of increasing the power and the range of mind and reason against the narrower impulses of the body. It is necessary therefore to apply the Biblical doctrine to the facts of experience in order to establish its relevance. This can be done most conveniently in terms of the application of a very comprehensive and profound Pauline text to the moral and spiritual experience of men: "I am crucified with Christ: nevertheless I live; yet not I, but Christ liveth in me: and the life which I now live in the flesh I live by the faith of the Son of God who loved me, and gave himself for me."[1]

It will be well to consider the implications of this description of the process of regeneration in order:

1. "I am Crucified with Christ"

We have previously noted that St. Paul is fond of interpreting the destruction of the old life and the birth of the new in the symbolism of the death and resurrection of Christ. The first assertion of his interpretation is that the old, the sinful self, the self which is centered in itself, must be "crucified." It must be shattered and destroyed. It cannot be redeemed merely by extending the range of mind against the inertia of the body. The Christian doctrine of grace stands in juxtaposition to the Christian doctrine of original sin and has meaning only if the latter is an accurate description of the actual facts of human experience. It will not be necessary to reconsider this doctrine here.[2] But it may be helpful to restate the human situation very briefly in terms of the doctrine. The plight of the self is that it cannot do the good that it intends.[3] The self in action seems impotent to conform its actions to the requirements of its essential being, as seen by the self in contemplation. The self is so created in freedom that it cannot realize itself within itself. It can only realize itself in loving relation to its fellows. Love is the law of its being. But in practice it is always betrayed into self-love. It comprehends the world and human relations from itself as the center. It cannot, by willing to do so, strengthen the will to do good. This weakness is partly due to finiteness. The propulsive powers of the self, with its natural survival impulse, do not suffice to fulfill the obligations which the self as free spirit discerned. But the weakness is not merely one of "nature." It is also spiritual. The self never follows its "natural" self-interest without pretending to be obedient to obligations beyond itself. It transcends its own interests too much to be able to serve them without disguising them in loftier pretensions. This is the covert dishonesty and spiritual confusion which is always involved in the self's undue devotion to itself.[4]

The self in this state of preoccupation with itself must be "broken" and "shattered" or, in the Pauline phrase, "crucified." It cannot be saved merely by being enlightened. It is a unity and therefore cannot be drawn out of itself merely by extending its perspective upon interests beyond itself. If it remains self-centered, it merely uses its wider perspective to bring more lives and interests under the dominion of its will-to-power. The necessity of its being shattered at the very center of its being gives perennial validity to the strategy of evangelistic sects, which seek to induce the crisis of conversion.[5] The self is shattered whenever it is confronted by the power and holiness of God and becomes genuinely conscious of the real source and center of all life. In Christian faith Christ mediates the confrontation of the self by God; for it is in Christ that the vague sense of the divine, which human life never loses, is crystallized into a revelation of a divine mercy and judgment. In that revelation fear of judgment and hope of mercy are so mingled that despair induces repentance and repentance hope.

2. *"Nevertheless I Live"*

The Christian experience of the new life is an experience of a new selfhood. The new self is more truly a real self because the vicious circle of self-centeredness has been broken. The self lives in and for others, in the general orientation of loyalty to, and love of, God; who alone can do justice to the freedom of the self over all partial interests and values. This new self is the real self; for the self is infinitely self-transcendent; and any premature centering of itself around its own interests, individually or collectively, destroys and corrupts its freedom.

The possibility of a reconstruction of the self is felt to be the consequence of "power" and "grace" from beyond itself because the true analysis of the plight of the self revealed it to be due to impotence rather than to lack of knowledge. The current and contemporary ideas of salvation by knowledge (even as the gnostice ways of salvation in the ancient world) rest upon a dualistic interpretation of human personality, which separates mind from body, and spirit from nature. They obscure the unity of selfhood in all its vital and rational processes. Wherever this dualism prevails "spirit" is devitalized, and physical life is despiritualized.

The assertion, "nevertheless I live," may be taken to refute two alternative schemes of salvation. In the one the self is indeed invaded by "spirit" as "power" but it is not the "Holy Spirit" and therefore it destroys the self. In the other the spirit of the self seeks to extend itself into its most universal and abstract form until all power, and ultimately the self itself, is lost.

The possession of the self by something less than the "Holy Spirit" means that it is possible for the self to be partly fulfilled and partly destroyed by its submission to a power and spirit which is greater than the self in its empiric reality but not great enough to do justice to the self in its ultimate freedom. Such spirit can be most simply defined as demonic. The most striking, contemporary form of it is a religious nationalism in which race and nation assume the eminence of God and demand unconditioned devotion. This absolute claim for something which is not absolute identifies the possessing spirit as "demonic"; for it is the nature of demons to make pretensions of divinity; just as the devil "fell" because he sought the place of God. The invasion and possession of the self by spirit, which is not the Holy Spirit, produces a spurious sense of transfiguration. The self is now no longer the little and narrow self, but the larger collective self or nation. But the real self is destroyed. The real self has a height of spiritual freedom which reaches beyond race and nation and which is closer to the eternal than the more earthbound collective entities of man's history. Such demonic possession therefore destroys and blunts the real self and reduces it to the dimensions of nature.

However terrible the consequences of modern demonic possessions, particularly in political life, they furnish the useful lesson of proving that human life is actually subject to power and not merely to mind. Modern political religions captured men partly because our liberal culture had become devitalized and "rationalized" to the point where salvation or the fulfillment of life was universally regarded as no more than the extension of mind. Men felt certain that they possessed themselves; and sought in the complacency of their self-possession to extend the range of the self and to make it more inclusive. But a self which possesses itself in such a way never escapes from itself. Human personality is so constructed that it must be possessed if it is to escape the prison of self-possession. The infinite regression of its self-transcendence represents possibilities of freedom which are never actualized in self-possession; for self-possession means self-centeredness. The self must be possessed from beyond itself.

Yet such possession of the self is destructive if the possessing spirit is anything less than the "Holy Spirit." For in that case spirit represents some partial and particular vitality in life and history and therefore does not deserve the unconditioned devotion which is consequent upon being thus possessed. According to the Christian faith, Christ is the criterion of the holiness of spirit. He is the criterion of holiness because the revelation of God in Christ is on the one hand an historical focus of the divine, through which the mystery of the divine becomes morally and socially relevant to human nature, involved in finiteness and unable to comprehend the eternal. On the other hand it is the unique character of the revelation of God in Christ that it makes the divine and eternal known in history without giving any particular or partial force, value or vitality of history a sanctity or triumph which its finite and imperfect character does not deserve. Christ is thus both the criterion of the holiness of spirit and the symbol of the relevance between the divine and the human.

The Pauline word, "nevertheless I live," is set not only against the fulfillment of self by demonic possession through which the self is really corrupted and destroyed; it also marks the contrast between Christian conceptions of fulfillment and mystic doctrines of salvation in which the final goal is the destruction of the self. We have previously considered the tendencies towards self-destruction in various types of naturalistic, idealistic and mystic philosophies and religions.[6] We need only to emphasize at this point that the contrast between mystic-idealistic and Christian conceptions of self-fulfillment is determined by the "existential" character of the self in Christian doctrines. The self is a unity of finiteness and freedom, of involvement in natural process and transcendence over process. There is, therefore, not one particular level of the self, either in its consciousness or its reason, which can be extricated from flux and thereby achieve redemption. But on the other hand the unity of the self is so conceived in the Christian faith that it is not destroyed in the process of its fulfillment. Mystic doctrines of salvation might be expressed in a paraphrase of the Pauline word: "The Christ in me has been resurrected; therefore I have ceased to live."

According to these doctrines the real self is never threatened, judged, crucified or destroyed in any first step of salvation. Yet it is destroyed and lost in the final step. According to these doctrines there are various selves, and more particularly two: one immersed in finiteness and the other transcending it; yet neither is a real self.

According to the Christian doctrine the sinful self must be destroyed from beyond itself because it does not have the power to lift itself out of its narrow interests. It cannot do so because all of its transcendent powers are intimately and organically related to its finiteness. It is tempted by this situation to pretend emancipation; but this pretension is its sin. Yet when the sinful self is broken and the real self is fulfilled from beyond itself, the consequence is a new life rather than destruction. In the Christian doctrine the self is therefore both more impotent and more valuable, both more dependent and more indestructible than in the alternate doctrines.

3. "Yet not I; but Christ Liveth in Me"

The last of the Pauline assertions about the reconstruction of the self in the experience of conversion and "self-realization" could be defined as a "negation of a negation"; for the denial that the self has been destroyed is now made subject to another denial on another level. Just what does St. Paul mean by this final denial "Yet not I; but Christ liveth in me"?

There is an ambiguity in this final explication of the relation of the self to Christ which may well be an expression of the double aspect of the Christian experience of grace, to which we have previously alluded and with which all the Christian ages are concerned. The "yet not I" could be intended to assert merely the "priority of grace," to be a confession by the converted self that its new life is the fruit, not of its own power and volition, but of an accretion of power and an infusion of grace. It could also be intended as an affirmation that the new self is never an accomplished reality; that in every historic concretion there is an element of sinful self-realization, or premature completion of the self with itself at the center; that, therefore, the new self is the Christ of intention rather than an actual achievement. It is the self only by faith, in the sense that its dominant purpose and intention are set in the direction of Christ as the norm. It is the self only by grace, in the sense that the divine mercy "imputes" the perfection of Christ and accepts the self's intentions for achievements

The double negation could mean either one or the other of these two affirmations. But why could it not mean both? Is it not fundamental to Pauline thought that these two aspects of grace are always involved, in varying degrees of emphasis in the various interpretations of the life of the spirit? And is it not the testimony of human experience that in the final experience of "love, joy and peace," it is not possible to distinguish between the consciousness of possessing something which we could not have possessed of ourselves and the consciousness of not possessing it finally but having it only by faith?

1. Gal 2:20.
2. We have sought to do this in Vol. I, chs. VII-IX.
3. "For to will is present with me: but how to perform that which is good I find not" (Rm 7:18).
4. Described by St. Paul in the words: "Their foolish heart was darkened" (Rm 1:21).
The Augustinian definition of the plight of the self as a "defect of the will" is correct in pointing to the necessity of an accession of power from beyond the self; but it is incorrect, or at least subject to misinterpretation, in so far as it suggests mere weakness, rather than spiritual confusion as the cause of the vicious circle of self-centeredness.

5. There is of course no absolute necessity for a single crisis. The shattering of the self is a perennial process and occurs in every spiritual experience in which the self is confronted with the claims of God, and becomes conscious of its sinful, self-centered state.

6. Cf. Vol. I. ch. III.

The Awakening to Conversion

The first thing that we have to say is that Christians (and therefore those who are sanctified by *the* Holy One) are those who waken up. As they awake they look up, and rise, thus making the counter-movement to the downward drag of their sinfully slothful being. They are those who waken up, however, because they are awakened. They do not waken of themselves and get up. They are roused, and are thus caused to get up and set in this counter-movement. Thus strictly and finally this awakening as such is in every sense the source in whose irresistible flow they are set in the obedience of discipleship.

But this awakening is also—and here the metaphor breaks down—an awakening and therefore a rising from the sleep of death; the sleep from which there can be no awakening except in the power of the mystery and miracle of God.

For the moment we will postpone our investigation of the jolt or shock which initiates it, thus making it in its totality a divine action which seizes and dominates, while it does not exclude, all creaturely factors and their motions. Our first question must be simply concerning the awakening as such, and the meaning and content of this event. No matter what may be its origin and goal, which factor may be first and which second, or where the preponderance may lie, it does at any rate take place. And it takes place all at once. It does not take place in stages. It does not take place in such a way that first one thing happens with its own particular meaning and content, and then another with a different meaning and content; the divine on the one side and the human on the other. Nor does it take place on two different levels, so that we are forced to look first at what happens on the top deck as it were, and then at what happens on the lower; the gift and work of God in the one case, and the task and action and abstention of man in the other. This awakening and waking of man is one event with one meaning and content. In the first instance, therefore, it must concern us in its unity as such. We call it the awakening of man to conversion.

Let us go right to the heart of the matter at once and say that this rising up of man takes place in his conversion. The sleep from which man is awakened according to Scripture consists in treading a wrong path on which he is himself perverted, and can never be anything else. Thus awakening from this sleep, and the rising which follows, is far more than a vertical standing up. It makes no odds whether we go this false path erect or stooping. As Scripture sees it, waking and rising from sleep is turning round and going in the opposite direction. That God awakens us to this is the problem set for the Church, and therefore for us, by Holy Scripture. It cannot be exchanged for the (in themselves) very interesting problems of improvement or reformation or more noble effort in our further progress along the same path. It is not a question of improvement but alteration. It is not a question of a reformed or ennobled life, but a new one. And the alteration and renewal mean conversion—a term which we cannot avoid for all its doubtful associations. As it emerges in Holy Scripture, the human reality which is inseparably connected with, and determined by, the reality of God and Jesus Christ is the awakening of man to convert. The movement which we see made by the men of the Bible, or which is always aimed at, is *this* movement. We cannot say—for it simply would not be true— that we see in the Bible converted men. What we can and must say is that we see men caught up in the movement of conversion. If conversion is not behind them, it is also not in the mists before them. They are at the very heart of the movement. They had moved away from God. And it is saying too much to claim that they have moved right back to God. But what we must say is that they can no longer proceed without God. On the contrary, they are compelled to rise up and come to Him, and are now in the process of doing so. This is the movement of conversion. And the awakening to this movement which in some way comes to these men and characterizes them is the reality which impinges upon us, and becomes our own problem. in and with the reality of God and of Jesus Christ.

Conversion, and therefore life in this movement, means renewal. In relation to a life which is not engaged in this movement, it is the new life of a new man. Conversion means the turning on an axis. The life of the old man, which is not engaged in this conversion, also involves movement. But it has no axis—and that is why it is not engaged in conversion. It moves straight ahead, and this means straight ahead to the descent—the plunge—to death. It is a life which is encircled by death. The difference between the life of the one who is engaged in conversion and that of others is not that the former moves itself, but that it has an axis on which to turn. It is properly this axis which makes this man a new man, giving him a part in its own movement. But the axis which makes his life a movement in conversion is the reality which is not concealed from him, but revealed as the truth, that God is for him and therefore that he is for God. God is for him as a proprietor is for his possessions, protecting and guarding and cherishing them but also controlling them, answering for them but also disposing them according to his own purposes. And he himself is for God as possessions stand under the protection and control, the responsibility and disposition, of their owner. This is the axis which, when it is established in his life, makes it a life in conversion. For with this twofold "for"—the second grounded in the first—he is told both to halt and to proceed. His former movement is halted; and he is told to proceed in the opposite direction. And the two moments, which belong together in an indissoluble unity, constitute his conversion. Revealed to him as

truth, the reality that God is for him and he for God sets him
in this movement, in the *conversio* which is as such his *renovatio*.
In the dynamic of this twofold principle—because God is for him
and he for God—he can and may cease to proceed in the old
direction and turn round and begin to move the other way.

We continue at once that in conversion we have to do with a
movement of the whole man. There are in his being no neutral
zones which are unaffected by it and in which he be another
than the new man involved in this process. By the establishment
of his life on this axis everything that he is and has is brought
under its influence. If anything is not brought under its influence,
and thus remains in the continuity of his previous being as the
old man, he can be and have and do it only *per nefas*. This is the
case because in the principle of his conversion and renewal, at
the center where his life is bound to this axis, we have to do with
God. That God is for him, and he for God, is a total reality
which asserts itself in his life in the power of total truth, setting
him wholly and not merely partially in this movement, placing
him wholly under the call to halt and proceed. We will try to
see what is meant by the totality of this movement in some of its
most important dimensions.

1. We cannot interpret the conversion and renewal of man
merely in terms of a relationship between him and God, to the
exclusion of any relationship with his brother. To be sure, we are
dealing with the fact that God is for him, and he for God; with
this reality as a revealed truth which forcefully sets him in motion.
But he is not a man without his fellow-men. How can this truth
set him in motion if, as he makes the movement, it does not en-
croach at once upon his relationship with his fellows, necessarily
involving the perishing of the old and the emergence of a new
thing in this relationship? It would not be the conversion of the
whole man if it did not commence and work itself out at once
in this relationship.

2. Again, we cannot try to see and realize the conversion of
man in a new movement and activity (whether purely inward or

purely outward). Because God is for him, and he for God, it is a
matter of his heart, his thinking, his will, his disposition and also
of his consequent action and abstention on the same ultimate basis.
It is a matter of his disposition and action together; of the two
as a totality. Conversion in a separate inner or religious sphere,
or conversion in a purely cultic or moral, political or ecclesiastical sphere, is not the conversion of man as it is set in motion
by God. The conversion in which he returns to this peace embraces in this sense too the whole man.

3. We cannot make the conversion of man into a purely private
matter, as though it were only a concern of the individual, the
ordering of his own relationship to God and his neighbor, of his
inward and outward life, of his own achievement of pure and
essential being. It is right to emphasize its personal character, its
singularity, and the isolation in which this individual must perish
as the man he was, and can and may become new. But we must
remember at this point the basis on which alone, if it takes place,
it is an affair of the individual. The biblical individual is not self-
ishly wrapped up in his own concerns. It is a matter of God—
that God is for him and he for God. But to say God is to make
mention of the name of God which is to be hallowed, the kingdom of God which is to come, the will of God which is to be
done on earth as it is done in heaven. That God, the Subject of
this universal mystery, and in this action, is for him, and that
engaged in this action he for his part is for God—this is the axis
on which the individual moves as he turns from his own way to
God. His conversion and renewal is not, therefore, an end in
itself, as it has often been interpreted and represented in a far
too egocentric Christianity. The man who wants to be converted
only for his own sake and for himself rather than to God the Lord
and to entry into the service of His cause on earth and as His
witness in the cosmos, is not the whole man. When we convert
and are renewed in the totality of our being, we cross the threshold of our private existence and move out into the open. The
inner problems may be most urgent and burning and exciting,

but we are not engaged in conversion if we confine ourselves to them. We simply run (in a rather more subtle way) on our own path headlong to destruction. When we convert and are renewed in the totality of our being, in and with our private responsibility we also accept a public responsibility. For it is the great God of heaven and earth who is for us, and we are for this God.

4. We cannot understand the conversion of man as a matter for only one period in his life, which others will follow in which he can look back on what has happened *quasi re bene gesta,* or in which he might have to repeat it at this or that specific point, the prior or intervening times being periods in which he does not live in conversion, either because he is already converted, or is in need, and capable, of conversion but is only moving towards it. If it is the revealed truth that God is for him and he for God which necessitates his conversion and sets him in this movement, the movement is one which cannot be interrupted but extends over the whole of his life. It is neither exhausted in a once-for-all act, nor is it accomplished in a series of such acts. Otherwise how could it be an affair of the whole man? It becomes and is the content and character of the whole act of his life as such. Certain moments in the totality of the fulfillment of this act, certain impulses and illuminations, disturbances, changes and experiences which we undergo at particular times, may have the meaning and character of a particular recollection of its total content. But sanctification in conversion is not the affair of these individual moments; it is the affair of the totality of the whole life-movement of man. To live a holy life is to be raised and driven with increasing definiteness from the center of this revealed truth, and therefore to live in conversion with growing sincerity, depth and precision.

We may sum up as follows. By the revealed truth that God is for him and he for God, the whole man is set in the movement of conversion. It is for this that he is awakened in sanctification, and it is in this that his raising of himself consists. In every dimension we have to do with the whole man, as already explained in detail.

In the light of this conclusion, we must now go on to make a second main proposition—that in this movement we have to do with a warfare, or, to put it a little more precisely and less dramatically, with a quarrel, or falling-out.

We cannot overlook the fact that in the fulfillment of this movement a man finds himself under a twofold determination.

The first consists in the powerful summons to halt and advance which is issued, and by which he is set in this distinctive movement, in virtue of the fact that God is for him and he for God, and that this fact is clearly and powerfully revealed to him. In this determination he is the new man; the man who is impelled by the Spirit of God, to use the phrase of Rm 8:14. In this determination he repents and renounces what he previously was and did, leaving his old way, abandoning himself as he was, boldly enterprising a completely new and different being and action, entering a new way, affirming and apprehending himself in the future which thereby opens up for him—and all this, commensurate with the powerful cause which sets him in this movement, in the unqualified totality of his existence and being as a man.

But the second determination under which he finds himself consists in the fact that it is still he himself who is wholly placed in this movement and constituted the one who makes it. It is he himself, i.e., the one for whom this call to halt and advance previously had no meaning or power. As he gives himself to enter this way, he comes from the old way. He repents, but he does so as the one who previously knew nothing of repentance. He boldly enterprises a new being, but he does so as one who previously had no boldness to do so. He affirms and apprehends himself in the future indicated by this cause which effectively moves him, but he does so as the one who has also his past. Even in the turn which he executes, at the very heart of the present of this happening he is never without his past. Today, already impelled by the Spirit, he is still in the flesh of yesterday. He is already the new man, but he is still the old. Only in part? Only to a limited extent? Only in respect of certain relics? The older theology was right when in relation to the sinful past of man as it still persists in the present of conversion it referred to the remains or relics of the old man, of the flesh and its sinful action. It is only as sorry remains that the being and action of man under this second determination can be seen and understood in the light of the first determination. But it was an unfortunate delusion if this remnant was regarded as fortunately smaller in relation to something other and better. On the contrary, if we are just a little honest with ourselves (as we will be in serious conversion), we cannot conceal the fact that it is again the whole man with whom we have to do in this residuum; that it is still the whole man who under this second determination is in puzzling contrast with himself under the first. The man who today is confronted by that call to halt and advance, who today is set in that movement, in the totality of his exisence and being, by the powerful truth that God is for him and he for God, is also today, and again in the totality of his existence and being, the sinful man of yesterday. Thus in the today of repentance we have not only to do with the presence of certain regrettable traces of his being and action of yesterday. No, the one who is under the determination and in the process of becoming a totally new man is in his totality the old man of yesterday.

The situation can be understood, therefore, only in the following terms. In the twofold determination of the man engaged in conversion we have to do with two total men who cannot be united but are necessarily in extreme contradiction. We are confronted with two mutually exclusive determinations.

Luther's *simul* (*totus*) *iustus, simul* (*totus*) *peccator* has thus to be applied strictly to sanctification and therefore conversion if we are to see deeply into what is denoted by these terms, and to understand them with the necessary seriousness. It is certainly hard to grasp that the same man stands under two total determinations which are not merely opposed but mutually exclusive; that the same man, in the *simul* of today, is both the old man of yesterday and the new man of tomorrow, the captive of yesterday

and the free man of tomorrow, the slothful recumbent of yester-
of seeing and understanding the matter. Static and quantitative
day and the erect man of tomorrow. But there is no easier way
terms may seem to help, but they are not adequate to describe
the true situation. They involve a separation into constituent elements. It is true that the situation seems to cry out for this separation. It seems to be much more illuminating if, instead of saying
that the whole man is still the old and yet already the new, in
complete and utter antithesis, we say that he is still partially the
old and already partially the new. But if we put it in this way
we mistake the matter. For the new man is the whole man; and so
too is the old. And conversion is the transition, the movement, in
which man is still, in fact, wholly the old and already wholly the
new man. We are badly advised if we abandon this statement because we fear the severity of the antithesis. To do so, and thus
to proceed to transform and divide the *simul* into a *partim-partim*,
in which the old man of the past is sharply and a little triumph-
antly separated from the new man of the future, is to leave the
sphere of the *vita christiana* as it is actually lived for a psychological myth which has no real substance. The *vita christiana* in
conversion is the event, the act, the history, in which at one and
the same time man is still wholly the old man and already wholly
the new—so powerful is the sin by which he is determined from
behind, and so powerful the grace by which he is determined
from before. It is in this way that man knows himself when he is
really engaged in conversion.

But now we must go on to emphasize no less sharply that the
conversion in which he is simultaneously both, is an event, an act,
a history. The coincidence of the "still" and "already" is the content of this *simul*. Because this "still" and "already" coincide in
him, it is not the *simul* of a balancing or co-ordination of two
similar factors. Nor are the positions of the two moments which
are simultaneously present—the old and the new man—in any sense
interchangeable. On the contrary, they are wholly and utterly
dissimilar. There is an order and sequence in this *simul*. There is

direction—the movement to a goal. The old and the new man are simultaneously present in the relationship of a *terminus a quo* and a *terminus ad quem*. Thus conversion, in which at one and the same time we are still the old man and already the new, and both wholly and altogether. is neither a juggling nor a movement in a circle. In accordance with the fact that it is initiated by the divine command to halt and advance, the man engaged in it finds that—with no possibility of interchange—he is wholly denied as the old man of yesterday and wholly affirmed as the new man of tomorrow; that he is wholly taken out of identity with the former and wholly set in identity with the latter; that he is in no sense taken seriously by God as the former but taken with unqualified seriousness by God as the latter; that as the former he is wholly given up to eternal death and as the latter wholly taken up into eternal life. When he is simultaneously the old and the new man, and both in totality, he is not only forbidden to be this in neutrality, in a static equipoise of the two; he finds that this is quite impossible in practice. He can be the two only in the whole turning from the one to the other. We speak of this turning when we speak of his conversion. And we emphasize the serious and radical nature of it when we speak of the twofold, total determination of the man engaged in it.

In these circumstances the thought of falling-out is perhaps the best to describe the situation. To begin with, it indicates that the coincidence of the "still" and the "already," of the old man and the new, of the *homo peccator* and the *homo sanctus*, cannot remain. It is true that there is no present in which we can look beyond this *simul*, in which the man engaged in conversion is not wholly under the power of sin and wholly under that of grace. Yet he is not merely not authorized by the content of the two determinations coinciding in this *simul*, nor is he merely prohibited, but he is positively prevented from understanding this *simul* as something lasting and definitive. To his own salvation, he has no continuing city. If it is true that we can never at any time see beyond this *simul*, it is equally true that this *simul*, in virtue of its dynamic as a moment in the history of God with man and man with God, points beyond itself, impelling to the only possible decision between the two determinations which now coincide in man. He cannot remain what he still is *in toto*. He can no longer be this in face of what he already is *in toto*. And what he already is *in toto*, he may become and be in such a way that he is this alone (excluding what he still is *in toto*). What in this *simul* is still present in conjunction as a twofold determination of one and the same man cannot by its very nature remain in this conjunction. Its whole will and movement and impulse is to fall out or to fall apart, and to do so in the direction unequivocally characterized by the radically different content of this twofold determination; not dualistically in a division or re-stabilized co-existence of an old man and a new, a sinner and saint; but monistically in the passing and death and definitive end and destruction of the one in favor of the development and life and exclusive, uncompromised and inviolable existence of the other. In the quarrel in which a man finds himself engaged in conversion—as he who is still wholly the old and already wholly the new man—he has not fallen out with himself partially but totally, in the sense that the end and goal of the dispute is that he can no longer be the one he was and can be only the one he will be.

We must now speak more specifically of the basis and origin of conversion, of man's awakening to it, and of the power which sets and keeps it in motion as his falling-out with himself. At the beginning of this discussion we described it as an axis which establishes itself in the life of man, or on which his life is established, so that he has to follow its movement in his own life and being, its turning automatically making his life a life in conversion. We called this dynamic principle the power of the reality that God is for him, and he for God, as this reveals itself to him and shows itself to be the truth. Some elucidations are now needed in respect of this center of the problem.

We must (1) abandon the figure of the axis with the magical or mechanical or automatic associations which it might conjure up, and call the thing intended by its proper name. When Paul speaks of a man led to conversion by the Spirit of God, it is not at all the case that he is betrayed into the sphere and influence of an overwhelming impulse with the alien movement of which he has to cooperate and by which he *nolens volens* sets himself in totality under that twofold determination as an old and new man, and therefore in that dispute with himself. It is true, of course, that it is by the omnipotence of God that he is awakened to conversion and set in this movement. But the omnipotence of God is not a force which works magically or mechanically and in relation to which man can be only an object, an alien body which is either carried or impelled, like a spar of wood carried relentlessly downstream by a great river. It is a matter of God's omnipotent mercy, of His Holy Spirit, and therefore of man's liberation, and therefore of his conversion to being and action in the freedom which he is given by God. To be sure, there is a compulsion. He *must* pass from a well-known past to a future which is only just opening up, "to a land that I shall shew thee"; from himself as the old man to himself as a new man; from his own death to his own true life. There is necessarily a compulsion. No question of a choice can enter in. He is not merely set in, i.e., before a decision. He makes the decision, looking neither to the right hand nor to the left, nor especially behind. But the compulsion is not a mere compulsion. It is not abstract. It is not blind or deaf. We have to realize that mere compulsion is basically evil and demonic. The compulsion obeyed in conversion is not of this type. It is the compulsion of a permission and ability which have been granted. It is that of the free man who as such can only exercise his freedom. The omnipotence of God creates and effects in the man awakened to conversion a true ability. He who previously vegetated to death under a hellish compulsion, in a true comparison with the driftwood carried downstream, may now live wholly of himself and be a man. The coming, the opening up of this "may" is the revelation of the divine summons to halt and proceed; the power which makes his life, life in conversion. Be-

cause and as he is given this permission and ability, he necessarily
stands at this point. He *must* leave those things which are behind,
and reach forth unto those things which are before, pressing
toward the mark (Ph 3:13f.). It is for this that he is freed, and
free. In this freedom there has been taken from him once and for
all any mere choosing or self-deciding. In the exercise of this
freedom—still as the man he was, already as the man he will be—he
fulfills his conversion.

But as we enquire (2) concerning the specific character of the
basis and origin of conversion, and therefore the particular nature
of the awakening of man to it, we must take a step backwards.
The dynamic principle of this movement is the truth, revealing
itself to man, that God is for him, and that—in virtue of the fact
that God is for him—he is for God. It is this truth which frees
him for God, and therefore for that dispute with himself. It is this
truth which kills and makes alive. Thus in its origin and basis, at
the superior place where it is set in motion, the conversion of man
is a decision of God for him which not only makes possible a
corresponding decision of man for God, the free act of his obedience, but makes this act and obedience real, directly causing it to
take place. If in this basis and origin the order were different,
and the truth revealed to man were that man is for God, and
therefore God for man, the truth would not make us free. It would
simply be a demand that man should be what he is not free to be.
It would then have nothing to do with *vivificatio*. For how can
the man who is against God become a new man merely by being
asked to make a decision which is quite alien to him and to be for
God? But it could also have nothing to do with *mortificatio*. It
might startle and frighten man, but it could not and would not
in any way raise him out of his existence as a sinner, or even
affect this existence. It would simply be an abstract law—a law
without any *locus* in a life fulfilling and embodying it, but merely
advancing the arid claim that it is the law of God, and that as
such it has the right to demand that man should be for God, and
thus fulfill the condition under which God will also be for him.

This abstract law has never yet led a man to conversion, even by killing him, let alone by making him alive. It has no power to do either. For it is not the living God, nor His quickening Spirit, who places man under this law. The revealed truth of the living God in His quickening Spirit has its content and force in the fact that it is He first who is for man, and then and for that reason man is for Him. God precedes therefore, and sets man in the movement in which he follows. He says Yes to him when man says No, and thus silences the No of man and lays a Yes in his heart and on his lips. He loves man even though he is an enemy (Rm 5:10), and thus makes him the friend who loves Him in return. As it is revealed to man that this is how matters stand between him and God—and this is what is revealed to him by the Holy Spirit—he comes to have dealings with the living God and the quickening Spirit. He is awakened to conversion. He is plunged into the dispute with himself in which he dies as an old man and rises again as a new. In short, it is unequivocally and exclusively by the Gospel, the revealed grace of God, that conversion is effectively commanded as a radical termination and a radical recommencement. But effectively means as a gift of freedom, and therefore as the law of his own free act apart from which he has no freedom to choose any other. The law which he obeys has its *locus* in his life as it is freed by the Gospel. As the "law of the Spirit of life" (Rm 8:2), it frees us, but in so doing it genuinely binds and engages us. It makes the divine summons to halt and advance quite unavoidable. It makes quite natural and self-evident the being in transition from what we still are to what we are already.

Finally (3), we have to ask concerning the superior place itself and as such where it is a real fact, and can thus emerge as potent truth in the work of the Holy Spirit, that God is for man and man for God. Everything that we have so far said depends ultimately upon whether we can say that this is not a mere suspicion, or hypothesis, or construct, or axiom of philosophical metaphysics, or dogma of theology, but that it is really the case with unassailable objectivity. In other words, the event of revelation which has been our starting-point in all these discussions must be merely the manifestation of a real event which takes place with incontestable objectivity. It is in relation to this climax that—to look back for a moment from the point we have just reached—all our previous statements have been made: about the primacy of the Gospel in virtue of which the decisive work of that event of revelation is the new life, the *vivificatio*, of man; about the liberation imparted to him in it; about the force and depth and teleology of the dispute in which he fulfills this liberation; about the totality with which, awakened to repentance, he finds himself claimed and impelled. How do we know all these things? How is it that we can treat them as a reality, and interpret this reality only as has actually been the case? On what basis have we thought and spoken about the totality of conversion, and reached our detailed decisions, partly for and partly without and even against Calvin, by whom we have especially tried to orientate ourselves in this field?

The answer is quite simple. We have merely taken seriously what Calvin called the *participatio Christi*, making it the ultimate foundation of his whole doctrine of sanctification. The actual event which is an event of revelation in virtue of the enlightening work of the Holy Spirit, and as such sets in motion the conversion of man, is the Christ-event. Jesus Christ is the climax, the superior place, where it is properly and primarily and comprehensively real, where it originally takes place, that God (*vere Deus*) is for man, and man (*vere homo*) is for God. If the conversion of man is the movement which is initiated and maintained from the point where this is primarily and comprehensively real, this is only to say that it has its basis and origin in this climax, in Jesus Christ.

[Major deletions have been made in this edited version.]

The Concept of Conversion

JOHN E. SMITH

The first point to be noticed is that while the linguistic approach demands that attention be directed to the meaning or use of terms, linguistic philosophers for the most part would deny that they are engaged in either etymological analysis or lexicography. They would emphasize instead that their concern is with the *concept* of, in this case, conversion, and that, although the clue to discovering the meaning of this concept is through analysis of the language used in situations where the concept is relevant, the aim of linguistic analysis is neither the origin of terms nor their natural history as this might be found in an historical dictionary. On the other hand, etymology does contribute something to the understanding of our subject and we can best begin with an indication of the root meanings attached to the term from which the English word "conversion" derives.

"Conversion" comes to us from "conversus" which is the past participle of "convertere," which has the basic meaning of "to turn round." The religious sense of the term as "turning to God" is present from the beginning. It is clear from studying the use of the term over several centuries that the *spatial* connotation of "revolving," "reversing" and changing direction was basic; the religious use stems from this as the "direction" or "orientation" of a man's life, that is, what a man "turns to" or "turns toward" for guidance, direction and assistance. In Souter's *Glossary of Later Latin to 600 A.D.*, "conversio" is listed as meaning both the revolution of the celestial bodies and the turning of the sinful man to God. There seems to be no indication in the etymology at least that the change or turning is sudden or catastrophic, although there is ground for holding that the turning is an "about face" in the sense that the reality or state *to which* we turn is in some opposition to the reality or state *from which* we turn. For example, according to Souter, "convert to" could mean "turning away from" the world and turning to God by becoming a monk. The important point for our purpose is that the specifically religious sense of the term is equally primitive with the spatial connotation of "conversus" and cognate terms.

If we turn from etymology to what is sometimes referred to as the technical use of the terms under consideration, we find a broad range of experience reflected. Unfortunately, little is to be gained in the way of understanding any one technical use by attending to any other, except in a most general way. The term "conversion" has a more or less clearly defined meaning in the domains of *theology, law, logic, mathematics,* and *psychology,* and it is frequently found among the terms used in the empirical sciences as when, for instance, we speak of *converting* a temperature reading from the Fahrenheit scale to the Centigrade scale, or of *converting* grams into ounces. The basic connotation running throughout these technical uses is "change," "transformation," "transposition" in accordance with a principle or rule. Thus, in logic, "conversion" means a certain exchange in the position of the subject and predicate terms of a proposition, while leaving certain other features of the proposition unaltered. "Conversion" as a technical term in law refers to the assumption by one party of rights over certain properties that rightfully belong to another; conversion is therefore an actionable matter that may involve larceny or even crime. While all these specialized meanings involve the common core meanings indicated above and thus serve to elucidate the complexity of the concept of conversion, these specialized meanings do not contribute significantly to our understanding in the religious context.

Turning from technical uses of the term, we find two other

domains of use that may be of more help—first, the use of the
term "conversion" in a variety of ordinary situations involving
the relations between persons, their beliefs and attitudes, and
second, the ordinary or commonsensical meaning attached to the
term by those who believe that they are reflecting the *religious*
meaning when they use it. The latter use expresses the meaning
of conversion as understood by the layman and in popular religious discourse.

Let us consider several situations belonging to our common
experience in which we have occasion to use the terms "convert,"
"converted," "conversion." No claim is here made to complete-
ness, but I believe it will be generally admitted that the instances
chosen are typical and expressive of recurrent experience. Consider, first, the use of the term "convert" as a noun; we say, "Jones
is a recent 'convert' to our way of thinking." Here the term
"convert" means the person himself and in so naming him we
mean to indicate, first, that he previously had a different viewpoint or standpoint from the one he now has, secondly, that he
has "changed his mind" in some fundamental way so that he now
thinks in a new way or holds a new set of beliefs, and thirdly,
that he was "won over" by argument or in some way induced to
change. It is important to notice that the use of the term does not
restrict the content or the subject matter in any respect; the "way
of thinking" may be about economics, about government, about
art, and it need not be about religion in any sense, although it
seems clear that most people would think of the term "convert"
as borrowed from the religious context.

Consider a second situation in which the same term is used,
this time as a verb; one says, "He spoke with such passion and
argued so earnestly that I know he was trying to convert me."
Here the meaning of "to convert" is to exert influence, to play
a part in, to be a significant factor in, leading a person to abandon a previous view and adopt the view presented by the speaker.
A fundamental presupposition of this use of the term is that the
change in question, or the achieving of the desired result is some-

thing that can be brought about by speaking, arguing, persuading on the part of another person. The change in question need not be a matter of ideas, doctrines or beliefs alone; we may also say, "He was trying to convert me to his way of life," and such a change would involve far more than the adoption of new beliefs or doctrines.

Consider still a third situation relevant to the theme; one says, "You need not labor the point; in speaking to this group with regard to that issue, you are already speaking to the *converted*." Here the meaning of the key term centers on the state of those who listen; no arguments are necessary concerning the belabored point because the hearers are already confirmed in, adhere to, accept, do not question, the view which the speaker would have had to defend were his hearers of a different persuasion. "Converted" is this use means being already settled in a state of belief, such that effort is no longer required in order to bring your hearers to that position.

In the foregoing examples, the main emphasis has fallen on beliefs, points of view, doctrines held or believed in, by individuals or groups; let us consider a case where reference is made to the person as a whole, his state, his character, his condition and not merely his beliefs. In a situation where two people have experienced a deep and serious misunderstanding, one might say, "You must learn to understand Tom, you see he is a new man, he has undergone some sort of *conversion* since you last saw him." Here again the primary connotation is that of change or transformation, but the change now appears difficult to locate and determine. The person is in some sense changed, but the change seems not to be a difference *in* this or that feature of the person's life, but a change *of* person as if a new being now dwelt where another had lived before. The implication is not that there is a new person, *simpliciter*, as in the case of a second and different person taking the place of the other; in speaking of the person as having undergone a conversion we mean to say that it is the *same* person who has undergone the change. The change, that is, is referred to an abiding person, but the change is so radical and so completely alters the being of the person that we are inclined to speak of a "new" person being involved.

At least one significant result emerges from a consideration of the foregoing instances; when the term "conversion" (and related words) is used to describe persons and their experiences, the term may refer to either a *partial* or a *total* transformation. The change may be described as a determinate *alteration in* some identifiable feature of a person's life and experience, or it may be thought of as a more radical transformation involving a *change of* total personality. It may be that upon further reflection this distinction would have to be modified; perhaps the two are not separable. However, as far as linguistic use is concerned, it is clear that we ordinarily consider it possible for a person to change his mind about some disputed issue for example, or to adopt a new attitude to some person or place, without at the same time becoming a totally new person.

A second set of linguistic uses relevant for a discussion of "conversion" is found in the attempts of the ordinary man, so-called, including the religious layman, to express his understanding of this phenomenon as it figures in the religious situation. Behind these uses is the assumption that the term bears a religious meaning or is meant to refer to what happens within the confines of the religious life. It would, I believe, be generally admitted that the term calls to mind a revivalistic context and a conservative theological tone. Theological liberalism, among clergy and laity alike, has invariably looked askance at the language of "conversion" because of its individualistic and often sentimental connotations. We most frequently associate conversion with an evangelical crusade, with a preaching mission, with situations in which the religious content is presented in a rhetorical, persuasive or moving way under the express motive of leading the individual to arrive at a decision, to make a confession, to accept, to "come to terms with" (as we say) the religious truths and realities that are set before him. And frequently along with the aim of inducing a decision, there is also the invocation of God or the religious power to bring the change into being. Conversion understood in this revivalistic or evangelical context means a change in and for an individual, and it points to an intensely personal *experience* which, in the popular imagination, has always been associated with the voices, visions and such demonstrations of emotion as were scornfully described by Charles Chauncy in the days of Jonathan Edwards as the "late religious commotions in New England." An inseparable part of the meaning of "conversion" and related terms in this context is that the person must be aware in some vivid way of being "moved," of "being reached," of "being called," of "being saved," of being brought out of—to use the wonderfully expressive language of Jonathan Edwards—"a cold and lifeless frame" into a new and intensely vital condition. It is surely no accident that the early Wesleyans—whether this was true for Wesley himself or not—could not understand how conversion could take place for an individual without his *knowing* that it has taken place; in short, they could not divorce conversion from the *experience* and knowledge of being changed.

Despite the strong emphasis that has always been placed on doctrine in the traditions of Protestant piety, it is clear that conversion understood in the popular, revivalistic sense does not mean primarily a change of doctrine or theology, but rather a change of heart, a change in nature, a change in the self sufficiently deep and lasting to bring about a change of conduct and bearing in the world. Much of the anti-intellectualism of evangelical piety centers in the understanding of conversion as something that can happen only to those who "have the Spirit" and who do not identify religion with learning that comes from books or indeed with any form of sophistication. The records are filled with the opinions expressed by revivalistic preachers according to which conversion can only be retarded by the presence of theological sophistication.

The extent to which the transformations envisaged by revivalistic piety are understood, from the standpoint of ordinary experience, as having been brought about "miraculously" as a work of the Spirit and entirely apart from any effort or will on the part of the individual, remains uncertain. Here ordinary experience and ordinary use fail us, and they do so simply because they reflect no more than ordinary understanding which does not penetrate the surface. Ordinary understanding does not probe the basic issues—the nature of the self, of faith, of God and of the Holy Spirit. If we want to develop a consistent position, we shall have to pass beyond the analysis of language and of use to a reflective analysis of experience itself, involving both description of what is actually encountered and the drawing of the appropriate logical consequences. At this juncture we may turn to what I regard as a more difficult, but in the end more fruitful, contribution of philosophy to the formulation of religious truth and the resolution of theological problems.

Every religious doctrine involving reference to God, to the world and to man, though it finds its primary content in some tradition of revealed experience and interpretation, is logically related to secular knowledge, to knowledge gained from sources other than the revealed tradition. The relation is necessary in the sense that in speaking about a religious doctrine such as conversion, for example, we cannot avoid introducing a general theory of the human person, some understanding of the relation between the human mind and man's capacity for action (including the act that is in faith), not uniquely derived from officially religious sources. As a result, a number of problems arise concerning the proper relation of this secular knowledge, especially philosophy, to the formulation of religious truth.

I do not sympathize with the current view according to which there exist, in the sphere of theology, clear answers to perplexing questions of human existence, which answers can be communicated to the modern man if only we succeed in finding some commonly accepted language in which to express them. Such a view conceives the relation between theology and secular knowledge as wholly external. The fact is that, given the present state of human knowledge, and especially the widespread skepticism that exists concerning the possibility of truth in religion, theological answers are, for most people, not answers at all but new *questions* and *problems*. This means that theological interpretations can make their impact on the modern scene only in dialectic with other alternatives. This dialectic is a more arduous undertaking than is supposed by those who assume a ready-made religious truth and then look about for an accepted language in which to express it.

A critical understanding of conversion as a phenomenon of the religious situation demands a solution to several perplexing questions. These are questions that must be faced by every theory of conversion's having a claim on our understanding because these questions belong to the generic structure of human life in the world, a structure in which the religious and the non-religious alike are involved.

At present, the most important contribution that can be made from the side of philosophy to the theological cause is to formulate critical questions not in the fashion of those who pose difficulties in order to explain religion away, but in the fashion of those who want to see the religious point of view expressed in the most intelligible way, which means in the way that "makes most sense" not only, or even especially to critics, but primarily to those who are earnestly seeking to discover what the purpose of human life may be. In order to understand the profound and absolutely essential religious concept of conversion, it will be helpful if we proceed in what philosophers are wont to call "transcendental" fashion, and ask, what conditions must be satisfied if we are to speak intelligibly about conversion as an event, whether momentary or extended, in the life of a person. I shall propose some three conditions that must be satisfied by any doctrine of conversion in the religious sense. If these conditions are indeed universal, we shall have a touchstone for estimating the validity of a particular theory.

1. The first condition concerns an adequate theory of the

human self, both in the descriptive and normative senses. It makes no sense to speak of a changed life, a new self, etc., unless we have a defensible theory expressing what it means to be a self. Whether conversion in the religious sense is understood primarily as a change in belief, as a change in the nature of the person, or as a change in attitude, the change involved is unintelligible unless there is an *enduring* self lasting in some sense through change, and marked by unity, identity and uniqueness. The self of the classical empiricist tradition consisting of a series of momentary experiences more or less loosely bound together by memory is inadequate for understanding a change in the person as profound as is implied in conversion. The existentialist self in some of its versions at least, despite the marked elements of truth expressed in the general approach, too radically identifies the self with its freedom and capacity to project itself anew in every moment, to account for any sort of stability or abiding character of self-hood. In view of the fact that religion concerns the self in its depth and as a whole, no theory of the self will be adequate which does not allow for these features. Momentary selves will not do; there must be a larger, deeper, time-spanning self through which the center and character of the person can be identified. Conversion means a change that affects the person in his center, either in the sense that he undergoes an exchange of centers or that an element—belief, attitude, concern—that was previously peripheral now becomes central.

2. A second and closely related problem concerns the capacity of the self to be a questing self and to have a concern for itself, its ground and goal focused by self-knowledge. Conversion as a hoped for change in the person involving acknowledgment of a man's separation from God and his ultimate turning back to God would be unintelligible unless the self is seeking for a truth and reality which it knows it does not have. Such seeking may take many forms, depending on the sensitivity of the individual. The quest may be calm and largely speculative, or it may be fraught with anxiety. The divided, unhappy self brought to a *crisis* by despair

or the absolute sense that life cannot go on without a major transformation, longs to find release and a new form of existence. On
the other hand, a self with little or no capacity for concern or
with little self-understanding will never understand what conversion means because he does not understand the human predicament to which conversion is the resolution.

3. The third condition concerns the freedom of the self. Quite
apart from the complexities of the theory of freedom stated in
metaphysical terms, everyone is aware that man is different from
a star or a stone in his capacity to reflect, use language and, as it
appears at least, make choices and decisions. No religious truth
is consistent with man as we know him, unless it takes account
of man's freedom. The point is crucial for any doctrine of conversion. Conversion cannot be understood as a wholly "objective"
transaction taking place entirely beyond the consciousness of the
individual because such a view leaves faith, concern, decision,
repentance—in short all the "existential movements" involving a
measure of freedom—out of account; man might be converted in
this objective way, but he would become a puppet in the process.
On the other hand, it is essential to the repentance and dependence
upon God contained in the idea of conversion that some change
take place which is *beyond the power of the finite human will to
effect.* Thus conversion transcends human will and consciousness
while still remaining related to both. Unless man has the freedom
to become aware of separation from God and to repent, and unless
he has the freedom to *accept* the offered release, conversion becomes unintelligible. The self is thus *active* and *passive* in the conversion situation; passive in receiving what it cannot bring about,
but active in seeing the need for salvation, in opening himself to
the possibility and in accepting the gift when it comes.

To recapitulate, conversion is unintelligible without an adequate theory of the self that allows for the three conditions speci-
fied—the *enduring self* existing with a center beyond the frag-
mentary moments of experience; the *questing self* capable of eval-
uating itself and of understanding man's predicament and how

it is to be resolved in religious terms; the *free self* capable of opening itself to the possibility of the divine power and of accepting its own limitations when confronted with that power.

Part Two

HISTORICAL AND BIBLICAL PERSPECTIVES

The Idea of Conversion

A. D. NOCK

Man is born into a world in which there are some objects and processes which are to him fully comprehensible and others which are not. When he releases his hold on a stone which he has held in his hand and it falls to the ground, the result is always the same, and there is nothing to excite any feeling of dependence on unknown forces. Birth, however, and growth and sexual relations and death and success in fishing or hunting and agriculture are all matters in which man is not his own master and appears to be dealing with something uncanny. This distinction is fundamental, and we can observe it in the behavior of animals. Where man differs from the animals—so far as we yet know—is that throughout as much of his evolution as is known to us he has normally not remained supine but has striven to take a positive attitude and assume a definite line of conduct towards these mysteries. What he says and does rests on the assumption that the secret workings of nature are capable of being influenced by his actions, and commonly on the further assumption that these secret workings are due to forces which operate in virtue of wills and emotions comparable with those which prompt his own operations.

What he thus says and does makes up religion. Our evidence does not allow us to penetrate into the beginnings of this form of conduct; at the earliest stages of human evolution known to us such activity is already determined by a tradition which embodies the collective wisdom of the community. Like many other aspects of social organization, it is often thought to rest upon some original revelation or revelations, given by higher powers, or upon the communing of specially gifted persons with these powers; and like these other institutions it is commonly conceived as possessing an inherent fixity. In fact, however, it is not exempt from the law of change, but such change is gradual and is not liable to be considerable unless new needs or new cultural contacts arise. Those who follow such a tradition have no reason to interest themselves in other traditions, and no impulse to commend their own tradition to others. It serves their own needs, and the members of other social units have traditions which serve theirs. Within the group itself pressure may be put upon individuals who are lax in their participation in time-honored observances, but that is a domestic matter, and in the last resort a question of public order and well-being. It was so, as we shall see, with the Greeks.

Such a religion is part of the whole scheme of life which each man inherits. It has for him the emotional value attaching to a thing in which he has grown up, often intensified by the solemnity of the puberty ceremonies in which he has learned the weightier matters of the law. But it makes no sudden imperious demands—except on any who feel a vocation to be shamans or medicine men—and it asks of him action and not belief. The situation changes when a prophet emerges. By the term prophet we mean a man who experiences a sudden and profound dissatisfaction with things as they are, is fired with a new idea, and launches out on a new path in a sincere conviction that he has been led by something external and objective. Whereas in religions of tradition the essential element is the practice and there is no underlying idea other than the sanctity of custom hallowed by preceding generations, in prophetic religions the reason is all-important and the practice flows from it and is in a sense secondary even if indispensable.

The prophet has a message which he feels an inward and instant impulse to deliver. He can do nothing else; the truth has been vouchsafed to him, and his fellows have need of it.

So the prophet preaches to those who will hear, and some of them are prepared to stake all on the truth and fundamental importance of his preaching. That is the first stage. Of these disciples some are so eager in their adhesion that they seek to convey to others what they have come to regard as saving truths. That is the second stage. From this an institution may develop, in which the experience of what is in time a distant past is mediated to generations yet unborn, as a thing ever fresh, and can harden into a tradition as rigid as the order from which the prophet revolted.

We have so far considered the two opposing poles of man's spiritual history. One is the system of religious observances of a small social unit with elementary needs and interests and no important contacts with other cultures which have either material or intellectual superiority or a cult and belief capable of exciting curiosity and attention—of a unit in which, as a playwright says, nothing happens except hearing three o'clock strike and waiting for it to strike four. The other is the religion of a prophetic movement in the first ardor of the founder. In the first there is no religious frontier to cross, no difficult decision to make between two views of life which make its every detail different; in the other the individual stands before a choice which means either the renunciation of his past and entry into kingdom, which if the promises made for it are true—and that cannot be proved or disproved—is wholly other here and will be wholly other hereafter, or the refusal of this dream as chimerical.

He cannot wed twice nor twice lose his soul.

Between these two opposing terms, one wholly static and one wholly dynamic, there is a middle country—that of the changes in belief and worship due to political development or cultural interplay. As society advances to more complex forms a particular center may glorify itself by glorifying its gods and representing its gods as deserving the homage of all the members of the new larger unit; this was so in Egypt, where the rise of Ra and Osiris to national significance is due to their local priesthoods. Conquest and invasion have notable effects. We expect that under the circumstances the conquered will accept the religion of the conquerors, because our views are formed by the ideas which we have of the sequel of Christian and Mohammedan invasions, but what happened then was peculiar in that the religion of the races possessing military ascendancy was in each case prophetic and militant in origin and type. In the ancient world the conquerors were liable not indeed to accept the dogmas of the conquered—for there were in general no dogmas to accept—but to incorporate deities and rites of the conquered in their own system. A conspicuous example is afforded by the Indo-Germanic invasion of Greece. Not merely were the conquerors inferior in point of civilization to the conquered, but it could appear to them, as to later Greeks, that the gods of a region were, so to speak, permanent residents who had a natural right to the worship of any human occupants and whom in any event it would be unwise to neglect. Further complication is introduced by the conditions of a time in which men of different races and religions are able to move freely over a large range of territory, whether for trade or otherwise. When this is so, we find in big cities and elsewhere groups of expatriated folk living in alien surroundings. Such groups retain their religious, as their other cultural traditions, often indeed with changes due to intermarriage and various contacts; and those among whom they find themselves are equally exposed to this blending of strains. Exclusiveness in religion is confined to the prophetic type, and it is natural that there should be give and take outside it. To take an early example, the connection between Egypt and Byblos resulted in borrowings on both sides. The contacts thus produced by these foreign groups are the most important, for they led not only to borrowing but to fusion and to new developments; but there were others, as for instance those due to military service abroad and to slavery. Naaman heard of Jehovah through his Hebrew handmaid.

These external circumstances led not to any definite crossing of religious frontiers, in which an old spiritual home was left for a new once and for all, but to men's having one foot on each side of a fence which was cultural and not creedal. They led to an acceptance of new worships as useful supplements and not as substitutes, and they did not involve the taking of a new way of life in place of the old. This we may call adhesion, in contradistinction to conversion. By conversion we mean the reorientation of the soul of an individual, his deliberate turning from indifference or from an earlier form of piety to another, a turning which implies a consciousness that a great change is involved, that the old was wrong and the new is right. It is seen at its fullest in the positive response of a man to the choice set before him by the prophetic religions.

We know this best from the history of modern Christianity. Here it takes two forms, the turning back to a tradition generally held and characteristic of society as a whole, a tradition in which the convert was himself reared but which he has left in scepticism or indifference or violent self-assertion; and the turning away to an unfamiliar form of piety either from a familiar form or from indifference. Psychologically the two have much in common, since the man who returns with enthusiasm will commonly feel that he has never before fully grasped the import of the faith of his childhood. The bottles are old but the wine is new.

The features of such conversion have been classified by William James as a passion of willingness and acquiescence, which removes the feeling of anxiety, a sense of perceiving truths not known before, a sense of clean and beautiful newness within and without and an ecstasy of happiness; these emotions are sometimes, and in fact often, accompanied by hallucinatory or by quasi-hallucinatory phenomena. This type of experience is very well known. We must not, however, expect to find exact analogies for it beyond the range of countries with a long-standing Christian tradition, for in them even when the fact of conversion appears wholly sudden and not led up to by a gradual process of gaining conviction, even when the convert may in all good faith profess that the beliefs which have won his sudden assent are new to him, there is a background of concepts to which a stimulus can give life. When John Wesley preached to the miners in Kingswood few of them can have been obsessed by a sense of sin or filled with a desire for supernatural grace, and yet those ideas were somewhere under the level of consciousness as a heritage from generation after generation of Bible-reading and sermon-hearing forefathers. Such conversion is in its essence a turning away from a sense of present wrongness at least as much as a turning towards a positive ideal. To quote James:

> Now with most of us the sense of our present wrongness is a far more distinct piece of our consciousness than is the imagination of any positive ideal that we can aim at. In a majority of cases, indeed, the sin almost exclusively engrosses the attention, so that conversion is "a process of struggling away from sin rather than of striving towards righteousness."

Primitive religion seeks to satisfy a number of natural needs, to set a seal on the stages by which life is marked and to ensure the proper working of the natural processes and sources of supply on which its continuance depends; it provides also an outlet for certain emotions of humility, dependence, and self-dramatization. Prophetic religion has to create in men the deeper needs which it claims to fulfill.

Acts 16:30 represents the jailer at Thessalonica as saying to Paul and Silas "What must I do to be saved?," but this is in a story told from the Christian point of view. If such a man used phraseology of this sort, he could have meant only "What am I to do in order to avoid any unpleasant consequences of the situation created by this earthquake?" *Soteria* and kindred words carried no theological implications; they applied to deliverance from perils by sea and land and disease and darkness and false opinions, all perils of which men were fully aware.

Prophetic religion, therefore, does not in general find in men's minds anything like the same unconscious sympathy which modern revivalism has used. Yet it naturally finds men's minds in a measure prepared; it is difficult to see how else it would make serious headway. The receptivity of most people for that which is wholly new (if anything is) is small; tradition suggests that it

was long before Zarathustra obtained much following. The originality of a prophet lies commonly in his ability to fuse into a
white heat combustible material which is there, to express and
to appear to meet the half-formed prayers of some at least of his
contemporaries. The teaching of Gotama the Buddha grows out
of the eager and baffled asceticism and speculation of his time,
and it is not easy even now to define exactly what was new in
him except his attitude. The message of John the Baptist and of
Jesus gave form and substance to the dreams of a kingdom which
had haunted many of their compatriots for generations.

We cannot understand the success of Christianity outside
Judaea without making an effort to determine the elements in
the mind of the time to which it appealed.

It the first place, there was in this world very little that corre-
sponded to a return to the faith of one's fathers as we know it.
Except in the last phase of paganism, when the success of Christianity had put it on the defensive and caused it to fight for its
existence, there was no traditional religion which was an entity
with a theology and an organization. Classical Greek has no word
which covers religion as we use the term. *Eusebeia* approximates
to it, but in essence it means no more than the regular performance of due worship in the proper spirit, while *hosiotes* describes
ritual purity in all its aspects. The place of faith was taken by
myth and ritual. These things implied an attitude rather than a
conviction. Where there was a conviction it was to be found in
those who wished to innovate or to deny, in the men who inaugurated or supported new movements, and in the men who denied
the validity of traditional views—occasionally of all views—of the
supernatural. Some such denial was common among men of speculative tendencies. Recantation was less common but not unknown. Horace tells how he had been sparing in his attentions
to the gods, but was converted by a thunderclap out of a clear
sky, a phenomenon for which he could not give a scientific explanation (*Odes* i. 34).

In the second place, the feelings which we associate with
conversion or with the acceptance of prophetic religion were

seldom excited by the new forms of belief and worship to which
men turned. These were as a rule supplements rather than alternatives to ancestral piety. This is obvious with regard to all the
worship paid to new deities in the ordinary ways—by sacrifice,
by attendance at processions, by making vows in distress and
paying them after relief was obtained. It needs some explanation
as far as ceremonies of initiation are concerned. What did they
offer? Orphism at an earlier date had indeed maintained that all
men have an inherited guilt which dooms them to a weary round
of reincarnations unless by use of its means of salvation they win
release. But the initiations which were sought in the world in
which Christianity spread promised something like this: "We
assume from the fact of your approach to us that you are not in
too bad a state. We will of course give you a preliminary rite
or rites of disinfection which will ensure the requisite ritual
purity. That is to be followed by our holy ceremony, which will
confer on you a special kind of blessedness which guarantees to
you happiness after death." This blessedness was secured by a
rite in which the initiate went through a symbolic anticipation
of what was to take place hereafter; it was a piece of sympathetic
magic which ensured safety by a simulation here and now. Death
and rebirth have this meaning and no other—with the exception
of a curious sacrament of auto-suggestion in *Corpus Hermeticum*,
xiii, in which the powers of evil are driven out of a man and the
powers of good take their place, and of the *taurobolium* in which
he received a new vigor. Consequently, there is no idea that the
sacramental experiences of the initiate would make it easier for
him to live a good life here and now. Further, apart from Orphism
and the ancient mysteries of Eleusis, it was never maintained that
these rites were essential requisites of happiness hereafter—they
were valuable safeguards, on which you could depend—and the rites
were actions efficient in themselves as rites and not as the expression of a theology and of a world-order sharply contrasted with
those in which the neophyte had previously moved.

Let us set against this the claims of Judaism and Christianity.

Judaism said in effect to a man who was thinking of becoming a proselyte: "You are in your sins. Make a new start, put aside idolatry and the immoral practices which go with it, become a naturalized member of the Chosen People by a threefold rite of baptism, circumcision, and offering, live as God's Law commands, and you will have every hope of a share in the life of the world to come." Christianity said: "You are in your sins, a state inevitable for you as a human being and aggravated by your wilfulness. No action of your will enable you to make a new start, no effort of yours will enable you to put aside your guilt in God's eyes, and you are doomed to endless suffering hereafter. Turn to us, stake everything on Jesus the Christ being your savior, and God will give to you the privilege of making a new start as a new being and will bestow upon you grace which will enable you so to live here as to obtain a share in the life of the world to come. By using our sacraments you will here and now triumph over death and will have a foretaste of the joys which await you in heaven. Christ became man that you may become as God."

This contrast is clear. Judaism and Christianity demanded renunciation and a new start. They demanded not merely acceptance of a rite, but the adhesion of the will to a theology, in a word faith, a new life in a new people. It is wholly unhistorical to compare Christianity and Mithraism as Renan did, and to suggest that if Christianity had died Mithraism might have conquered the world. It might and would have won plenty of adherents, but it could not have founded a holy Mithraic church throughout the world. A man used Mithraism, but he did not belong to it body and soul; if he did, that was a matter of special attachment and not an inevitable concomitant prescribed by authority.

There was therefore in these rivals of Judaism and Christianity no possibility of anything which can be called conversion. In fact the only context in which we find it in ancient paganism is that of philosophy, which held a clear concept of two types of life, a higher and a lower, and which exhorted men to turn from the one to the other.

[Major deletions have been made in this edited version.]

Conversion and Grace in The Old Testament

DOM MARC-FRANCOIS LACAN

"The Old Testament is the libretto of a spiritual itinerary, the history of a vocation, the equivalent of a catechumenate. The themes of journey and way are central in it."[1]

Now to follow a way is not only to walk, but to walk in the right direction; and this is where the themes of sin and conversion enter the scene. The sinner has turned in the wrong direction, so he walks in vain: "the way of the wicked is doomed" (Ps 1:6). The condition for salvation is a turning around, a conversion, which directs man's journey toward God.

The Old Testament is at once both the story of man's conversion and the history of his vocation. For, from the beginning, God's call has collided with man's infidelity; from the beginning, man, doubting God and his love, has not sought, but fled, his presense. In order to bring unfaithful man back to the right direction, God must make him realize that he has gone astray, calling. "Adam, where are you?" (Gn 3:9). This call is implicitly an invitation to a return, an invitation to a change of interior attitude, an invitation to conversion.

Throughout the history of salvation, God teaches man to transform himself; it is through this necessary conversion and its continuous renewal that man succeeds in responding to his vocation and his mission. The Old Testament tells us how this education was carried out.

In sketching this divine pedagogy in broad strokes, we will underline the major lessons which emerge from it: the conversion

4

to which God invites us is a grace; it is necessary to receive it as
a grace and to become a witness to this grace.

I. An Exemplary Conversion: David

Our starting point will be the conversion of David recounted
in the Second Book of Samuel. David is a man called by God to
the high mission of ruling the chosen people, whose God is the
only true king. In this mission, David demonstrates his fidelity.
A wise, valiant, and devout king, he remains humble in success,
as indicated by his behavior at the time of the entrance of the
Arc into Zion (2 S 6); also, God promises to remain faithful to
David's descendants (2 S 7).

However, David yields to a temptation which involves him in
a series of grave faults. Not only does he violate the divine law
by taking another man's wife and by bringing about the husband's
death, but, in order to commit these unjust deeds, he abuses the
power conferred on him by his royal mission, the mission which
imposes on him the duty of bringing about the reign of justice
by overseeing the observance of God's law (2 S 11).

a) The Revelation of Sin and the Call to Conversion

These faults remain secret for some time, and David's conscience does not seem to trouble him. The passion which motivated
him to act with cunning and cruelty continues to blind him. The
word of God, whose messenger is the prophet Nathan, must make
him recognize that he has sinned, that he has committed an act
which has outraged God (2 S 12:14). David has scorned God,
for he knew that what he was doing was offensive to God; even
more, he knew why such acts offend God, as he proves by his
reaction to Nathan's story about the theft of a poor man's lamb.
By means of this story, Nathan forces David to pass a judgment
which at once both defines his sin and condemns it; the rich man
who had stolen the poor man's lamb deserved death because he
had not had pity (2 S 12:5-6). But this was only a question of a

lamb. What is to be said when it is a question of a man from whom his king takes both his wife and his life?

Once David's conscience has been awakened, the prophet emphasizes the gravity of his fault: the crying injustice suffered by Uriah was committed by a man whom God had filled with his gifts. Then Nathan declares the terrible punishment: the child born to David and Uriah's wife, Bathsheba, is to die. Now without this divine initiative denouncing his sin and declaring his punishment, David, this man of upright heart, whom God had chosen and who had been faithful to his vocation, whom God loved and who had responded to divine favors with a humble piety, would have remained in his sin, for it is precisely sin which is the source of blindness.

At the same time that it is an offense to God, sin is also a failure to acknowledge God. True knowledge of God implies gratitude to him and confidence in him. The more man sins, the more he closes himself to true knowledge of God; and the less he knows God, the less he is capable of discerning what offends God. More and more his conscience becomes dull and his heart hard, unless God intervenes, unless the word of God awakens his conscience by proclaiming a misfortune, a just punishment for his sin and a sign of God's judgment.

b) Confession of Sin and the Humble Confidence of the Converted

To this divine judgment, David responds: "I have sinned against Yahweh" (2 S 12:13). By this admission David recognizes that he had turned away from Yahweh, and turns back to Him. His response is at once a confession of his fault and a conversion towards God. This response is significant because it underscores the essence of sin: David sinned because he acted "against God." He was therefore no longer "with him."

By his humble admission, David returns to God and takes up again in his presence the attitude of humility which had formerly opened him to God's gifts and which now opens him to his pardon. Granted to him immediately, this pardon is a divine seal which proves the authenticity of his conversion (2 S 12:13).

David's conversion has another important aspect which the continuation of the account will show. As we have noted, sin causes the sinner to lose the sense of God. The converted person finds this sense again in his conversion, which is nothing else than the reception of divine light, towards which God's judgment obliges the sinner to turn. In this light, the converted person knows the God who judges him, but who also calls him to salvation.

This is why David, in saying, "I have sinned against Yahweh," not only humbly admits his fault and makes possible the pardon which purifies him, but also recognizes again who his God is. And to the mercy of this God, he responds with an attitude of total trust; as an expression of this confidence, he opens himself actively to the pardon in prayer accompanied by fasting (2 S 12:15-19).

David's confession of his fault is also a confession of his God, a proclamation of the goodness of this God whose mercy calls to conversion and whose compassion arouses confidence. In return, the confidence of the converted person is praise of the mercy which has called him and brought him back. David's trust proves how profound his knowledge of God is and how perfect has been the conversion which results in such knowledge and trust.

We should especially note David's behavior at the moment Nathan announces God's pardon to him, a pardon which implies, however, a punishment; the death which David is spared will strike the child born of his sin. Faced with this verdict, David does not despair of saving his child's life, which he attempts to do through ardent pleading and severe penance. David's officers see in his behavior only the expression of a father's suffering; in reality, it is the expression of his limitless trust in divine mercy (2 S 12:22). Also, when the child dies, David, to everyone's amazement, ceases his penance and accepts this death with perfect submission to the will of God (2 S 12:20-23).

David's conversion allows us to discern the essential elements of an authentic conversion. God initiates it: conversion is a grace. It is a grace of light which reveals to the sinner both his sin and the goodness of the one he has offended. The converted person receives the grace by humbly admitting his sin, and by opening himself with confidence to the goodness which wants to pardon him.

II. THE GRACE OF CONVERSION

Throughout the course of his people's history, God teaches the same lessons which we have just drawn from the typical case of David. The people whom God freely chose are constantly unfaithful to him; but, through his prophets, God never ceases to remind them of his Covenant's law. Conversion, then, is a return to this law, but a return which is possible only if God changes man's heart. The grace of this change will inaugurate a new Covenant announced by the prophets.

The history of Israel, enlightened by the prophetic preaching, thus disposes the people to receive conversion as a grace. On the one hand, indeed, the prophets' call to conversion serves only to emphasize Israel's infidelity without succeeding in converting it; the people recognize their sin as well as their powerlessness to liberate themselves from its hold. On the other hand, the promises of the prophets emphasize the fidelity of God who will convert a small "remnant" in order to accomplish his plan of salvation; the people recognize that conversion will be the gratuitous gift of God's love.

a) *Conversion, the Demand of the Old Covenant*

"It did not take them long to stray from the way which I prescribed for them" (Ex 32:8). In this reproach to Moses, God defines man's constant attitude. It was Adam's attitude at the very beginning of human history (Gn 3); and it has been Israel's attitude since the origins of its existence as a people, inaugurated by the Covenant of Sinai. The adoration of the golden calf (Ex 32) is only a rather expressive form of the permanent infidelity denounced by Moses: "You have rebelled against Yahweh since the day he first knew you" (Dt 9:24).

But God continues to chastise his people in order to lead them back to him. In the Book of Judges, the history of Israel develops as a succession of phases whose cycle is always the same: the people forsake Yahweh (Jg 2:12) and Yahweh delivers them over to their enemies (Jg 2:14); "the children of Israel cry to Yahweh and Yahweh raises up for them a savior" (Jg 3:9; cf. 3:15; 6:7; 10:10-16).

In the time of the Kings, history unfolds according to the same rhythm, up to the destruction of the Northern Kingdom, which the author of the Book of Kings justifies by reason of the hardening of the people who had refused to listen to the prophets (2 K 17:13-18). The prophets' call to conversion was not short on vigor, however.

One has only to read Amos to hear "Yahweh roar from Zion" (Am 1:2). He announces the "visit" of Yahweh to his people; it is precisely because Yahweh has known this people in a completely special way, making them his own by the Covenant, that he is going to punish them for their iniquities (Am 3:2). But these punishments are in vain; the evocation of each one always ends with the bitter statement: "And you have not returned to me, oracle of Yahweh" (Am 4:6, 8, 9, 10, 11).

Worship continued to go on, however:

> Offer your sacrifices each morning
> and your tithes on the third day, . . .
> announce your voluntary offerings, make them public,
> for this is what makes you happy, sons of Israel
> (Am 4:4-5).

But at the same time:

> . . . They have sold the virtuous man for silver
> and the poor man for a pair of sandals,

. . . they trample on the heads of ordinary people
and push the poor out of their path (Am 2:6-7).

Because of this injustice, God declares that he despises the
feasts, pays no heed to the sacrifices (Am 5:21-22), and is going
to change the feasts into mourning like that over the loss of an
only son (Am 8:10). It is necessary to be converted, and conversion consists in "seeking God" (Am 5:4).

To seek God does not mean going to places of worship such
as Bethel, Gilgal, or Beersheba (Am 5:5); rather, it means seeing
to it that justice prevails (Am 5:15). He who seeks God, by pursuing the good and despising evil, will live (Am 5:6, 14, 15).
Without this conversion, "let Israel prepare itself to meet its God"
(Am 4:12)! It will be a fearsome meeting with a God who will
pardon no longer (Am 7:8; 8:2). It would be impossible to specify
more pointedly the moral character of the conversion demanded
by the Covenant; rituals are useless if there is no change in
morality.

And for morality to change, there must be a change of heart.
Isaiah cries this out in the Kingdom of Judah, where his preaching
takes up again the calls which Amos had addressed to the Northern Kingdom. It would really be necessary to cite the very moving first chapter of Isaiah in its entirety; but a few lines will give
something of its tone:

> They have abandoned Yahweh, despised the Holy One
>   of Israel . . .
> Where shall I strike you next? . . .
> from the sole of the foot to the head there is not a
>   sound spot . . .
> You may multiply your prayers,
> I shall not listen. . . .
> Cease to do evil . . .
> search for justice, help the oppressed . . .
> But if you persist in rebellion,
> the sword shall eat you instead (Is 1:4-6, 15-17, 20).

Let us add the complaint which Jesus will later repeat:

> This people . . . honors me only with lip-service,
> while its heart is far from me (Is 29:13; cf. Mk 7:6).

This is what will draw down on Judah the punishment which
has already struck Israel. As the author of the Book of Kings puts
it, the sins of Manassas have wearied Yahweh (2 K 21:10-15;
23:26-27). However, Josiah, who succeeded Manassas, rivaled
David in fidelity, and promoted the Deuteronomic reform (2 K
22:2; 23:1-25). But that was not enough to win God's pardon, for
the attempted reform did not survive Josiah. And if the reform
did not last, it was because it had not been deep enough. It had
destroyed the high places and had centralized worship in Jerusalem in the hope of purifying it, but the Deuteronomist demanded more than this cultic reform.

What he demanded was a circumcision of the heart, an undivided fidelity inspired by a limitless love for God (Dt 10:12-17).
And this is what Jeremiah preached. If he recalled the fundamental prohibition of the worship of strange gods (Jr 11:9-12),
he above all proclaimed the uselessness of worship without fidelity
to the moral demands of the Law (Jr 7:8-11, 21-28).

Certainly, to turn away from God is a great evil, and Jeremiah
denounces this abomination in many refrains:

> Does a nation change its gods?
> —and these are not gods at all!
> Yet my people have exchanged their Glory
> for what has no power in it.
> You heavens, stand aghast at this,
> stand stupified, stand utterly appalled
> —it is Yahweh who speaks.
> Since my people have committed a double crime:
> they have abandoned me, the fountain of living water,
> only to dig cisterns for themselves,
> leaky cisterns that hold no water (Jr 2:11-13).

But let one return to Yahweh, and he will keep the magnificent promises made to Abraham; otherwise, eternal destruction.

> If you wish to come back, Israel—it is Yahweh who speaks—
> it is to me you must return.
> Do away with your abominations
> and you will have no need to avoid me.
> If you swear, "As Yahweh lives!"
> truthfully, justly, honestly,
> the nations will bless themselves by you,
> and glory in you (Jr 4:1-2; cf. Gn 12:3).

> Circumcize yourself for Yahweh . . .
> lest my wrath should leap out like a fire,
> and burn with no one to quench it,
> in return for the wickedness of your deeds (Jr 4:4).

But what does it mean to return to Yahweh? Above all, it means "to do what is right and to seek the truth" (Jr 5:1).

Such is the "way of Yahweh" (Jr 5:5) which priests and prophets must know and teach; but they have departed from it themselves. Greedy and practicing fraud, they too are among the ungodly (Jr 6:13; 23:11). One can know Yahweh only by returning to him along the way Josiah followed:

> He practiced honesty and integrity . . .
> He used to examine the cases of poor and needy . . .
> Is not that what it means to know me?—it is Yahweh
> who speaks (Jr 22:15-16).

The only true glory is in following this way, which is to imitate God himself:

> Let the sage boast no more of his wisdom,
> nor the valiant of his valor,
> nor the rich man of his riches!
> But if anyone wants to boast, let him boast of this:
> of understanding and knowing me.
> For I am Yahweh, I rule with kindness,
> justice and integrity on earth;

yes, these are what please me
—it is Yahweh who speaks (Jr 9:22-23).

Following such a way supposes a conversion of heart which
Josiah's reform did not achieve. Far from being converted, their
hearts appeared incapable of transformation. Jeremiah reports it
with grief:

> Why does this people persist in apostasy,
> in continuous apostasy?
> They cling to illusion,
> they refuse to come back . . .
> Not one repents of his wickedness saying: What
>   have I done? . . .
> My people do not know the ruling of Yahweh!
> They feel no shame,
> they have forgotten how to blush (Jr 8:5-7, 12).

Thus the prophet clashes with a basic corruption which appears
incurable despite the trials intended to purify the people:

> The wound of the daughter of my people wounds me too,
> all looks dark to me, terror grips me. . . .
> Then why does it make no progress,
> this cure of the daughter of my people?
> They are corrupt, incapable of repentance. . . .
> Look, I will now test them in the crucible
> —but how am I to deal with their wickedness?
>   (Jr 8:21-22; 9:4-6).
> They are all corrupt. . . .
> In vain: the smelter does his work,
> but the dross is not purged out (Jr 6:28-29).
> Can the Ethiopian change his skin,
> or the leopard his spots?
> And you, can you do what is right,
> you so accustomed to wrong? (Jr 13:23).

And that is not all. Not only is Jeremiah faced with infidelity
and corruption; not only has he to lament the death of a devout

king which jeopardizes the attempted reform; but he also runs into an obstacle with which Jesus will later collide: an erroneous understanding of religion which confuses a religious sense with fidelity to institutions. As a result of such confusion, the conscience of sinners, already warped by their vices, ends up in self-destruction.

How do you convert someone who thinks he is righteous and whose "tranquility is based simply on the possession of Israel's privileges? After all, to possess the Law and the Temple, the royal house of David and the body of the prophets, the secrets of authentic worship, and circumcision, all these elements of the Covenant in which one takes pride, is not this the guarantee that one is on the right path?"[2]

Jeremiah must criticize all these institutions in order to redeem the divine demands of the Covenant from the worthless accretions of human traditions. This is the only way of restoring a sense of sin to the people and of opening them to the grace which alone can save them. We will cite only the diatribe against the Temple, by which Jeremiah, at the risk of his life (Jr 26:8), shakes the false confidence which gives Israel a good conscience:

> Put no trust in delusive words like these: This is the sanctuary of Yahweh, the sanctuary of Yahweh, the sanctuary of Yahweh!

> What! Come presenting yourselves in this Temple that bears my name, saying: Now we are safe—safe to go on committing all these abominations! Do you take this Temple that bears my name for a robbers' den?

> Since you . . . have refused to listen when I spoke so urgently, so persistently, or to answer when I called you, I will treat this Temple that bears my name, and in which you put your trust, . . . just as I treated Shiloh (Jr 7:4, 10-11, 13-14).

And the exile will place the divine seal on the prophet's word. Is it necesary then to despair of the conversion of this people which is constantly unfaithful to the Covenant?

b) Conversion, Grace of the New Covenant

Give up hope? Not at all. Exactly the opposite, in fact, for to
be converted is to hope, to trust in Yahweh, to fully expect his
grace:

> Heal me, Yahweh, and I shall be really healed,
> save me, and I shall be saved,
> for you alone are my hope (Jr 17:14; cf. 31:18).

Such is the attitude to which the divine teaching strains to lead
the people of the Covenant in order to make them a witness to
grace among the nations. But this attitude will be achieved in
only a small number, a *remnant*.

Isaiah had already spoken of this "remnant" when he announced a punishment which would have been avoided if the
people had relied on God:

> For thus says the Lord Yahweh, the Holy One of Israel:
> Your salvation lay in conversion and tranquility,
> Your strength, in complete trust;
> and you would have none of it (Is 30:15).

The destruction is thus determined; only a remnant will escape:

> This remnant . . . will truly rely on Yahweh, the Holy One
> of Israel.
> A remnant will return, the remnant of Jacob, to the
> mighty God (Is 10:20-22).

This remnant will be a humble and modest people which Yahweh
will allow to stand (Zp 3:12-13). Why will it be spared? Because of Yahweh's eternal love for Israel (Jr 31:3). Before Jeremiah, Hosea had celebrated this love of Yahweh for his unfaithful
spouse. Hosea had invited the unfaithful to return to Yahweh in
order to be healed by him (Ho 6:12); he had talked about true
conversion:

> Turn again, then, to your God,

> hold fast to love and justice,
> and always put your trust in your God (Ho 12:7).

To be converted is to become faithful. To succeed in this, a person must rely on God in perfect trust. These themes of Hosea were taken up again and deepened by Jeremiah.

At the time of the first deportation to Babylon, Jeremiah writes to the exiles about what God is going to do for them: they are the people whom God will bring back from exile, for they will be converted to God with all their heart. This conversion will be the fruit of a gift with which God will favor them: he will give them a new heart, a heart capable of knowing him (Jr 24:6-7). The true "remnant," therefore, are not those who escaped deportation and remained in Jerusalem, but those whom the exile has disposed to conversion, those whose hearts have been changed by the effect of a free gift.

From then on, conversion takes on a personal character, which appears even more clearly in the announcement of the new Covenant. This announcement rings out at the very moment when the destruction of Jerusalem seems to consecrate the destruction of the people unfaithful to the Covenant and to put in question God's fidelity to this people. God remains faithful to his people; but his people are not those who broke the Old Covenant; his people are a converted people, a people whose faults have been pardoned and who have received the gift of knowing and loving God's Law (Jr 31:31-34).

By this gift, a new Covenant is inaugurated and a new people constituted. This people is still called "house of Israel," but nothing prevents others from entering this house, for the only condition for entry is to have received a new heart from God. Did Jeremiah grasp the universality of the new Covenant? Whether he did or not, it is affirmed in a text which, if it is not from Jeremiah, was inserted into his book by the exiles, among whom his oracles kindled conversion and nourished hope:

> When that time comes, Jerusalem shall be called:

> The Throne of Yahweh; all the nations will gather there
> in the name of Yahweh and will no longer follow the
> dictates of their own stubborn hearts (Jr 3:17).

Thus the nations, too, are called by the grace of conversion.

In addition to Jeremiah there is another voice which makes
the call to conversion resound in the ears of the exiles, emphasizes the personal character of conversion, and proclaims that it
is a grace. This is the voice of Ezekiel, whom God has placed as
a sentinel responsible for his people; if he does not warn sinners,
he must give account to God for their loss (Ezk 3:16-21; 33:1-9).
One can understand then the pounding insistence with which
Ezekiel hammers his listeners on the theme of their personal responsibility.

Let no one pretend that his conversion is impossible: neither
his heredity nor his past life can prevent the sinner from being
converted, any more than they can guarantee perseverance to the
just man; a turning around is always possible. To all, the Lord
addresses the same threat of death and the same promise of life,
so that the just man might remain just and the sinner might be
converted. No one dies except by his own fault, for God does not
take pleasure in anyone's death; rather, he wants life, and the
conversion which is its condition (Ezk 18:1-32; 33:10-20).

When Ezekiel invites the sinner to "make a new heart and a
new spirit for himself" (Ezk 18:31), one could wonder whether
he is teaching that conversion is a grace. For does this not seem
to say that the sinner can be converted by his own strength? If
such were Ezekiel's thought, his call would be welcomed by few
sinners; they would tell him that he was demanding the impossible. But Ezekiel's thought cannot be that the Lord has anticipated the dispositions of those to whom he was going to speak:
"Son of man, the house of Israel will not listen to you, for it will
not listen to me. The whole house of Israel has only hard heads
and callous hearts" (Ezk 2:7).

Can the prophet expect a spontaneous conversion from such
listeners? No, but he can invite them to welcome the grace which

make a conversion possible, a conversion which is necessary even though they are incapable of it by themselves. To invite hardened sinners to "make a new heart and a new spirit for themselves" is to ask them to receive the gift which God wants to present to them, the gift which Ezekiel proclaims to them at the same time that he declares the pardon of their faults:

> I shall pour clean water over you and you will be
> cleansed. . . . I shall give you a new heart, and put a
> new spirit in you; I shall remove the heart of stone
> from your bodies and give you a heart of flesh instead.
> I shall put my spirit in you, and make you keep my laws
> and sincerely respect my observances. . . . You shall be my
> people and I will be your God (Ezk 36:25-28).

Thus, for Ezekiel, conversion is indeed a grace, a grace capable of healing even the most hardened heart, a grace of resurrection. In order to convince his listeners of this, and to arouse in them a hope which will receive this grace, the prophet presents them with a dramatic, unforgettable vision: dried bones are strewn on the ground of a plain; and then, at the word of Yahweh, vivified by his spirit, they rise up, a vast army (Ezk 37:1-14). God will bring this resurrected people back to its land, thereby manifesting his holiness to the nations: they will know that he is Yahweh (Ezk 37:14, 28; 39:27).

Here Israel's conversion seems to prime the conversion of the nations. In the Book of the Consolation of Israel and at the end of the Book of Isaiah, the universal call is explicitly affirmed; the grace of conversion is offered to everyone (Is 45:22); thanks to a mysterious Servant of God (Is 49:5-6), all can have access to the eternal covenant which unites God with his people (Is 54:1-3; 55:5-7; 56:3-8).

In post-exilic Judaism not everyone will understand this universality of the call to conversion; a narrow particularism will win the day and still be alive at the time of the apostolic preaching. The Acts of the Apostles, while witnessing to universality, show the astonishment of Jewish-Christians at the conversion of pagans and the gift of the Spirit which consummates it (Ac 10: 45; 11:18). The chosen people is jealous of its privileges, though it received them in order to be, among the nations, the prophet of the salvation which God offers to all, the prophet of the conversion which is the condition of this salvation.

The Book of Jonah reminds Israel of its prophetic mission. Jonah, who refuses to preach conversion to Nineveh; Jonah, who gets angry upon seeing Nineveh converted and pardoned by God; this Jonah is the symbol of the jealous Israel who has understood nothing of God's plan. Jonah wants the death of the sinner; God wants his conversion. Not without some humor, God shows Jonah that his jealousy, which betrays a profound misunderstanding of divine goodness, is also ridiculous. God, who calls all sinners to be converted, is always ready to pardon anyone who welcomes his call and the grace it conveys (Jon 4:2; cf. Ex 34:6).

III. CONVERSION, ACCEPTANCE OF GRACE

God has the initiative in the conversion of the sinner, and this conversion is impossible without the divine call which kindles it. But if this call implies the offer of transforming grace, it remains that it is also an invitation to a free choice, and that the grace offered must be accepted. What does the Old Testament tell us about this acceptance?

a) The Urgency of Conversion

The threats of the prophets emphasized first of all the urgency of conversion. When God speaks, one must hasten to answer him; if not, it will be too late:

> See what days are coming . . .
> They will stagger from sea to sea,
> wander from north to east,
> seeking the word of Yahweh
> and failing to find it (Am 8:11-12).

Now is the time to seek God, by seeking justice and humility, so as to be sheltered on the day of God's wrath; for:

> The great day of Yahweh is near,
> near, and coming with all speed. . . .
> A day of wrath, that day,
> a day of distress and agony (Zp 1:14-15; cf. 2:3).

The time of mercy must not be missed:

> Seek Yahweh while he is still to be found,
> call to him while he is still near.
> Let the wicked man abandon his way,
> the evil man his thoughts.
> Let him turn back to Yahweh who will take pity on him,
> to our God who is rich in forgiving (Is 55:6-7).

Echoed in the psalms, this prophetic call thus resounds endlessly throughout the worship:

> My people refused to listen to me,
> Israel refused to obey me. . . .
> If only my people would listen,
> if Israel would follow my ways,
> at one blow I would defeat their enemies
> and strike at all who attack them.
> While I would feed you on pure wheat
> and satisfy you with the wild rock honey (Ps 81:11,
> 13-14, 16).

Thus, to deliver his people and fill them up, Yahweh awaits only their conversion. On the contrary, if this conversion is delayed, the danger is serious: God will loathe those whom he had chosen freely:

> If only you would listen to him today,
> Do not harden your hearts as at Meribah . . .
> when your ancestors challenged me, tested me . . .
> For forty years that generation repelled me . . .

And so, in anger, I swore that not one
would reach the place of rest I had for them (Ps 95:7-11).

The authors of the wisdom literature also take up this prophetic
teaching on the urgency of conversion. In Proverbs, Wisdom
herself speaks:

> Pay attention to my warning:
> now I will pour out my heart to you,
> and tell you what I have to say.
> Since I have called and you have refused me . . .
> and rejected all my warnings,
> I, for my part, will laugh at your distress . . .
> when it bears down on you like a whirlwind.
> Then they shall call to me, but I will not answer,
> they shall seek me eagerly and shall not find me
> (Pr 1:23-28).

Ben Sirach sums up the whole tradition when he says to his
disciple:

> Do not delay your return to the Lord,
> do not put it off day after day;
> for suddenly the Lord's wrath will blaze out,
> and at the time of vengeance you will be utterly destroyed
> (Si 5:7).

b) The Prayer and Witness of the Converted

This urgent conversion consists in accepting divine pardon
and opening oneself to the grace which will renew the heart. The
converted person is the man who humbly acknowledges his need
of pardon and who confidently asks for the grace of his transformation; he is the man who prays with humility and trust.
These dispositions, of which we considered David a model, are
also the dispositions of the "poor," whose prayer is expressed in
so many psalms.

Among these psalms, the *Miserere* remains the psalm of conversion *par excellence*. There is first of all a confession; the psalm-

ist reveals his sense of sin, his opposition to God's will, his rupture with God:

> For I am well aware of my faults,
> I have my sin constantly in mind,
> having sinned against none other than you,
> having done what you regard as wrong.
> You are just when you pass sentence on me,
> blameless when you give judgment (Ps 51:3-4).

When this confession comes from a humble heart, God accepts it as a sacrifice:

> My sacrifice is this broken spirit,
> you will not scorn this crushed and broken heart
> (Ps 51:17).

From this contrite heart there springs forth also a confident prayer disclosing the sense of a God rich in mercy who wants the sinner's salvation:

> Have mercy on me, O God, in your goodness,
> in your great tenderness wipe away my faults;
> wash me clean of my guilt,
> purify me from my sin.
> God, create a clean heart in me,
> put into me a new and constant spirit,
> do not banish me from your presence,
> do not deprive me of your holy spirit (Ps 51:1-2, 10-11).

The psalmist learned from Jeremiah and Ezekiel that his purification and renewal are the work of God, the effect of the gift of his spirit. He expects his salvation from the goodness of God, and his trusting prayer is already a witness to this goodness which gratuitously saves him. But this witness is not enough for him. Converted by such goodness, he has only one desire: that sinners be converted and that their savior be praised; thus his prayer ends up in praise:

> I shall teach transgressors the way to you,
> and to you the sinners will return.
> Lord, open my lips,
> and my mouth will speak out your praise (Ps 51:13, 15).

The grace of conversion, welcomed by prayer, manifests its efficacy by making the converted person a witness. And his testimony must consist not only in words of praise, but also in a faithful life.

This is the lesson an anonymous prophet gives, upon return from exile, to a community discouraged by difficulties. This community gives itself over to penitential practices, such as fasting, in order to manifest its desire for conversion and to draw God's blessing upon itself. Now these practices, though humbling, are not sufficient to make man pleasing to God. The true seeking of God, says the prophet, consists in following God's ways by practicing justice (Is 58:3). And he adds:

> Look, you quarrel and squabble when you fast
> and strike the poor man with your fist.
> Fasting like yours today will never make
> your voice heard on high.
> Is not this the sort of fast that pleases me
> —it is the Lord Yahweh who speaks—
> to break unjust fetters
> and undo the thongs of the yoke,
> to let the oppressed go free, and break every yoke,
> to share your bread with the hungry,
> and shelter the homeless poor,
> to clothe the man you see to be naked
> and not turn from your own kin?
> Cry, and Yahweh will answer; call, and he will say,
> "I am here" (Is 58:4, 6-7, 9).

Such is the sign of perfect conversion; such is the witness that God expects from those to whom he has given the grace of conversion. This witness consists in imitating the one who said:

> For I am Yahweh, I rule with kindness,

justice and integrity on earth;
yes, these are what please me (Jr 9:24).

In order that all men can be converted and become imitators of God, and in order that they may follow ways which please God and lead into his presence, he who will seal the new and eternal Covenant in his blood must come.

c) The Suffering and Conversion of the Just

We have just brought to mind the sufferings of Christ and, with them, the mystery of the suffering of the Just One.

We have already seen the role of suffering in the conversion of the sinner. It has a two-fold aspect. Suffering is a punishment by which God arouses the sinner's conscience; it is also a pain that God imposes on the converted person in reparation for his offense and for the scandal he has caused (cf. 2 S 12:14).

This double role of punishment and expiation appears in the penitential liturgies and in the psalms which express their sense. In order to convert the sinner, the Lord "watches over the disasters" (Dn 9:2; Ba 2:7), that is to say over the fulfillment of the threats made to sinntrs. Under these blows from God, the sinner admits that he is submerged in sin and calls to his aid the God of his salvation (Ps 38:3-6, 19, 22-23). And the converted psalmist blesses God for having humbled him in order to bring him back from his strayings (Ps 119:67, 71). The guilty people humbles itself under the hand which punishes it, and imposes voluntary sufferings on itself: by "fasting, tears, cries of mourning," it comes back to its God and expects that God will return to it (Jl 2:12-13).

But, inversely, God's people are astonished when they suffer misfortunes which do not seem justified by any infidelity (Ps 44:10-23). And the suffering of the just causes scandal. It puts God's justice on trial. In the Book of Job, the sages make themselves advocates of God, accusing the unfortunate just man of being a sinner. But Job does not accept this traditional interpretation of suffering. If, in his ordeal, he blesses God (Jb 1:21; 2:10), Job still tells his friends not to defend God with untruths; they would do better to be silent and have pity on him (Jb 13:5-8; 19:21).

As for himself, like Jeremiah (Jr 12:1-2), Job turns toward God. He stands as a living interrogation before the God who strikes him, despite his fidelity. To Job's moving plea (Jb 29-31), God only responds with some questions of his own; or rather he invites Job to listen to the question which creation poses to him: "Who therefore is he to doubt the Creator?" (Jb 38-41). Job admits that this question silences him (Jb 40:4-5) and he is sorry for having spoken (Jb 42:6). He is converted. Not that he admits having been unfaithful, but he realizes that his fidelity does not give him the right to ask for an account from God, that God has the right to have one serve him "for nothing" (Jb 1:9).

This is true justice, the justice of faith. In order that Job might comply with this justice, God permitted his faith to be tested by suffering (Jb 1:6-11; 2:1-5); by this trial, Job is led to abandon himself totally to God. And in this consists the conversion of the just. The opposite of the Man who doubted, of Adam the sinner, Job is the Man fully converted, the just man who lives in faith (cf. Hab 2:4).

The source of this conversion, as we have said, is the grace of the Lord merited by the sufferings of the Just One (Ac 3:14) who, according to the prophecy of Isaiah, will accomplish God's plan (Is 53:10), justifying the multitude of sinners by taking away their sins and bearing their punishment (Is 53:4-6, 10-12). And this Just One will be the Lord himself who, in order to save us, will take the condition of a servant.

---

1. A. Gelin, "L'espérance dans l'ancien Testament," *Lumieère et Vie* 8 (January-March, 1959), 3.
2. A. Gelin, *Jérémie* (Paris, 1952), p. 61; Chapter Four focuses on the critique of institutions.

Conversion and Kingdom in the Synoptic Gospels

DOM MARC-FRANCOIS LACAN

Introduction: The Call of John the Baptist

The expectation of the Kingdom of God excited the people of Israel with a definite enthusiasm. God had chosen this people and become their King through the Covenant. The Book of the Consolation of Israel (Is 40-55) celebrates the approach of this longed-for Reign with unequalled power and brilliance. To be established thanks to an eternal Covenant, this Reign demands of sinful man a profound conversion.

> My people will therefore know my name;
> that day they will understand that it is I who say,
> "I am here."
> How beautiful on the mountains, are the feet of one
> who brings good news, who heralds peace, brings
> happiness, proclaims salvation, and tells Zion, "Your God
> is King!" (Is 52:6-7).
> With you I will make an everlasting covenant
> out of the favors promised to David.
> Seek Yahweh while he is still to be found,
> call to him while he is still near.
> Let the wicked man abandon his way,
> the evil man his thoughts.
> Let him turn back to Yahweh who will take pity on him,
> to our God who is rich in forgiving;
> for my thoughts are not your thoughts,
> my ways not your ways—it is Yahweh who speaks
> (Is 55:3, 6-8).

Now, in the synoptic gospels, it is important to note that John
the Baptist, whose preaching is the "beginning of the Good News
of Jesus Christ" (Mk 1:1), is presented as realizing the fundamental theme of the Book of the Consolation, as proclaimed in its
prologue. According to the three evangelists, John the Baptist is
"the voice of one crying in the desert: Prepare the way of the
Lord, make straight his path" (Mk 1:3; cf. Mt 3:3; Lk 3:4; Is
40:3). By citing this verse, the evangelists invite us to refer to its
immediate context in the Book of the Consolation, which ex-
plains why it is necessary to clear the Lord's way:

> Then the glory of Yahweh shall be revealed
> and all mankind shall see it. . . .
> Shout with a loud voice, joyful messenger to Jerusalem.
> Shout without fear, say to the towns of Judah, "Here is
>   your God."
> Here is the Lord Yahweh coming with power,
>   his arm subduing all things to him (Is 40:5, 9-10).

Thus John the Baptist realizes a prophecy in which conversion
and God's reign are closely united. Indeed, his mission is defined
as a call to conversion (*metanoia*):

> John the Baptist appeared in the wilderness, proclaiming
> a baptism of repentance for the forgiveness of sins.
> All Judea and all the people of Jerusalem made their
> way to him, and as they were baptized by him in the river
> Jordan they confessed their sins (Mk 1:4-5; cf. Mt 3:5-6;
> Lk 3:3).

To be baptized by John is to admit that one is a sinner, to declare
that one wants to be converted, to dispose oneself to receive the
pardon which God alone can give. Baptism of water is not the
sign of this pardon, but the sign of the conversion which leads
to pardon (Mt 3:11).

But, at the same time that John calls to conversion—and this
in itself does not distinguish him from previous prophets—he also

proclaims a presence, and in so doing inaugurates the Gospel, giving a unique character to his mission.

"Someone is following me, someone who is more powerful than I am, and I am not fit to kneel down and undo the strap of his sandals. I have baptized you with water, but he will baptize you with the Holy Spirit" (Mk 1:7; cf. Mt 3:11; Lk 3:15-16). The baptism of the one who is coming will not only be the sign of a conversion, but the sign of the gift of the Spirit. Evoked here is the prophecy which is the high point of the Book of Ezekiel (36:23-27). By this purification, which is the work of the Holy Spirit, the Reign of God, complete and universal in renewed hearts, will be established. He who is coming and whose presence John proclaims will not only call to conversion, he will give conversion its perfection; he will establish the Reign whose coming demands a perfect conversion.

The mission of the Precursor, therefore, already establishes the link between man's conversion and the Reign of God. We hear Jesus proclaim this link in the synoptic Gospels; and in this proclamation we will see the dimensions of Christian conversion. In order to uncover these dimensions, we will look successively at the gospels of Mark, Matthew, and Luke. If they all have common fundamental themes, each presents these themes in its own perspective. It is important to place oneself in these perspectives in order to see the theme of Christian conversion in all its nuances, to discover its nature, source, and fruits.

I. THE NATURE OF CONVERSION ACCORDING TO SAINT MARK

John preached conversion, and his preaching drew down on him the persecution of the powerful who found themselves condemned by it and who refused to be converted. He is imprisoned (Mk 1:14) and will be beheaded (Mk 6:16-29), thus fully accomplishing his mission as precursor, as the new Elijah (Mk 9:11-13).

When prison has put an end to John's preaching, Jesus proclaims the Good News: it consists in a fact and a demand. "The time has come . . . and the kingdom of God is close at hand." Such is the fact. The demand is: "Repent, and believe the Good News" (Mk 1:15).

This verse contains in germ the drama which unfolds throughout the whole of Mark's gospel, the drama of men encountering Jesus and of their choice when confronted by him. The unfolding of this drama will make us progressively recognize the nature of the conversion demanded by the presence of the Kingdom of God.

a) The Conversion of Faith

To be converted (*metanoein*) is not only to repent for one's sins, but also to bring about an interior transformation which blossoms out in a change of conduct, in a new orientation of life; a spiritual or moral "about face."

The sinner has turned away from God; he has been seduced by covetousness which has stifled God's voice (cf. Mk 4:19); he no longer has ears to hear. How will he come to realize that he is headed in the wrong direction? How will he be able to repent for having estranged himself from God and for continuing in this estrangement? The Kingdom of God is for him a mystery which he cannot understand because he is outside this Kingdom (Mk 4:11-12).

In order that the sinner may "turn around," an intervention from God is necessary; it will give thet sinner a new means of meeting the one from whom he has turned, and of submitting to his attraction. Without this intervention from God, without its efficacious pull which will determine the sinner's new orientation, the sinner will never cease following his covetousness and never repent for his sins. The primordial element of conversion, therefore, is not an effort at moral reform, a flight from evil; it is, rather, an encounter with an envoy from God and the acceptance given to his word.

This point throws light on the meaning of Jesus' call: it both invites one to conversion and indicates its fundamental act, which arouses all the others, namely, the act of faith. To be converted is first of all to believe in the Good News which Jesus proclaims. And what is this news? The presence of the Kingdom of God. This is indeed news capable of causing whoever hears it proclaimed to "turn around," on the condition that he believe in the one who proclaims it.

The Gospel of Mark lets us see how Jesus arouses faith in him, how he reveals little by little that the Kingdom is present in his person. The coming of the Kingdom is the arrival of Jesus. To accept the Kingdom is to accept him, Jesus, in faith.

But all do not accept him; some harden their hearts. Faith implies certain conditions; there are attitudes to be adopted, others to be rejected. Faith, with its conditions, constitutes the first aspect of conversion, its principle; we will examine this first. Then we will see what transformations faith in Jesus demands; these transformations are the second aspect of conversion, its achievement.

b) The Principle of Conversion: Faith and its Conditions

The voice of John has aroused the attention of Israel: someone is going to come after John, someone who brings the Holy Spirit (Mk 1:7-8). John's preaching was an invitation to open one's ears and one's heart. Everyone did not respond in the same way to this invitation. Mark shows us this from the very beginning of his gospel. As soon as he has related the proclamation which inaugurates Jesus' preaching, he gives us an example of perfect docility. Jesus calls four fishermen to follow him: "And at once [Simon and Andrew] left their nets and followed him. . . . And [James and John], leaving their father Zebedee in the boat with the men he employed. . . . went after him" (Mk 1:17, 18, 20). Later it will be the same with the publican Levi (Mk 2:14).

But the attitude of some of the scribes is exactly the opposite. Jesus has already aroused admiration by the power of his word; the authority of his teaching is confirmed by this power; with a word, he delivers the possessed and cures the sick (Mk 1:27, 31, 34). Therefore, "everybody is looking for [him]," and "people from all around would come to him" (Mk 1:37, 45). However, when Jesus declares to a paralytic who has been brought to him, "My child, your sins are forgiven," the reaction of the scribes is to close their hearts up: "He is blaspheming. Who can forgive sins but God?" (Mk 2:7).

Are they at least going to change their attitude when they see Jesus read their hearts and give them, by curing the paralytic, clear proof that "the Son of Man has authority on earth to forgive sins" (Mk 2:8, 11)? Not at all. They merely watch and criticize the young rabbi and his disciples (Mk 2:16, 18, 24). Malevolence inspires them. One sabbath, Jesus enters a synagogue where there is a man with a withered hand: "And they were watching him to see if he would cure him on the sabbath day, hoping for something to use against him" (Mk 3:2). Jesus makes a last effort to make himself understood. "Then he said to them, 'Is it against the law on the sabbath day to do good, or to do evil; to save life, or to kill?' But they said nothing. Then, grieved to find them so obstinate, he looked angrily round at them, and said to the man, 'Stretch out your hand.' He stretched it out and his hand was better. The Pharisees went out and at once began to plot with the Herodians against him, discussing how to destroy him" (Mk 3:4-6).

From now on, it is settled. They will declare Jesus possessed by an unclean spirit; they will attribute to the prince of devils the works which manifest the presence of the Holy Spirit in Jesus. Jesus declares this blasphemy an eternal sin because it is a refusal of light, a refusal which renders conversion impossible (Mk 3:22-30). For men thus disposed, miracles are useless; Jesus declares this, sighing from deep within his heart (Mk 8:11-12), and he puts his disciples on guard against this deep attitude which he calls the yeast of the Pharisees (Mk 8:15).

At the foot of the cross, ridiculing the crucified, they will give a final proof of this attitude of refusal in the face of truth. "The chief priests and the scribes mocked him among themselves.

. . . 'He saved others,' they said, 'he cannot save himself. Let the Christ, the king of Israel, come down from the cross now, for us to see it and believe' " (Mk 15:31-32). They lie in saying that they would believe if they were to see. For they have just attested that Jesus saved others, thus recalling the miracles they have seen; now, despite that, they have not believed. Why?

The question is a serious one. Jesus responded to it the day the disciples were trying to keep the little children away from him. "But when Jesus saw this he was indignant and said to them, 'Let the little children come to me; do not stop them; for it is to such as these that the kingdom of God belongs. *I tell you solemnly, anyone who does not welcome the kingdom of God like a little child will never enter it* " (Mk 10:14-15). This fundamental disposition is a *sine qua non* condition for conversion and, therefore, for admission into the Kingdom of God; it is necessary to be like children, to be open. The emotion which Jesus shows on this occasion underlines the importance of the lesson.

Jesus denounces obstacles to this openness of heart to the gift of God. The parable of the sower discloses how the Word is prevented from bearing fruit (Mk 4:14-19); wealth is one of the most frequent obstacles, and many episodes in the gospel illustrate the teaching of the parable in a concrete way. The Gerasenes are so attached to their pigs that instead of reflecting on the meaning of the miraculous event which deprives them of the pigs, they beg Jesus to go away (Mk 5:15-17). The rich young man, who has only to become poor in order to follow Jesus, goes away full of sadness instead of casting off his riches. And Jesus says emphatically: "How hard it is for those who have riches to enter the kingdom of God" (Mk 10:21-25).

But if wealth is an obstacle, it is one only to the degree that it makes a man satisfied. And there is a satisfaction, a self-sufficiency of the spiritual order more dangerous than that which comes from money. How will the man who has a good conscience because he believes himself to be in possession of truth and justice be open to this gift which Jesus brings, to this free gift without which one is outside of the Kingdom and incapable of being converted?

This is the key to the attitude of the Pharisees. They are in possession of a tradition, which, as the practical and detailed commentary on the Mosaic Law, is their rule of life. They forget to ask themselves if the same spirit which animates the divine Word animates the commentary which ought to help them to understand this Word properly and to observe it better. But, by reason of this tradition, the Pharisees even change the Law of God, to the point of nullifying it (Mk 7:6-13). Jesus vigorously reproaches them for this, but what he especially denounces is the fundamental hypocrisy, already branded by Isaiah (Is 29:13), which reduces worship to external rites.

This external observance is the Pharisees' touchstone of justice. They believe themselves to be just by reason of this observance; anxious about the rites of purification, they are not concerned about the purity of their hearts. Their fidelity to these rites renders them satisfied with themselves instead of supporting in them an awareness of being sinners in need of conversion.

In order to awaken this need of conversion, Jesus invites his listeners to a first turning around: they must change their conception of purity. The purity to be sought after is purity of the heart (Mk 7:18-23). Now whoever examines his heart is no longer self-satisfied; he realizes his sin and his need of salvation. It is for this man, and for all who need to be saved, that Jesus has come; he has come to call sinners to conversion (Mk 2:17).

To these sinners Jesus brings deliverance, provided that they recognize themselves as sinners and believe in him. This humility and faith, both of which the Pharisees refused, constitute the principle of conversion; wherever Jesus finds them, he exercises his saving mission. The example of the pagan who obtains the healing of his daughter through his confident supplication and humble response is particularly enlightening (Mk 7:25-29). His humble faith seems to force the hand of Christ.

This indeed is why Jesus never ceases inviting those who come to him to believe; his salvific power will thus be free to act. "Everything is possible for anyone who has faith," he says to the father of the epileptic child (Mk 9:23). In order to be saved, one must believe that everything is possible with God (Mk 10:27) and pray with faith (Mk 11:22-24).

c) The Completion of Conversion: The Demands of Faith

By making Peter's confession the center of his gospel, Mark highlights two key points: that Jesus expects us to believe in him, and that this faith is the fundamental conversion to which he calls us.

Slowly, by his preaching and miracles, throughout controversies and opposition, Jesus reveals himself to his disciples as the one whom John announced; he is not John raised from the dead, nor a prophet like the others, as the crowd thinks (Mk 6:14-16). Who is he, then? Peter answers: You are the Christ (Mk 8:29).

If this affirmation is the center of Mark's gospel, it is not, however, its summit; it is rather the hinge which joins the gospel's two stages. Indeed faith in Christ is the acceptance of the Kingdom; it is the principle of the conversion which gives access to the Kingdom; but it demands also that one follow Christ up to the end in order to enter into the eternal Kingdom.

To follow Christ means that we let Christ complete our conversion, that we let his word reshape our thoughts, that we let his example refashion our conduct, and that we let his love completely transform us and make us his witnesses so that all might believe and be saved (cf. Mk 16:15-16).

Thus, hardly has Peter proclaimed his faith when Jesus reveals its mysterious content to him. This Christ which he has just confessed will accomplish his mission by undergoing suffering and death and by rising from the dead (Mk 8:31). Immediately Peter shows how imperfect his conversion is: he dares to reprove Christ (Mk 8:32). In order to make him realize how deep a spiritual transformation faith requires, Christ rebukes him by calling him Satan: for. like Satan, Peter puts himself in opposition to God's plan: "Because the way you think is not God's way but man's" (Mk 8:33).

What, then, are the thoughts of God? The answer is found in a teaching of Jesus which the three Synoptic Gospels link with the account of Peter's confession. "Anyone who loses his life for my sake, and for the sake of the gospel, will save it" (Mk 8:35). To follow Jesus, therefore, is to walk in a direction diametrically opposed to that which men spontaneously follow; but, by this very fact, one becomes a witness of the Gospel, a witness of Christ, and a witness of the salvation which he has come to bring about.

Practically speaking, what is this way in which it is necessary to follow Christ in contempt of human wisdom? In order to tell us, Jesus employs an image which foretells how he himself will bring about our salvation. For him it will not be an image, but the reality of having to carry the cross on which he will die. What does this teaching which Jesus gives to the crowd mean for us in our daily lives: "If anyone wants to be a follower of mine, let him renounce himself and take up his cross and follow me" (Mk 8:34). One can understand the meaning of this image by listening to the lesson Jesus gives his disciples on two occasions when they show themselves to be all too human in their thoughts and desires, each concerned with being the greatest among them. Jesus teaches them the law of his Kingdom and the continual conversion that it demands: "If anyone wants to be first, he must make himself last of all and servant of all" (Mk 9:35; cf. 10:42-44). By doing this, he will be imitating the Son of Man, who "did not come to be served but to serve, and to give his life as a ransom for many" (Mk 10:45).

The rule of conduct thus given is tied to a conversion in the concept of messianism. Temporal messianism, which underlies the Pharisees' perfidious question about the tribute to Caesar, is rejected. Jesus teaches with perfect clarity that to render to Caesar that which is Caesar's does not prevent one from following the way of God by rendering to God what is due to him (Mk 12:14-17), that is to say, by being obedient to the law of the Kingdom, which consists in the full love of God and neighbor (Mk 12:28-33).

And, finally, a last conversion remains to be carried out. Jesus suggests it in questioning the Pharisees on the Messiah, the Son of David: If David calls the Messiah his Lord, how can one say that the Messiah is the son of David (Mk 12:37)? The answer, which no one can give, was, nevertheless, already in the parable of the unfaithful winegrowers; the last messenger sent by the owner of the vineyard, this vineyard which is Israel, is his beloved Son (Mk 12:6). The Son of man is therefore the Son of God. Jesus will testify to this, at the decisive hour, before the Sanhedrin (Mk 14:62), which will cry blasphemy (Mk 14:64).

And this affirmation of Jesus demanded a revolution in the religious thought of the Israelite, as it still demands of anyone who has a sense of God and his transcendence. Is there not an unbridgeable abyss between the God who is the Holy One of Israel and creator of the universe, on the one hand, and man, his sinful creature, on the other? A man can be said to be a son of God in a metaphorical sense, as a way of expressing a divine choice favoring a privileged people or individual. But is it conceivable that a man could say he is God and call God his father in the strong sense of the term? If one can admit the possibility, what is to be said when this alleged Son of God lets himself be crucified?

Nevertheless, this is the mystery one must believe in order to have access to salvation. This is the Good News which one must bear witness to in the whole universe (Mk 16:15-16), attesting that the one who was crucified is risen (Mk 16:6) and is seated at the right hand of God (Mk 16:17). We can understand better now why Jesus proclaimed "Be converted," before saying "Believe in the Good News" (Mk 1:15). It is impossible for someone to believe unless he is ready to relinquish his own thoughts in order to be open to the thoughts of God.

Who gives us the power of this conversion, of this supreme *metanoia?* The very one who calls us to it, the one whose word reveals the mystery of the Kingdom to us, the one whose death gives all men access to this Kingdom. Mark shows the efficacy of this death by quoting the words of the centurion facing Jesus just after he has died: "Truly this man was the Son of God" (Mk 15:39). The pagan who says this—whatever be the value of the words he uses—witnesses to his intimate transformation; he attests that the man who has just been crucified because he said he was the Son of God is nevertheless worthy of faith. He believes what this man has said; he believes that this man is the Son of God, in the sense in which he has said it.

Every man who relives the drama of Jesus by hearing Mark's testimony can, if he does not close his heart as the Pharisees did, believe as the centurion did. His faith will be the principle of a total conversion which will give him access to the Kingdom, that is to say, to Life (cf. Mk 9:43, 45, 47).

II. The Fruits of Conversion according to Saint Matthew

One finds in Matthew the same teachings as in Mark; the texts themselves are sometimes parallel. But the perspective has changed. In Mark, Jesus is the King in whom the Kingdom is present, the King who comes to seek the sinful man and invite him to a choice. Faith is the fundamental conversion to which Jesus calls him; in addition, Mark reveals all the demands of this faith.

In Matthew, Jesus is always the King; but he teaches the community of those who believe in him, the community which is his Kingdom on earth; his teaching is oriented toward making this community a missionary community whose witness arouses the conversion of men of all nations (Mt 28:19-20). The listener whom Matthew aims at is not the man outside the Kingdom, but the one within it, "the son of the Kingdom" (Mt 13:38); this disciple will be reminded of the conversion by which he has entered the Kingdom, of course, but this is in order to invite him "to produce the fruits" which this conversion demands, according to the expression employed by John the Baptist in castigating the Pharisees (Mt 3:8).

The axis of Matthew's gospel is the proclamation of Christian justice which is the fruit of conversion and the requirement of faith. Now, this justice is nothing other than a permanent conversion; Jesus defines the just man in a word: he is the one who "seeks," who has never stopped "seeking the kingdom of God and his justice" (Mt 6:33).

This is why Matthew insists so much on the condemnation of the Pharisee's false justice (Mt 5:20); it serves as a contrast to the true justice of which Jesus is the unique model. The Pharisees are like a mirror in which the Christian can contemplate what he would become himself, if he were to give up his effort at conversion.

a) The False Justice Which Renders Conversion Sterile

"But if you are repentant, produce the appropriate fruit, and do not presume to tell yourselves, 'We have Abraham for our father,' because, I tell you, God can raise children for Abraham from these stones. Even now the axe is laid to the roots of the trees, so that any tree which fails to produce good fruit will be cut down and thrown on the fire" (Mt 3:8-10). Thus speaks John the Baptist to the Pharisees who rely on their privilege as sons of Abraham, which makes them sons of the Kingdom; now, John tells them, and Jesus will tell them again, if their faith is sterile they will be cast outside (Mt 8:10).

The pharisaical attitude branded by Jesus is before all else that of the satisfied man. Such is the son who contents himself to say yes to his father, but does not obey him by going to work in his vineyard (Mt 21:30). Such is the rabbi who is contented to teach others and place a heavy burden on their shoulders, without lifting a finger himself to lighten the burden, without making his life consistent with his word (Mt 23:3-4). Such is the hypocrite who is satisfied with external acts of virtue, inspired by his desire to be admired, without doing anything which the purification of his heart demands (Mt 23:5, 23-28). The best acts, almsgiving, prayer, and fasting (Mt 6:2, 5, 16), are corrupted by the pride which inspires them. And this appearance of justice with which the Pharisees satisfy themselves makes them incapable of conversion.

Jesus' call to conversion finds the Pharisees deaf; for Jesus surely has them in mind first and foremost when he says: "their ears are dull of hearing, and they have shut their eyes, /for fear they should see with their eyes, /hear with their ears,/ understand with their heart,/ and be converted/ and be healed by me" (Mt 13:15). Signs, even that of Jonah, are fruitless for those who are deliberately blind (Mt 12:38-41). Confronted with the sign of the Resurrection itself, they coldly invent a deliberate lie to deny it (Mt 28:11-15).

The believer, who is converted by a free gift of God, must take care then not to sterilize in himself the grace he has received by being proud of it. On the contrary, he must give witness to this grace in order to invite all men to receive it as he has. That is true justice.

b) The True Justice Which is Permanent Conversion

The model of true justice is Jesus, who defines himself in saying to his disciples: "Shoulder my yoke and learn from me, for I am gentle and humble in heart (Mt 11:29).

He gives a luminous example of this humility by beginning his preaching with the reception of John's baptism. John protests that this reverses their roles. But Jesus states that this is why he has humbled himself in taking our condition; this is why he will further humble himself in his passion when he will take our sins upon himself (Mt 26:28) and make us just. The baptism is the symbol of the passion (cf. Mk 10:38; Lk 12:50) by which justice will be accomplished.

To be humble like the Lord, man must "change and become like little children" (Mt 18:3). But conversion is not an act to be done once and for all. For, once one becomes like a little child, he must remain such. To become a child is to become spiritually poor (Mt 5:3), to hunger and thirst for justice (Mt 5:6). It is not a passive attitude which one settles into, but a humble and confident ardor which one must renew, an enthusiasm which results from a sense of our calling and at the same time from a sense of our powerlessness to respond to this calling by ourselves.

"To become a child" is to recognize our impotence and, by that very recognition, to open ourselves to the grace which will make us capable of responding to our calling, capable of reaching true justice by accomplishing the will of the Father who is in heaven (Mt 7:21). This will is that we might be perfect as the heavenly Father is perfect (Mt 5:48). What a transformation that supposes! One can understand why conversion must be unceasing. But the goal of this conversion is not our perfection. The heart of this conversion is the seeking of God's glory, the desire that the Father who is in heaven be glorified by all men (Mt 5:16). Here humility and love blend in the filial attitude which is the fruit of a permanent conversion and the perfection of Christian justice.

This permanent conversion will manifest itself in our relations with our neighbor. To be perfect like the Father is to be merciful like him. The beatitude of the merciful is connected with that of those who thirst for justice (Mt 5:6-7). The merciful cooperate in the arrival of the justice for which they thirst, the justice which consists in the glorification of the Father and the establishment of his Reign, the primary object of their prayer (Mt 6:9-10). Indeed, the merciful reveal the face of their Father (Mt 5:45); but their conduct supposes a transformation of the human concept of justice.

To love those who love us is just. But those who hate and persecute us? Not to give them evil for evil seems already more than is demanded by justice as expressed in the talionic law (Mt 5:38; cf. Ex 21:24). But to pray for them with a prayer inspired by love supposes that man is renewed, that his ways have become those of God. Brotherly love, even of enemies, will manifest itself by a pardon renewed as often as necessary (Mt 18:22);

Jesus tells Peter this, and he reinforces his teaching with the parable of the merciless servant (Mt 18:23-25). The Lord's Prayer echoes this parable and engraves its lesson in the hearts of the disciples; in the midst of the requests of this prayer, the Lord has inserted an affirmation: "As we have forgiven our debtors." One who would refuse to make this affirmation his own could not invoke God as his Father nor expect his prayer to be granted (Mt 5:12, 14, 15).

This conversion of the moral life is rooted in a conversion in our way of perceiving. This fact is thrown into relief by a page of Matthew's that is peculiarly his own, a solemn page which he places at the end of the eschatological discourse, just before the account of the Last Supper and the Passion: the impressive fresco of the Last Judgment. There the Justice of God is revealed, a salvific justice which casts out of the Kingdom only those who have not imitated the mercy of the Father; there it is revealed that the Judgment is already taking place throughout our life, determined by our attitude toward the least of men; in order that this attitude may be "just," Jesus invites us to see himself, the King of the eternal Kingdom, the Son of Man who is also the Son of God (Mt 25:31, 34), in the least of these little ones who are his brothers (Mt 25:40, 45). Everything we do for these little ones, everything we refuse them, we do for him, we refuse him.

The whole of the Christian life, therefore, is a conversion. Without this conversion we cannot be witnesses of the Father's mercy. Sleep lies in wait for us, like the virgins of the parable who have let their lamps go out (Mt 25:5; cf. 5:15-16), like Peter and the disciples at the hour of the agony (Mt 26:40). The spiritual sleep which the satisfied fall into is a permanent temptation which one cannot resist unless he follows Jesus' advice: "Watch and pray" (Mt 26:41).

III. THE SOURCE OF CONVERSION ACCORDING TO SAINT LUKE

We know on what conditions one becomes a son of the Kingdom, and on what conditions one continues to be such. The word "conversion" sums up these conditions; it expresses the transformation which is the heart of the Christian life; this transformation makes children of us, gentle and humble like Jesus, seeking without ceasing, like him, the glory of the Father.

It should be noted that the word "conversion," as well as the corresponding verb, is more frequent in Luke than in Mark and Matthew put together.[1] This is a significant insistence, although the theme of conversion is also expressed in many texts which do not employ the word itself.

To understand Luke's own distinctive perspective, we must recall the link which connects his gospel to the Acts of the Apostles: the gift of the Spirit. This gift is the goal of Jesus' work, as related in the gospel; this gift, accomplished on the day of Pentecost, is the principle of the Church's blossoming, as related in the Acts. Jesus, filled with the Spirit (Lk 4:1), comes in order to communicate this Holy Spirit to us, which is the Father's gift *par excellence* (Lk 11:13), and to bring fire to the earth (Lk 12:49). By undergoing the baptism of the Passion (Lk 12:50), Jesus realizes God's plan: he baptizes us in the Holy Spirit and fire (Lk 3:16) in order that "all mankind shall see the salvation of God" (Lk 3:6; cf. Is 40:5).

Luke particularly insists on the universality of salvation; and at the end of his gospel, he defines the apostolic mission as the "preaching to all nations, in the Name of Christ, of conversion in view of the pardon of sins" (Lk 24:47; cf. Mt 28:19). That is to say that if salvation is universal, conversion is its necessary condition.

Because salvation is universal, Luke's gospel is one of joy; because conversion is the condition of salvation, Luke's gospel is one of absolute renunciation. But how can joy and renunciation, two so different moods, coexist? In order to understand this, we must, with Luke's help, discover their common source: the mercy of the Father. It is this mercy which kindles our conversion by filling us with divine joy, thus making us capable of every renunciation.

a) Conversion, Condition of the Joy of Salvation

Luke puts the demands of faith in even greater relief than Mark and Matthew through his way of formulating them. Conversion is necessary: "I say to you, if you do not repent, you will all perish" (Lk 13:3, 5). Conversion is urgent: the barren fig tree is going to be cut down if it does not bear fruit (Lk 13:6-9). Conversion demands a universal renunciation: "None of you can be my disciple unless he gives up all his possessions" (Lk 14:33). And without regrets: "Once the hand is laid on the plough, no one who looks back is fit for the kingdom of God" (Lk 9:62). Total self-denial is demanded day in and day out: "If anyone wants to be a follower of mine, let him renounce himself and take up his cross every day and follow me" (Lk 9:23).

The starting point of such a total conversion is the sense of sin, which inspires the humble prayer of the publican: "God, be merciful to me, a sinner" (Lk 18:13). The severity of this conversion is tolerable only if the sense of salvation comes to fill with joy the hearts of the converted who know their names are written in heaven (Lk 10:20). This joy, which made John leap in his mother's womb (Lk 1:41), also fills Zacchaeus when Jesus, received in the house of this "sinner," arouses his conversion and proclaims his salvation (Lk 19:5-9).

But without conversion, there is no true joy. Thus the wealth which prevents conversion is declared a misfortune (Lk 6:24). Thus pride, which renders one self-satisfied and removes the awareness of sin, deprives one of salvation; the proud Pharisee needs forgiveness as much as the publican whom he scorns, but he does not receive the pardon obtained by the publican's humble prayer (Lk 18:10-14).

Those who refuse to follow the way of conversion must weep for themselves, for they are like dry and barren trees (Lk 23:28). And Jesus weeps over Jerusalem which would not understand his call to the conversion that is the condition for peace (Lk 19:41-44).

b) The Mercy of the Father, Source of Conversion and Joy

In order to triumph over the hardening of men's hearts, it is necessary to reveal to them the mystery of God's love, the mercy of his Fatherly heart. This revelation is Luke's distinctive mission: he is the evangelist of mercy.

God's love manifests itself through the sending of his beloved Son (Lk 3:22) who comes to call sinners to conversion (Lk 5:32): "For the Son of Man has come to seek out and save what was lost" (Lk 19:10). At what price? The triple announcement of the Passion, reported in the three Synoptic Gospels, says it clearly (Lk 9:24, 44; 18:31-33). And, after the Resurrection, Jesus emphasizes again that his Passion was part of the plan of salvation announced by the Scriptures (Lk 24:25-27, 44-46).

When Jesus, on the cross, asks his Father's pardon of his executioners who "do not know what they are doing" (Lk 23:34), is he not praying for all sinners who do not realize from what love they are closing themselves off? In any case, it is to reveal this love to them that he has come and given his life. How Jesus did this is shown by Luke in some of his most distinctively personal pages, which are without doubt the most poignant in the Gospel.

There is first of all the woman, a public sinner, who was transformed because she had faith in Jesus, because she believed in the salvation that he proclaimed (Lk 7:50). She was moved by love, and gave Jesus a testimony of this love, which was also an expression of her humble repentance. Faced with the Pharisee who despises this woman and is not even moved by her unsettling humility, Jesus declares that this woman is pure; the mercy which aroused her conversion, in which she had faith and to which she responded with so much love, has completely forgiven and renewed her (Lk 7:37-48).

Even more poignant in its brevity is the dialogue between Jesus and the repentant thief crucified with him. What faith and humble trust there is in the thief's appeal: "Remember me, Jesus, when you come into your kingdom" (Lk 23:42). The solemn response reveals what an all-powerful love the converted heart opens itself to: "Indeed, I promise you, today you will be with me in paradise" (Lk 23:43).

The mystery of infinite mercy is revealed in this dialogue; in order to grasp its depth, it is necessary to contemplate the drama of Calvary in the light of three parables which Luke groups together on a truly singular page (Lk 15).

The first of these three parables speaks of the sheep which Matthew told us *had gone astray* (Mt 18:12-14); Matthew focused on the sheep which must recognize its guilt. Luke focuses on the shepherd whose heart suffers because one of his hundred sheep *"is lost"* (Lk 15:4). This loving shepherd sets out in search of this unique, irreplaceable sheep. "And when he has found it, would he not joyfully take it on his shoulders and then, when he returns home, call together his friends and neighbors, saying, 'Rejoice with me'. . ." (Lk 15:5-6).

This is the revealing word: joy. When Jesus heard the words which expressed the conversion of the thief crucified with him, his good shepherd's heart rejoiced; and all of heaven was in joy with him. For "there will be more rejoicing in heaven over one repentant sinner than over ninety-nine virtuous men who have no need of repentance" (Lk 15:7). The parable of the lost drachma illustrates the same truth and the same mystery.

Is there not something there to open the most closed heart, making it a gushing spring of tears? The Savior's joy depends on the conversion of the sinner. The Son of Man came only to look for the sinner, and he poured out his blood in order to recover him (Lk 22:20); the sinner has only to let himself be carried and brought back to the fold, and the Savior will rejoice.

And not only the Savior, but also the Father, whose beloved Son he is. The parable of the prodigal son unrolls a film which displays the corruption and meanness of the human heart, and in which, once more, false justice appears worse than sin sincerely admitted. But the father is there; full of mercy, he goes out to meet the son who comes back to him (Lk 15:20) and who declares himself a sinner, unworthy of being called a son (Lk 15:21). With a word, the father reveals both the power of his forgiveness and the joy of forgiving: "We are going to have a feast, a celebration, because this son of mine was dead and has come back to life; he was lost and is found" (Lk 15:23-24). And to his other son, who is jealous of his converted brother, the father says: "It was only right we should celebrate and rejoice, because your brother here was dead and has come to life; he was lost and is found" (Lk 15:32).

The joy of the Father is to be merciful. And his mercy is the source of our conversion and our salvation. We are sons of the heavenly Father only if his mercy converts us, only if we convert ourselves in order to delight our Father, only if we find our joy in the conversion of our brothers, the condition of their salvation.

We must cooperate in this salvation by being merciful as our Father is merciful (Lk 6:36). This cooperation has as its condition a conversion in our whole way of perceiving, a conversion which Jesus invites us to in the parable of the good Samaritan. This same conversion in our way of perceiving others was at issue in Matthew's Last Judgment scene: we were invited to see Jesus in each of our brothers. In Luke's parable, Jesus invites us to view our brothers as he views them: with that love which tends toward sinners and sees their unhappiness, with that merciful love which desires the sinner's salvation and restores him to life by generously redeeming him.

We do not have to ask ourselves, therefore, "Who is my neighbor?" as if, among men, we could exclude some from our love. Jesus turns this question around; we must ask ourselves: "How will I show that I am a man's neighbor, whoever he may be?" (Lk 10:29, 36). The answer is undeniably clear: "By being merciful to him" (Lk 10:37). And Jesus completes this answer with a rule of action which will make us imitators of the Father and participants in his life: "Go, do this and life is yours" (Lk 10:28-36).

Conclusion: The Grace of Conversion and the Joy of the Converted

Such are the dimensions of Christian conversion. It is not simply a remorse for sin. Judas is overcome with remorse, but with the despairing remorse of the hopeless; he is not converted, for want of faith in the Savior's mercy (Mt 27:3, 5). The bitter tears of Peter are those of conversion, for Jesus "has prayed for Peter that his faith may not fail," and that, "once converted, he might strengthen his brothers" (Lk 22:32, 62).

Conversion is a grace, a grace of the resurrection of the sinner (Lk 15:24, 32) who becomes a child of God. This transformation, inaugurated by faith in Jesus, demands that man constantly follow Christ in the way of humility by seeking only God's glory, and in the way of love by being merciful to his brothers. The converted person is a witness to the grace whose source is the Father's mercy; he witnesses to it through his joy which is communion in the joy of the Father.

Where this joy prevails, the Father's Reign has been established, thanks to Jesus the Savior. From the Ascension, this joy fills the disciples' hearts. It overflows in praise, waiting for the hour when the power of the Spirit will make these converted in turn the converters of all the nations (Lk 24:47-53).

---

1. *Conversion*: Mark, once; Matthew, twice; Luke, five times. *To be converted*: Mark twice; Matthew, five times; Luke, nine times.

Part Three

PSYCHOLOGICAL PERSPECTIVES

The Divided Self and Conversion

WILLIAM JAMES

At the close of [the last lecture] we were brought into full view of the contrast between the two ways of looking at life which are characteristic respectively of what we called the healthy-minded, who need to be born only once, and of the sick souls, who must be twice-born in order to be happy. The result is two different conceptions of the universe of our experience. In the religion of the once-born the world is a sort of rectilinear or one-storied affair, whose accounts are kept in one denomination, whose parts have just the values which naturally they appear to have, and of which a simple algebraic sum of pluses and minuses will give the total worth. Happiness and religious peace consist in living on the plus side of the account. In the religion of the twice-born, on the other hand, the world is a double-storied mystery. Peace cannot be reached by the simple addition of pluses and elimination of minuses from life. Natural good is not simply insufficient in amount and transient, there lurks a falsity in its very being. Cancelled as it all is by death if not by earlier enemies, it gives no final balance, and can never be the thing intended for our lasting worship. It keeps us from our real good, rather; and renunciation and despair of it are our first step in the direction of the truth. There are two lives, the natural and the spiritual, and we must lose the one before we can participate in the other.

In their extreme forms, of pure naturalism and pure salvationism, the two types are violently contrasted; though here as in most other current classifications, the radical extremes are somewhat ideal abstractions, and the concrete human beings whom we oftenest meet are intermediate varieties and mixtures. Practically, however, you all recognize the difference: you understand, for example, the disdain of the methodist convert for the mere sky-blue healthy-minded moralist; and you likewise enter into the aversion of the latter to what seems to him the diseased subjectivism of the Methodist, dying to live, as he calls it, and making of paradox and the inversion of natural appearances the essence of God's truth.

The psychological basis of the twice-born character seems to be a certain discordancy or heterogeneity in the native temperament of the subject, an incompletely unified moral and intellectual constitution.

Now in all of us, however constituted, but to a degree the greater in proportion as we are intense and sensitive and subject to diversified temptations, and to the greatest possible degree if we are decidedly psychopathic, does the normal evolution of character chiefly consist in the straightening out and unifying of the inner self. The higher and the lower feelings, the useful and the erring impulses, begin by being a comparative chaos within us—they must end by forming a stable system of functions in right subordination. Unhappiness is apt to characterize the period of order-making and struggle. If the individual be of tender conscience and religiously quickened, the unhappiness will take the form of moral remorse and compunction, of feeling inwardly vile and wrong, and of standing in false relations to the author of one's being and appointer of one's spiritual fate. This is the religious melancholy and "conviction of sin" that have played so large a part in the history of Protestant Christianity. The man's interior is a battle-ground for what he feels to be two deadly hostile selves, one actual, the other ideal.

* * *

To be converted, to be regenerated, to receive grace, to experience religion, to gain an assurance, are so many phrases which denote the process, gradual or sudden, by which a self hitherto divided, and consciously wrong inferior and unhappy, becomes unified and consciously right superior and happy, in consequence of its firmer hold upon religious realities. This at least is what conversion signifies in general terms, whether or not we believe that a direct divine operation is needed to bring such a moral change about.

Now for a minuter survey of the constituent elements of the conversion process. If you open the chapter on Association, of any treatise on Psychology, you will read that a man's ideas, aims, and objects form diverse internal groups and systems, relatively independent of one another. Each 'aim' which he follows awakens a certain specific kind of interested excitement, and gathers a certain group of ideas together in subordination to it as its associates; and if the aims and excitements are distinct in kind, their groups of ideas may have little in common. When one group is present and engrosses the interest, all the ideas connected with other groups may be excluded from the mental field. The President of the United States when, with paddle, gun, and fishing-rod, he goes camping in the wilderness for a vacation, changes his system of ideas from top to bottom. The presidential anxieties have lapsed into the background entirely; the official habits are replaced by the habits of a son of nature, and those who knew the man only as the strenuous magistrate would not "know him for the same person" if they saw him as the camper.

If now he should never go back, and never again suffer political interests to gain dominion over him, he would be for practical intents and purposes a permanently transformed being. Our ordinary alterations of character, as we pass from one of our aims to another, are not commonly called transformations, because each of them is so rapidly succeeded by another in the reverse direction; but whenever one aim grows so stable as to expel definitively its previous rivals from the individual's life, we tend to speak of the phenomenon, and perhaps to wonder at it, as a "transformation."

These alterations are the completest of the ways in which a
self may be divided. A less complete way is the simultaneous
coexistence of two or more different groups of aims, of which
one practically holds the right of way and instigates activity,
whilst the others are only pious wishes, and never practically
come to anything. Saint Augustine's aspirations to a purer life,
in our last lecture, were for a while an example. Another would
be the President in his full pride of office, wondering whether
it were not all vanity, and whether the life of a wood-chopper
were not the wholesomer destiny. Such fleeting aspirations are
mere *velleitates*, whimsies. They exist on the remoter outskirts
of the mind, and the real self of the man, the center of his energies, is occupied with an entirely different system. As life goes
on, there is a constant change of our interests, and a consequent
change of place in our systems of ideas, from more central to
more peripheral, and from more peripheral to more central parts
of consciousness.

What brings such changes about is the way in which emotional
excitement alters. Things hot and vital to us today are cold tomorrow. It is as if seen from the hot parts of the field that the
other parts appear to us, and from these hot parts personal desire
and volition make their sallies. They are in short the centers of
our dynamic energy, whereas the cold parts leave us indifferent
and passive in proportion to their coldness.

Whether such language be rigorously exact is for the present
of no importance. It is exact enough, if you recognize from your
own experience the facts which I seek to designate by it.

Now there may be great oscillation in the emotional interest,
and the hot places may shift before one almost as rapidly as the
sparks that run through burnt-up paper. Then we have the wav-
ering and divided self we heard so much of in the previous lecture. Or the focus of excitement and heat, the point of view from
which the aim is taken, may come to lie permanently within a
certain system; and then, if the change be a religious one, we
call it a *conversion*, especially if it be by crisis, or sudden.

Let us hereafter, in speaking of the hot place in a man's consciousness, the group of ideas to which he devotes himself, and
from which he works, call it *the habitual center of his personal
energy*. It makes a great difference to a man whether one set of
his ideas, or another, be the center of his energy; and it makes
a great difference, as regards any set of ideas which he may
possess, whether they become central or remain peripheral in
him. To say that a man is "converted" means, in these terms,
that religious ideas, previously peripheral in his consciousness,
now take a central place, and that religious aims form the habitual
center of his energy.

In his recent work on the Psychology of Religion, Professor
Starbuck of California has shown by a statistical inquiry how
closely parallel in its manifestations the ordinary "conversion"
which occurs in young people brought up in evangelical circles
is to that growth into a larger spiritual life which is a normal
phase of adolescence in every class of human beings. The age is
the same, falling usually between fourteen and seventeen. The
symptoms are the same,—sense of incompleteness and imperfec-
tion; brooding, depression, morbid introspection, and sense of sin;
anxiety about the hereafter; distress over doubts, and the like.
And the result is the same—a happy relief and objectivity, as the
confidence in self gets greater through the adjustment of the
faculties to the wider outlook. In spontaneous religious awakening, apart from revivalistic examples, and in the ordinary storm
and stress and molting-time of adolescence, we also may meet
with mystical experiences, astonishing the subjects by their suddenness, just as in revivalistic conversion. The analogy, in fact,
is complete; and Starbuck's conclusion as to these ordinary youthful conversions would seem to be the only sound one: Conversion
is in its essence a normal adolescent phenomenon, incidental to
the passage from the child's small universe to the wider intellectual and spiritual life of maturity.

"Theology," says Dr. Starbuck, "takes the adolescent tendencies and builds upon them; it sees that the essential thing in ado-

lescent growth is bringing the person out of childhood into the new life of maturity and personal insight. It accordingly brings those means to bear which will intensify the normal tendencies. It shortens up the period of duration of storm and stress." The conversion phenomena of "conviction of sin" last, by this investigator's statistics, about one-fifth as long as the periods of adolescent storm and stress phenomena of which he also got statistics, but they are very much more intense. Bodily accompaniments, loss of sleep and appetite, for example, are much more frequent in them. "The essential distinction appears to be that conversion intensifies but shortens the period by bringing the person to a definite crisis."[1]

Now there are two forms of mental occurrence in human beings, which lead to a striking difference in the conversion process, a difference to which Professor Starbuck has called attention. You know how it is when you try to recollect a forgotten name. Usually you help the recall by working for it, by mentally running over the places, persons, and things with which the word was connected. But sometimes this effort fails: you feel then as if the harder you tried the less hope there would be, as though the name were *jammed*, and pressure in its direction only kept it all the more from rising. And then the opposite expedient often succeeds. Give up the effort entirely; think of something altogether different, and in half an hour the lost name comes sauntering into your mind, as Emerson says, as carelessly as if it had never been invited. Some hidden process was started in you by the effort, which went on after the effort ceased, and made the result come as if it came spontaneously. A certain music teacher, says Dr. Starbuck, says to her pupils after the thing to be done has been clearly pointed out, and unsuccessfully attempted: "Stop trying and it will do itself!"[2]

There is thus a conscious and voluntary way and an involuntary and unconscious way in which mental results may get accomplished; and we find both ways exemplified in the history of conversion, giving us two types, which Starbuck calls the *volitional type* and the *type by self-surrender* respectively.

In the volitional type the regenerative change is usually gradual, and consists in the building up, piece by piece, of a new set of moral and spiritual habits. But there are always critical points here at which the movement forward seems much more rapid. This psychological fact is abundantly illustrated by Dr. Starbuck. Our education in any practical accomplishment proceeds apparently by jerks and starts, just as the growth of our physical bodies does.

Of the volitional type of conversion it would be easy to give examples, but they are as a rule less interesting than those of the self-surrender type, in which the subconscious effects are more abundant and often startling. I will therefore hurry to the latter, the more so because the difference between the two types is after all not radical. Even in the most voluntarily built-up sort of regeneration there are passages of partial self-surrender interposed; and in the great majority of all cases, when the will had done its uttermost towards bringing one close to the complete unification aspired after, it seems that the very last step must be left to other forces and performed without the help of its activity. In other words, self-surrender becomes then indispensable. "The personal will," says Dr. Starbuck, "must be given up. In many cases relief persistently refuses to come until the person ceases to resist, or to make an effort in the direction he desires to go."

Dr. Starbuck gives an interesting, and it seems to me a true, account—so far as conceptions so schematic can claim truth at all—of the reasons why self-surrender at the last moment should be so indispensable. To begin with, there are two things in the mind of the candidate for conversion: first, the present incompleteness or wrongness, the "sin" which he is eager to escape from; and, second, the positive ideal which he longs to compass. Now with most of us the sense of our present wrongness is a far more distinct piece of our consciousness than is the imagination of any positive ideal we can aim at. In a majority of cases, indeed, the "sin" almost exclusively engrosses the attention, so that conversion is "*a process of struggling away from sin rather than of striving towards righteousness.*"[3] A man's conscious wit and will, so far as they strain towards the ideal, are aiming at something only dimly and inaccurately imagined. Yet all the while the forces of mere organic ripening within him are going on towards their own prefigured result, and his conscious strainings are letting loose subconscious allies behind the scenes, which in their way work towards rearrangement; and the rearrangement towards which all these deeper forces tend is pretty surely definite, and definitely different from what he consciously conceives and determines. It may consequently be actually interfered with (*jammed*, as it were, like the lost word when we seek too energetically to recall it), by his voluntary efforts slanting from the true direction.

Starbuck seems to put his finger on the root of the matter when he says that to exercise the personal will is still to live in the region where the imperfect self is the thing most emphasized. Where, on the contrary, the subconscious forces take the lead, it is more probably the better self *in posse* which directs the operation. Instead of being clumsily and vaguely aimed at from without, it is then itself the organizing center. What then must the person do? "He must relax," says Dr. Starbuck—"that is, he must fall back on the larger Power that makes for righteousness, which has been welling up in his own being, and let it finish in its own way the work it has begun. . . . The act of yielding, in this point of view, is giving one's self over to the new life, making it the center of a new personality, and living, from within, the truth of it which had before been viewed objectively."[4]

"Man's extremity is God's opportunity" is the theological way of putting this fact of the need of self-surrender; whilst the physiological way of stating it would be, "Let one do all in one's

power, and one's nervous system will do the rest." Both statements acknowledge the same fact.

To state it in terms of our own symbolism: When the new
center of personal energy has been subconsciously incubated so
long as to be just ready to open into flower, "hands off" is the
only word for us, it must burst forth unaided!

We have used the vague and abstract language of psychology.
But since, in any terms, the crisis described is the throwing of
our conscious selves upon the mercy of powers which, whatever
they may be, are more ideal than we are actually, and make for
our redemption, you see why self-surrender has been and always
must be regarded as the vital turning-point of the religious life,
so far as the religious life is spiritual and no affair of outer works
and ritual and sacraments. One may say that the whole development of Christianity in inwardness has consisted in little more
than the greater and greater emphasis attached to this crisis
of self-surrender. From Catholicism on to Lutheranism, and
then to Calvinism; from that to Wesleyanism; and from this, outside of technical Christianity altogether, to pure "liberalism" or
transcendental idealism, whether or not of the mind-cure type,
taking in the medieval mystics, the quietists, the pietists, and
quakers by the way, we can trace the stages of progress towards
the idea of an immediate spiritual help, experienced by the individual in his forlornness and standing in no essential need of doctrinal apparatus or propitiatory machinery.

Psychology and religion are thus in perfect harmony up to
this point, since both admit that there are forces seemingly outside of the conscious individual that bring redemption to his
life. Nevertheless psychology, defining these forces as "subconscious," and speaking of their effects, as due to "incubation," or
"cerebration," implies that they do not transcend the individual's
personality; and herein she diverges from Christian theology,
which insists that they are direct supernatural operations of the
Deity. I propose to you that we do not yet consider this diver-

gence final, but leave the question for a while in abeyance—continued inquiry may enable us to get rid of some of the apparent discord.

Revert, then, for a moment more to the psychology of self-surrender.

When you find a man living on the ragged edge of his consciousness, pent in to his sin and want and incompleteness, and consequently inconsolable, and then simply tell him that all is well with him, that he must stop his worry, break with his discontent, and give up his anxiety, you seem to him to come with pure absurdities. The only positive consciousness he has tells him that all is *not* well, and the better way you offer sounds simply as if you proposed to him to assert cold-blooded falsehoods. "The will to believe" cannot be stretched as far as that. We can make ourselves more faithful to a belief of which we have the rudiments, but we cannot create a belief out of whole cloth when our perception actively assures us of its opposite. The better mind proposed to us comes in that case in the form of a pure negation of the only mind we have, and we cannot actively will a pure negation.

There are only two ways in which it is possible to get rid of anger, worry, fear, despair, or other undesirable affections. One is that an opposite affection should overpoweringly break over us, and the other is by getting so exhausted with the struggle that we have to stop—so we drop down, give up, and *don't care* any longer. Our emotional brain-centers strike work, and we lapse into a temporary apathy. Now there is documentary proof that this state of temporary exhaustion not infrequently forms part of the conversion crisis. So long as the egoistic worry of the sick soul guards the door, the expansive confidence of the soul of faith gains no presence. But let the former faint away, even but for a moment, and the latter can profit by the opportunity, and, having once acquired possession, may retain it.

* * *

I might multiply cases almost indefinitely . . . to show you how real, definite, and memorable an event a sudden conversion may be to him who has the experience. Throughout the height of it he undoubtedly seems to himself a passive spectator or undergoer of an astounding process performed upon him from above. There is too much evidence of this for any doubt of it to be possible. Theology, combining this fact with the doctrines of election and grace, has concluded that the spirit of God is with us at these dramatic moments in a peculiarly miraculous way, unlike what happens at any other juncture of our lives. At that moment, it believes, an absolutely new nature is breathed into us, and we become partakers of the very substance of the Deity.

That the conversion should be instantaneous seems called for on this view, and the Moravian Protestants appear to have been the first to see this logical consequence. The Methodists soon followed suit, practically if not dogmatically. . . .

All this while the more usual sects of Protestantism have set no such store by instantaneous conversion. For them as for the Catholic Church, Christ's blood, the sacraments, and the individual's ordinary religious duties are practically supposed to suffice to his salvation, even though no acute crisis of self-despair and surrender followed by relief should be experienced. For Methodism, on the contrary, unless there have been a crisis of this sort, salvation is only offered, not effectively received, and Christ's sacrifice in so far forth is incomplete. Methodism surely here follows, if not the healthier-minded, yet on the whole the profounder spiritual instinct. The individual models which it has set up as typical and worthy of imitation are not only the more interesting dramatically, but psychologically they have been the more complete.

In the fully evolved Revivalism of Great Britain and America we have, so to speak, the codified and stereotyped procedure to which this way of thinking has led. In spite of the unquestionable fact that saints of the once-born type exist, that there may be a gradual growth in holiness without a cataclysm; in spite of the obvious leakage (as one may say) of much mere natural goodness into the scheme of salvation; revivalism has always assumed that only its own type of religious experience can be perfect; you must first be nailed on the cross of natural despair and agony, and then in the twinkling of an eye be miraculously released.

It is natural that those who personally have traversed such an experience should carry away a feeling of its being a miracle rather than a natural process. Voices are very often heard, lights seen, or visions witnessed; automatic motor phenomena occur; and it always seems, after the surrender of the personal will, as if an extraneous higher power had flooded in and taken possession. Moreover the sense of renovation, safety, cleanness, rightness, can be so marvelous and jubilant as well to warrant one's belief in a radically new substantial nature.

What, now, must we ourselves think of this question? Is an instantaneous conversion a miracle in which God is present as he is present in no change of heart less strikingly abrupt? Are there two classes of human beings, even among the apparently regenerate, of which the one class really partakes of Christ's nature while the other merely seems to do so? Or, on the contrary, may the whole phenomenon of regeneration, even in these startling instantaneous examples, possibly be a strictly natural process, divine in its fruits, of course, but in one case more and in another less so, and neither more nor less divine in its mere causation and mechanism than any other process, high or low, of man's interior life?

Before proceeding to answer this question, I must ask you to listen to some more psychological remarks. At our last lecture, I explained the shifting of men's centers of personal energy within them and the lighting up of new crises of emotion. I explained the phenomena as partly due to explicitly conscious processes of thought and will, but as due largely also to the subconscious incubation and maturing of motives deposited by the experiences of life. When ripe, the results hatch out, or burst into flower. I have now to speak of the subconscious region, in which such processes of flowering may occur, in a somewhat less vague way. I only regret that my limits of time here force me to be so short.

The expression "field of consciousness" has but recently come into vogue in the psychology books. Until quite lately the unit of mental life which figured most was the single "idea," supposed to be a definitely outlined thing. But at present psychologists are tending, first, to admit that the actual unit is more probably the total mental state, the entire wave of consciousness or field of objects present to the thought at any time; and, second, to see that it is impossible to outline this wave, this field, with any definiteness.

As our mental fields succeed one another, each has its center of interest, around which the objects of which we are less and less attentively conscious fade to a margin so faint that its limits are unassignable. Some fields are narrow fields and some are wide fields.

The important fact which this "field" formula commemorates is the indetermination of the margin. Inattentively realized as is the matter which the margin contains, it is nevertheless there, and helps both to guide our behavior and to determine the next movement of our attention. It lies around us like a "magnetic field," inside of which our center of energy turns like a compass-needle, as the present phase of consciousness alters into its successor. Our whole past store of memories floats beyond this margin, ready at a touch to come in; and the entire mass of residual powers, impulses and knowledges that constitute our empirical self stretches continuously beyond it. So vaguely drawn are the outlines between what is actual and what is only potential at any moment of our conscious life, that it is always hard to say of certain mental elements whether we are conscious of them or not.

I cannot but think that the most important step forward that has occurred in psychology since I have been a student of that science is the discovery, first made in 1886, that, in certain subjects at least, there is not only the consciousness of the ordinary field, with its usual center and margin, but an addition thereto in the shape of a set of memories, thoughts, and feelings which are extra-marginal and outside of the primary consciousness altogether, but yet must be classed as conscious facts of some sort, able to reveal their presence by unmistakable signs. I call this the most important step forward because, unlike the other advances which psychology has made, this discovery has revealed to us an entirely unsuspected peculiarity in the constitution of human nature.

Interpreting the unknown after the analogy of the known, it seems to me that hereafter, wherever we meet with a phenomenon of automatism, be it motor impulses, or obsessive idea, or unaccountable caprice, or delusion, or hallucination, we are bound first of all to make search whether it be not an explosion, into the fields of ordinary consciousness, of ideas elaborated outside of those fields in subliminal regions of the mind. We should look, therefore, for its source in the Subject's subconscious life.

If, abstracting altogether from the question of their value for the future spiritual life of the individual, we take [cases of instantaneous conversion] on their psychological side exclusively, so many peculiarities in them remind us of what we find outside of conversion that we are tempted to class them along with other automatisms, and to suspect that what makes the difference between a sudden and a gradual convert is not necessarily the presence of divine miracle in the case of one and of something less divine in that of the other, but rather a simple psychological peculiarity, the fact, namely, that in the recipient of the more instantaneous grace we have one of those Subjects who are in possession of a large region in which mental work can go on subliminally, and from which invasive experiences, abruptly upsetting the equilibrium of the primary consciousness, may come.

I do not see why Methodists need object to such a view. Pray go back and recollect one of the conclusions to which I sought to lead you in my very first lecture. You may remember how I there argued against the notion that the worth of a thing can be decided by its origin. Our spiritual judgment, I said, our opinion of the significance and value of a human event or condition, must be decided on empirical grounds exclusively. If the *fruits for life* of the state of conversion are good, we ought to idealize and venerate it, even though it be a piece of natural psychology; if not, we ought to make short work with it, no matter what supernatural being may have infused it.

Well, how is it with these fruits? If we except the class of preëminent saints of whom the names illumine history, and consider only the usual run of "saints," the shopkeeping church-members and ordinary youthful or middle-aged recipients of instantaneous conversion, whether at revivals or in the spontaneous course of methodistic growth, you will probably agree that no splendor worthy of a wholly supernatural creature fulgurates from them, or sets them apart from the mortals who have never experienced that favor. Were it true that a suddenly converted man as such is, as Edwards says, of an entirely different kind from a natural man, partaking as he does directly of Christ's substance, there surely ought to be some exquisite class-mark, some distinctive radiance attaching even to the lowliest specimen of this genus, to which no one of us could remain insensible, and which, so far as it went, would prove him more excellent than ever the most highly gifted among mere natural men. But notoriously there is no such radiance. Converted men as a class are indistinguishable from natural men; some natural men even excel some converted men in their fruits; and no one ignorant of doctrinal theology could guess by mere every-day inspection of the "accidents" of the two groups of persons before him, that their substance differed as much as divine differs from human substance.

The believers in the non-natural character of sudden conversion have had practically to admit that there is no unmistakable class-mark distinctive of all true converts. The super-normal incidents, such as voices and visions and overpowering impressions of the meaning of suddenly presented scripture texts, the melting emotions and tumultuous affections connected with the crisis of change, may all come by way of nature, or worse still, be counterfeited by Satan. The real witness of the spirit to the second birth is to be found only in the disposition of the genuine child of God, the permanently patient heart, the love of self eradicated. And this, it has to be admitted, is also found in those who pass no crisis, and may even be found outside of Christianity altogether.

1. E. D. Starbuck, *The Psychology of Religion,* pp. 224, 262.
2. *Ibid.,* p. 117.
3. *Ibid.,* p. 64.
4. *Ibid.,* p. 115.

[Major deletions have been made in this edited version.]

The Psychology of Conversion

"Religious conversion" is the name commonly given to the process which leads to the adoption of a religious attitude; the process may be gradual or sudden. It is likely to include a change in belief on religious topics but this will be accompanied by changes in the motivation to behavior and in reactions to the social environment. One or other of these directions of change may seem to play the predominant role in the conversion change; one may then speak of *intellectual*, of *moral*, or of *social* conversions. The distinctions between them are not, however, clear cut; every intellectual change has its implications for behavior and for social allegiances, and no one is likely to change his social allegiance in religion or his behavior motivation without some corresponding change in what he believes.

We may take as a typical account of a sudden conversion that of St. Paul, described in Acts 9. It will be remembered that Saul, an orthodox and zealous Jew, was active in persecution of the Christians. He went from Jerusalem towards Damascus with authority from the high priest to arrest the Christians there. On his way, he had a vision of light and an auditory experience of a voice, ostensibly that of Jesus Christ, reproaching him for his persecutions and directing him to go to Damascus where he would be told what to do. He then found himself blind until a few days later a man called Ananias laid his hands on him telling him that he would recover his sight and be filled with the Holy Ghost.

Then Saul recovered his sight, and after baptism, started preaching in the synagogues that Jesus was the son of God.

The story has interested psychologists particularly in its suddenness and in the intensified hostility to Christianity immediately preceding it. The visual experience of light at the moment of conversion is a not uncommon feature, although I know of no plausible psychological explanation. The psychogenic blindness relieved only at the moment of final surrender has also been considered to be of psychological interest although it is an unusual feature of conversion stories. The character of increased hostility to the finally accepted attitude has a psychological explanation if we assume that the final acceptance has already taken place at some level before the individual has become aware of it. There are mental processes that actively resist changes of belief. Such are the processes of "rationalization" which may provide reasons for continuing to hold a belief system after it has been undermined by contrary evidence or by the development of a new attitude. The affective bias towards maintaining an old system of thought may be strong; the holder may be unwilling to give up the comforts of certain conviction and to pass through the unpleasant and insecure condition of doubt. He may also be unwilling to give up the comfort and security he received from his membership of the social group to which he belonged by virtue of his old opinion. So it is understandable that his first reaction to a threat to an established belief system may be to produce new rationalizations in its support, and to show the behavior pattern of increased intolerance towards those who threaten his old belief. As the forces acting against the cherished belief system accumulate, however, the system may suddenly collapse and the arguments previously used in its support may be seen to be mere rationalizations. A similar process may occur in a non-religious setting, resulting in a change of mind to which we are inclined to apply the same name. The above is a psychological account of what takes place in a religious conversion and may be correct but this does not imply that it is complete; it may well be that more can be said about the process of religious conversion from a theological point of view.

The idea that the psychological process in such a religious change as a sudden conversion might be one in which changes in attitude were taking place slowly but outside the limits of consciousness was called by William James the theory of "subconscious incubation."[1] The type of psychological thinking that has developed from Freud's system of psycho-analysis has given these ideas greater plausibility and precision. Instead of regarding subconsciousness or unawareness as a more or less accidental property of some kinds of mental processes, this system of thought considers that there is an active process of *repression* by which, that which is painful or incompatible with the purposes of the main stream of consciousness is banished into a region called the *unconscious* from which it may influence behavior or conscious processes of thought but cannot be voluntarily made a part of the conscious stream of thought

In view of the psychological interest of the conversion process, it is not surprising to find that one of the earliest psychological studies of a religious phenomenon by the use of a scientific method of enquiry was a study of conversion. This is plainly a field in which strictly experimental methods cannot be used but Starbuck, at the close of the nineteenth century, started to study it by what were then somewhat novel methods, sending out to a number of people a typed set of questions and then classifying their answers and subjecting them to a process of numerical analysis.[2] To William James, this did not seem to be a promising way of approaching the problems of religion and he has recorded in his preface to Starbuck's book how he tried to discourage him from his project. He also records, however, that he was convinced that he had been wrong in condemning Starbuck's proposed methods of study which had justified themselves by their results.

Starbuck was particularly concerned with the commonest age for conversion. His figures confirmed the general impression that conversion is above all an adolescent phenomenon. He analyzed a number of reports of conversion experiences and condensed these into a typical experience which had three successive phases: dejection and sadness, a point of transition, and lastly, joy and peace. He made a comparative study of conversions that occurred in regular church activities and those that resulted from the activity of a professional evangelist. He found that more conversions occurred under the latter conditions but that a very much larger number of these lapsed within a period of six weeks, and that those who remained within the church congregation were predominantly those converted during the regular work of the church. Starbuck also made a numerical comparison of those who experienced sudden conversion with those who showed a more gradual spiritual growth without a conversion crisis. While there were differences in the religious lives of these groups, Starbuck's general finding was that the religious development of the two groups was, on the whole, remarkably parallel.

Although James paid tribute to the success of Starbuck's attempt to apply empirical methods to the study of religion, it must be admitted that Starbuck's use of these methods falls short of the standards that would be applied to such a study at the present day. Starbuck seems not to have considered sufficiently how far the response to a system of questions may be determined by the form of the questions asked; a critic might reasonably object that the investigator started with a clear picture of what a conversion experience was and asked his subjects how well their experiences conformed to that picture. In addition, he seems to have been insufficiently careful to ensure that his subjects were a representative sample of the population as a whole. Later studies of the use of questionnaire methods have shown how important is the use of an unbiased sample. Also he asserted differences when these may have been merely accidental differences in the figures obtained; he was working before modern methods of determining the significance of numerical differences had been developed. These defects do not detract from the merits of Starbuck as a pioneer in the application of empirical methods to the psychological study of religion; they are grounds for not regarding his detailed results as of lasting value. They do, however, raise questions which later workers may answer by the use of more adequate methods.

It can hardly be questioned that Starbuck was right in his emphasis on adolescence as the typical period for the occurrence of religious conversion. This does not, however, imply that we should accept the formula adopted by some writers on religion who say that conversion is a phenomenon of adolescence. Rather it seems to be the case that there is one kind of conversion with certain well-marked distinctive characteristics which takes place only during the period of adolescence and seems to be by far the most frequently encountered.

Exaggeration of pre-conversion sinfulness and of post-conversion virtue are characteristics of adolescent conversion. One can find numerous examples of these tendencies in Starbuck's records. A male convert of sixteen, for example, is reported to have said of his state before conversion: "My mind was in a state of great anxiety. The fleshly mind was all aflame, and my guilt was hideous to me. Because I belonged to church I felt myself a hypocrite."

The opposite tendency is illustrated by a female convert who said of her state after conversion: "I was a new creature in Christ Jesus. Everything seemed heavenly rather than earthly: everything was so lovely. I had a love for everybody. It was such a blessed experience. Going home I walked on the curbstone rather than walk or talk with ungodly people."

No doubt, when conversion stories are told for the purpose of edification, part of this exaggeration is to make the stories more edifying. The abandonment of sin, for example, is the more improving to an audience as the depth of the sin was greater. But there is probably more than this in the tendency. Pre-conversion sin may be described in terms more suitable for a hardened criminal than for an erring child because part of the emotional experience of his conversion is that his previous life appears so to him. Similarly there may be a real experience behind the exaggeration of post-conversion virtue and the appearance of exaggeration may arise from the inevitable difference between the point of view of the convert himself and that of other people around him. The convert judges himself subjectively by the rich emotional experience of his new life. Other people judge him from observation of his behavior and this may seem to them in many cases not to be strikingly better than it was before. The convert may be impressed by her new feeling of love for everybody; her neighbors may observe only the behavior reaction of walking on the curbstone in order to avoid contact with ungodly people.

Another striking feature of adolescent conversions that comes out strongly in reading Starbuck's collection of narratives is their tendency to follow a well-defined course. One notices too a much greater dependence than in adult conversions on personal influence, such as that of a preacher, as well as a marked tendency to impermanence. These characteristics suggest that they are largely a product of suggestion rather than a result of development in the convert's own spiritual life.

There is, however, another possible explanation of the conventional character of adolescent conversions. Not only may they follow a convention developed in the religious tradition in which they occur, but they may also resemble one another in being products of the same developmental fact. All psychological writers have agreed that the essential developmental fact underlying adolescent conversion is the system of conflicts which result from the emergence into consciousness of the impulses connected with the sex instinct.

Some writers have regarded adolescent conversion as merely the normal psychic change at adolescence which has been given a religious coloring. Starbuck has pointed out truly that one of the features of the beginning of the sex life is the arousal of altruistic sentiments, and he appears to regard the sense of sin which accompanies conversion as revulsion from the previous egocentric life.

This does not, however, seem to be borne out by what his adolescent converts themselves say, "The fleshly mind was all aflame" does not describe a reaction against egocentricity. It suggests rather a reaction against sexual feeling. Starbuck's adolescent converts must be regarded as products of the attitude towards sexuality of their time, in which sexual feeling tended to be regarded as intrinsically sinful and its appearance in one's own consciousness was productive of feelings of guilt. The typical adolescent conversion may be regarded psychologically as the sudden emergence into consciousness of a previously repressed system of feelings belonging to the sex instinct, which is now admitted into consciousness because it is sublimated, purified and directed to a religious end.

In support of this view of the nature of these adolescent conversions, it must be noticed that when adolescents of that period spoke of sin and temptation to sin, they nearly always meant sexual behavior or sexual thoughts. They were not concerned about the sins and imperfections that an older person might reproach himself for: lovelessness, self-centeredness, or indifference to the sufferings of others. This predominant interest in sex as the root of all imperfections is the result, no doubt, in part of the fact that the problem of how to adjust himself to the demands of the sex-life is necessarily a central problem of adolescent behavior, just as the central behavior problem of a much older man must be that of adjusting himself to the fact of approaching death. It is also, however, no doubt the product of a particular kind of education about sex: the adolescent had been taught to feel guilty about sex. Under the influence of Freud and modern educators we no longer believe it is right to attach guilt feelings to sex itself but only to particular forms of sex behavior. If modern education makes the adolescent feel relatively neutral about the fact of sex, this may well affect the form of adolescent conversion experiences. It may still be true that conversions will take place predominantly at adolescence, for adolescence will remain a time of stress however much attitudes may change towards the emerging sexual impulses. But their form may very well be changing as a result of the changing attitudes of adolescents towards their problems. It may be, for example, that diffused guilt feelings would be less common in adolescent conversions at the present

day than they were in the time of Starbuck. A more modern
research investigation of adolescent conversion along Starbuck's
lines would tell us how far these expected changes in the character of adolescent religious conversion are in fact taking place.

Although there is no doubt that the majority of conversions
take place at or about the period of adolescence, one cannot
unreservedly accept the formula "conversion is a phenomenon
of adolescence" since it is also a fact that many of the conversions
that have been of most importance in religious history are excep-
tions to this rule. A large number of great religious leaders have
been converted late in life; St. Paul, St. Augustine, Pascal and
Tolstoy are outstanding examples. There are considerable psychological differences between these conversions and the typical
adolescent conversion; it seems better, therefore, to treat them as
belonging to a different category from that of the ordinary conversion at adolescence. Many of those experiencing this non-
adolescent type of conversion have recorded an earlier conversion
experience which took the typical adolescent form; in other cases
the converted individual is reported to have been very religious
from childhood. Thus Pascal was first converted at the age of
twenty-three and his second conversion took place eight years
later. Evan Roberts, the leader of the Welsh revival at the beginning of this century, was religious from his boyhood and
devoted to prayer and Bible-reading. He was converted with soul
anguish in 1904, and after that time he had paroxysms and saw
visions. Al Ghazzali, who was a professor of Islamic theology
at Baghdad, describes how he passed from dogmatic religion
through a period of scepticism until he was redeemed by a light
which God caused to penetrate into his heart, and afterwards he
gave up his professorship and become a *sufi* (a Muslim mystic).[3]

The most striking difference between these later conversions
and the typical adolescent conversion is that they are not changes
from a non-religious to a religious attitude but from a merely
conventional acceptance of the socially approved pattern of
religious life to an attitude in which the religious motive becomes
dominant and in which religious belief and behavior become more

personal and even possibly idiosyncratic. Thus John Wesley lived as a devout Christian for more than a dozen years after his first conversion, and then underwent a second conversion experience at the age of thirty-five which led to the intense preaching activity of fifty years during which he traveled widely throughout the country and preached 40,000 sermons. Some of Wesley's biographers, in view of the fact that he was a Christian before, have been inclined to doubt the reality of this second conversion. It is, however, only one of many examples of a mature conversion generically different from an adolescent conversion, in which the change is from an ordinary religious life to an attitude in which religious motivation becomes dominant.

While in some cases of mature conversions, such as Wesley's, the re-direction is towards intensified external activity, there are also mature conversions which are turnings from a conventional religious attitude to the more interior religious life of the mystic. This class of mature religious conversions may be called that of "mystical conversions." The religious conversions of Al Ghazzali and Pascal were of this type. Typically, the subject of a mystical conversion is a conventionally religious person who lives the usual life of a devout person and may be much respected for his piety and good works. He himself is not satisfied and yearns for something more than his religious life is giving him. He may begin to cut himself adrift from his accustomed life. Then, after a period of unhappiness due to painful inner conflict, he passes through an experience which he may be unable to describe, but which contains a revelation in the light of which his subsequent life must be lived. He may become more or less cut off from his previous social environment and increasingly absorbed in an interior life unintelligible to other people. He may join a contemplative religious order whose members will understand and perhaps share his experiences, but, if he remains in the world, he may find that he is no longer respected. He may, at any rate in the early stages of his new life, find that he experiences such abnormal phenomena as visions and trances, which create scandal amongst those who previously thought well of him. . . .

... The mystical conversion of Pascal was typical in that he was devout before his mystical conversion. Before he was twenty-four, he is reported to have been enlightened by God through the reading of books of piety so that he 'understood perfectly that the Christian religion obliges us to live only for God and to have no other object than Him.' He had always been orthodox in religion and virtuous in life. Two further factors that affected his religious life were the influence of the puritanically inclined Jansenists and a chronic invalidism which limited his intellectual activity. He seems also to have been in love with a woman of rank whom he could not hope to marry.

But he felt dissatisfied with the things of the world and under the influence of his sister who was a nun, he decided at the age of thirty 'to leave altogether all the intercourse of the world, and to cut off all the superfluities of life, even at the peril of his health.' But the change was not yet complete. He had learned to despise the world but not to love God. His own efforts to redirect his will proved ineffective. In November 1654, he heard a sermon in which the preacher insisted upon the necessity for entire surrender to God. Shortly after this, Pascal fell into a trance in which he had a vivid impression of the presence of God, and seemed to be illuminated by a supernatural fire. This was his mystical conversion which initiated a new life of obedience and submission to the will of God. The record of this conversion experience was found, after his death on a paper worn over his heart:

The year of grace 1654. Monday, November the 23rd ... From about half past ten in the evening to about half past midnight. Fire.

God of Abraham, God of Isaac, God of Jacob. Not of the philosophers and of the learned. Certainty. Certainty. Feeling. Joy. Peace. God of Jesus Christ. *Deum meum et Deum vestrum.* Thy God shall be my God—Forgetful of the world and of all except God. One finds him only by the ways taught in the Gospel. Greatness of the human soul. Righteous Father, the world has not known thee, but I have known thee. Joy,

joy, joy, tears of joy . . . My God will you leave me? May I
not be separated from him eternally.

This is eternal life, knowing thee the only true God and
the one sent by you J.-C. Jesus Christ. I have been separated
from him: I have fled from him, renounced him, crucified him.
May I never be separated from him.[4]

In these moving but somewhat incoherent words, Pascal reminded himself of the experience which changed his life and
started him on the road of mystical development.

1. W. James, *The varieties of religious experience*, London, 1902.
2. E. D. Starbuck, *The psychology of religion*, London, 1899.
3. C. Field, *The confessions of Al Ghazzali*, London, 1909.
4. P. Faugère, *Pensées, fragments et lettres de Blaise*, Paris, 1897.

[Major deletions have been made in this edited version.]

Conversion: Sacred and Secular

WAYNE E. OATES

Conversion is not a uniquely religious experience, although it may be. Conversion is not limited to any one religion, although one form of religion may make more of the phenomenon as a religious experience than another form does. However, no one seems to deny that conversion, in whatever form it takes, is a profound psychological experience with far-reaching social and interpersonal effects when indeed it is profound. From the beginning of its efforts as a scientific study of religious experience, the psychology of religion has, as a discipline, been concerned with conversion. Conversion is an observable, behavioral phenomenon. It can be spoken of in both a sacred and a secular manner. In fact, the experience is being less and less referred to in a sacred manner. This is true even in the literature of the psychology of religion because of the more distinctly secular ways of speaking of the experience. Therefore, one of the things the reader will want to look for, hopefully, as these pages are being read, is the way in which this potentially religious experience is referred to in increasingly secular manners. To begin this study, we need to get some of the definitions of conversion clearly in mind.

What Is Conversion?

Conversion, strictly defined, is a noun referring to the act of being converted in any sense from one position or conviction to another, from one party or form of religion to another, from one group affiliation to another. More often than not, in the psychology of religion, the word *conversion* is used to refer to an abrupt change toward an enthusiastic religious attitude, with the highly emotional features being conspicuously evident, whether they are lasting or not.

In the biblical accounts of the New Testament, conversion as a noun is used only once, and that is in Acts 15:3 which refers to the "conversion of the Gentiles." The word is used as a verb to refer to the act of turning away from God, as it is in Galatians 4:9, but it is ordinarily used in speaking of man's turning to God, as in Acts 9:35 and 15:19. Regularly, the verb for turning, *epistrephein*, means to reverse one's direction in life, to change one's devotion or loyalty, or to repent or rethink one's way of life as one lives before and in relation to God. The words for *turning* are often associated with the words *repent* and *believe*. One turns from darkness to light (Ac 26:18), from idols to God (1 Th 1:9), from vain things to a living God (Ac 14:15). When one turns to the Lord, the veil is removed, says Paul in 2 Corinthians 3:16. To be converted is an inward but objective change in man in that he confronts and comes to terms with God. Conversion is not a ritual, an outward deed, or a purely subjective experience inasmuch as God is working in the processes of man's life to will and to do his good work. It leads to an observable new way of life, but this is the result of a spiritual transformation and fresh identification with God in Christ.[1]

The biblical teachings concerning conversion are descriptions of encounters with oneself in relation to God all along life's way. They are never associated with any particular ritual, but are distinctly personal changes of direction because of significant revelations of one's self and of God. Such would be the spirit of William James in his 1901-02 Gifford Lectures on Human Nature. As a professor of psychology at Harvard, he became the best-known and most-quoted psychologist of religion of our times. In his lectures, later published as a book, he says of religion in general:

> I prefer to ignore the institutional branch [of religion] entirely, to say nothing of the ecclesiastical organization, to

consider as little as possible the systematic theology and the ideas about the gods themselves, and to confine myself as far as I can to personal religion pure and simple.[2]

Against the backdrop of a previous chapter on the divided self, James begins a chapter on conversion with the following classical definition:

> To be converted, to be regenerated, to recieve grace, to expe-
> rience religion, to gain an assurance, are many phrases which
> denote the process, gradual or sudden, by which a self hitherto
> divided, and consciously wrong, inferior and unhappy, be-
> comes consciously right, superior and happy, in consequence
> of its firmer hold upon religious realities. This is at least what
> conversion signifies in general terms, whether or not we be-
> lieve that a direct divine operation is needed to bring such a
> moral change about.[3]

Inherent in this definition are several assumptions about conversion that have become "standard operating assumptions" of the
field of psychology of religion since James indelibly stamped it
with his influence.

First, a variety of terms is used by different persons to describe
conversion, depending upon their own ideological persuasion.
Some of these terms are distinctly theological and refer to divine
intervention. Others are more psychological and attempt empirical descriptions of human behavior, as such. To James they
are "so many phrases" to describe a common phenomenon.

Second, a self-psychology of personality is used as a working
hypothesis of human nature. This self is capable of being divided
and being united. The concepts of self-psychology are inherently
a value-oriented psychology. Values are the basis of conflict. The
self is not to be thought of in terms of selfishness or unselfishness,
but much in the sense that the Revised Standard Version translates
the words *life* or *man* from the words such as *psyche* and *soma*.
The self refers to a person-as-a-whole or "being," as in human
"being." The later self-psychologists such as Freud, Jung, Adler,
Rank, Sullivan, Horney, Fromm, Angyal, Lecky, Rogers, Maslow,

Snygg, and Combs gave more elaborate views of the self. An excellent symposium of many of these views is to be found in Clark
Moustakas's, *The Self*.[4] However, in principle and content, these
assumptions are implicit or explicit in the definition of conversion
by James, as well as in his chapter, "The Divided Self." If one will
disentangle his conception of the soul from Platonic theories of
its separateness from the body, and if one will lean hard on the
unity of the person as a whole in Hebrew psychology, then one
can say that the self in twentieth-century psychologies of personality is a near-equivalent for the word *soul* without some of its
Platonic and religious propaganda connotations.

Third, another built-in presupposition of James's definition
of conversion is *conflict within the self*. This conception falls
into step with Pauline and Augustinian religious experience and
theology. Paul said: "What I would, that I do not; but what I hate,
that I do." In his Confessions, Augustine said: "I said within myself: 'Come, let it be done now,' and as I said it, I was on the point
of resolve. I all but did it, yet I did not do it."[5] James says of
Augustine: "Augustine's psychological genius has given an account of the trouble of having a divided self which has never
been surpassed."[6] I would amend his words "having a divided
self" to "*being* a divided self," because the words James uses infer,
to me at least, that we *have* a self, when in reality we are—existentially—a self-as-a-whole. Platonic assumptions lurk in James's
wording. The issue in any event, however, is that of conflict
between the self that I am and the self I want to become, the life
that is and the better life that can be. The resolution of this conflict is the essence of the conversion experience. In this view,
if there is no conflict, there is not likely to be any conversion.

James presupposes that conversion may or may not be the
result of "direct divine operation." Thereby he established the
intention to speak of conversion in either supernatural or humanistic terms. James opens the way for a creative tension between
psychology as a behavioral science and religion as a distinctly
theological endeavor. When one settles this tension on one side
or another, he becomes either a psychologist or a theologian, but

not a psychologist of religion. To create an antiphony between behavioral science and "theological dynamics," to use Seward Hiltner's phrase, is the task of the psychologist of religion. When the creative tension is rejected in behalf of the firm certainties of a psychological system or a theological dogma, however valuable these are, then the boundary situation remains untouched and unexplored.

Fifth, James perceives conversion as a *process* related to time. It is a "process, gradual or sudden." We are keenly aware of this issue in the churches of the Great Awakening which were founded on the presuppositions of the reality of conversion as the primary, valid index to religious certitude before God. We are prone to assume that the more sudden or gradual a conversion is the more valid, religiously or psychologically, it is. We are likely to impute the "miraculous intervention of God" to the more sudden conversion and to describe the more gradual conversion to religious nurture and correct psychological development. In both instances, we are likely to have a distorted perception. The commitment of the psychological approach is to see the process of development in both the gradual and the sudden conversion. In either event, the element of process-in-time is there.

For these five bases of a psychological approach to religion, inherent in his definition of conversion, we are permanently indebted to William James. Hence, his definition of conversion has become somewhat normative for a working hypothesis of conversion. The task that is at hand now is to describe more recent approaches to the nature of conversion since James's pioneering work. These varying perspectives are not necessarily contradictory but tend to be mutually complementary of each other.

PERSPECTIVES OF CONVERSION

Conversion as the Rapidation of Growth

By rapidation we mean that a given process in human life and development is sped up by intervention from without. By placing plants in a hothouse and controlling the weather, nutriment, and care, plants grow and produce faster. By placing a person in an engineering program of education, the assumption is that he can become an engineer in ten years whereas it would take a lifetime by the apprentice-direct experience of working one's way up from a sweeper in an engineering company to the position of chief engineer. Rapidation as applied to conversion would mean, by analogy, that the experience of conversion hastens, steps up, intensifies, normal growth.

The earliest proponents of this interpretation were G. Stanley Hall and Edward D. Starbuck. Starbuck stated the point of view as follows:

> Theology takes the adolescent tendencies and builds upon them; it sees that the essential thing in adolescent growth is bringing a person out of childhood into the new life of maturity and personal insight. It accordingly brings those means to bear which will intensify the normal tendencies. It shortens up the period of duration of storm and stress. . . . [The essential distinction appears to be that] conversion intensifies but shortens the period by bringing the person to a definite crisis.[7]

Starbuck overidentified conversion with adolescence, probably because his sample of people were adolescents. However, the studies of Jung and Erikson have supplied data for correcting this overidentification. Carl G. Jung points out that the heavier crises of faith, often resulting in psychological illness, occur after the age of thirty-five. As a result, his primary concern was with the failure of meaning in adult lives, not the origins of neurosis in childhood trauma.

The developmental hypotheses of Erikson also suggest that other times of storm and stress are even more intense than those of adolescence, such as the search for intimacy in the face of loneliness in young adulthood, the crises between generativity and self-absorption in adulthood, and the struggle between integrity and despair in later maturity. Each of these times is a time of conflict for a divided self that needs unification in order to grow. The growth of the self toward love, care, and wisdom, to use

Erikson's "schedule of human virtues," may be slow or rapid. Are these not times calling for conversion? Could not conversion shorten the process of maturity by bringing a person to a definite crisis? I think it could; but if so, one would need a dynamic rather than a static view of conversion. Conversion would have to be seen as an ongoing process that occurs more than once, although the initial occurrence would be the time after which— before God—a person would never be the same again by reason of an initial, conscious covenant of faith in God.

Another assumption in Starbuck's concept of conversion as the rapidation of growth is that he seems to assume that conversion always results in growth toward maturity and *never* in regression to an infantile state. James distinguished between "the religion of sick souls" and the "religion of healthymindedness," giving a prelude to what we now know as the psychopathology of religion. This field has collected data to demonstrate that conversion does not always shorten the process of growth but also may rapidate an already-in-progress regression of the person to a more infantile state.

The rapidation view of conversion must be challenged at this easy assumption that all rapidation is forward in its movement toward greater growth and maturity. More recent authors have observed that rapidation may be backward or regressive. Leon Salzman, for example, describes religious conversions as being of two kinds: (1) the progressive or maturational type, and (2) the regressive or psychopathological type. The first results in "the positive fulfillment of one's powers with self-awareness, concern for others, and oneness with the world." It is a conjunctive, anxiety-relieving, integrating conversion that matures the person. The second kind of conversion may either "precipitate or be a part of the psychotic process." The latter kind of conversion is marked by exaggerated irrationality and intensity of beliefs and results in a high percentage of backsliding of converts. It regularly includes contempt, hatred, intolerance, compulsive proselytizing and the need for martyrdom and punishment for beliefs.[8]

Conversion as the Unification of a Divided Self

As has already been suggested in the discussion of James's definition of conversion, the unification of the divided self is an optimum result of conversion. The division of the self should not be mistaken as a pathological phenomenon such as is superficially and popularly referred to as a split personality or schizophrenia. Schizophrenia more technically refers to a break with reality, withdrawal of one's affections from real to fantasied objects, and so on. The *dissociated* personality comes much more near to describing the divided self. A more intensive treatment of the religious life of both the schizophrenic person and the dissociated person will be found in a later chapter on psychopathology and religion. The focus of this chapter, however, is upon the dimensions of the self in persons who have no clinically definable mental illness in the strict medical use of those terms. These persons are caught between the poles of several dilemmas that pull them in different directions.

The first dilemma of the divided self is a *dilemma of loyalties*. The average person between the ages of eighteen and twenty-five is caught between loyalty to the way he has been brought up and the way of life of close friends and associates his own age. He has a loyalty to his parents and a loyalty to his peers. A nineteen-year-old girl, for example, has a war of independence going on with her mother at the same time the majority of her associates are smoking marijuana, going to marijuana festivals, and getting arrested by the police. She has a strong and positive devotion to her father, a negative attitude toward her mother, and a desire to help her friends who are in prison and in mental hospitals because of selling and/or using drugs such as LSD, hashish, and heroin. The beginning of her discovery of peace within her conflicting loyalties will be what Horace Bushnell called "the expulsive power of a new affection." Here the power of a new relationship magnetically relocates "the habitual center of personal energies" and creates a higher thesis for the polar tension between her parental loyalty and peer-group loyalty. This can be the emergence of a new leader in her life, such as a pastoral counselor, a teacher, or an older friend. It can be the discovery of a new cause, such as a vocational interest. It can be the persuasion to accept a new set of beliefs embodied in a new peer group. In any one or all three events, she is recentered on a new affection that overcomes the conflict.

The second dilemma of the divided self is the *dilemma of authority*. Erikson calls this the leadership polarization. The conflictual self is at war over the authority of parents, wife or husband, employer and institution. Much of the religious conflict expressed by persons is at its roots a conflict over what they were taught by their parents. A self can be deeply divided over the ways in which parental religious teachings have both become a part of the self and at the same time are rejected by the self. The need to be dependent upon parents is at war with the call to be independent of them. Leaving father and mother and following one's religious leader is a pitched battle within the self. Leaving father and mother to be married may be a way to escape from the authority of parents. Once the escape is effected the mate becomes of no more use, which may issue in divorce or chronic resentment of the authority of marriage as an institution.

Again, the ways in which husbands and wives dominate each other and strive for power in the home is another source of conflict over authority. The resolution of this conflict in a shared recognition of the authority of God is a new basis of humility and a possible sparking of the conversion of a whole family as result.

The conflict between the authority of God and one's own authority is the inner core of the conflict over authority. As Nietzsche is reported to have said: "There is no God! If there were, how could *I* not be he!" This struggle is called *hybris* or self-elevation. The psychoanalysts called it primary narcissism. The central thrust of healthy conversion is to sensitize persons to their finitude, to enable them to accept their humanity, and to cause them to prophesy concerning the grace of God but to be aware that they do so "in part" at the same time.

The third dilemma of the divided self is *conflict over freedom and restriction.* The late Andras Angyal called this the tension between the autonomous and homonomous needs of a person.[9] This conflict comes to focus most vividly in the collision of the freedom impulses of a person with the strictures of institutional religion. This conflict issued in the conversion of Martin Luther to a kind of freedom—later called Lutheranism—from Catholicism. This dynamic change has been portrayed by Erikson in his *Young Man Luther.* Before Luther, the conversion of Augustine was from a loose kind of limitless freedom of a rather wild life to the ordered disciplines of Catholicism. Similarly, John Henry Newman was "converted" from Anglicanism to Catholicism. Yet it was John Bunyan who was imprisoned for preaching without the legal permission of the Church of England. Today, one sees people from the free church tradition of Baptists, Quakers, and so on being converted to the more binding ritual and liturgy of the Episcopal church and the devout Catholic priest being converted to less ordered and structured expressions of faith such as Quakerism, as was Gregory Zillboorg, the psychoanalyst.

The divided self is nebulous and vague until one sees it in terms of these dilemmas of loyalty and authority and of freedom and structure. Until one gets such specifics in mind, the thought of a divided self is just another cause for free-floating anxiety, circular thinking, and reunification. However, such specifics have a way of at least marking out the battlegrounds of conflictual selves and locating the arenas that call for responsible decision. Responsible decision is integral to thoroughgoing conversion, yet these decisions must have the strong meat of specific relationship, of the self-as-a-whole to itself, to others, to institutions, and to God. Without these specifics the new birth in conversion may turn out to be a pseudocyesis, that is, an imaginary birth rather than a real one. All of the premonitory symptoms of a real birth will be there, but as Socrates says, it will upon delivery be a wind-birth.

Conversion as a Change of Direction

Conversion in its New Testament sense, as well as words used in the Old Testament for the experience of transforming encounters with God, literally means a change of direction, a "wheeling about," a U-turn in life. In the life of the Apostle Peter, for example, there were many such turnings, and the Lord Jesus Christ told him that he would "turn again" after his, Jesus', death. Then he was to strengthen his brethren and enable them to do likewise (Lk 22:31).

This conception of conversion is the most easily communicated of all the conceptions mentioned in this discussion. The reason in my opinion, for this ease of communication is that it encompasses *both* the decision of a person to change his direction *and* the participation of God in the revelation of *which* direction to take. The experience may be gradual or sudden, dramatic or undramatic, or even unnoticeable by others. Yet the event takes place.

A vivid description of the turning of the spirit of man from bondage to freedom, from darkness to light, from the clutch of necessity to the risks of freedom, is found not only in biblical accounts but also in Plato's *Republic*.[10]

The main characteristics of the conception of conversion as a spiritual turning is its dynamic interpretation of life as a pilgrimage of the spirit over the long pull of the years as over against the concept of conversion as being solely the first and "stamping" encounter with God at the conscious level. In this view, there are many turnings in the way although there will probably be one initial one hundred eighty degree turn. The central act of conversion is the change of direction in life. In Prescott Lecky's theory of personality, the thrust of the self is to maintain consistency of values. When a new set of values is posed to an individual—or group, for that matter—conflict ensues over the ethical dissonance between the new way of life and the old way. Resistance to change must be overcome if a person is to grow, or, if not, to consolidate on a level already attained.[11] Responding affirmatively to the new value claims results in a conversion.

The spiritual turning of which we are speaking here is also pictured in the New Testament as a changing of the mind, a change of heart. These words are translated as "repentance" or "rethinking." The hearts of fathers are hardened, but they are "turned" to their children by the power of the good news of the coming of the Kingdom of Christ. Here is a turning from unteachablenes to openness and teachability, from suspicion to trustfulness. In the Old Testament the meaning of *repent* is to turn back, as if to retrace one's steps back to God and the covenants one has formed with God. One has strayed and lost his sense of direction. To repent is to get on the right road going in the right direction. To do this one has faith in God. In the New Testament that God is revealed in Jesus Christ. In the contemporary church, repentance is the integral part of being converted.

Conversion as an Act of Surrender

One of the students in my class did a careful word study of the spectrum of literature on conversion, paying attention to the terms used for conversion as well as the grammatical forms the word *conversion* takes when used as a verb. He concluded that the verb *convert* is regularly used in the passive sense: "To be converted," "was converted," "have been converted," and so on are examples. This observation reflects one whole set of assumptions about the nature of conversion, namely, conversion takes place as a result of an act of surrender, a certain giving up, a release of aggressive discharges of personal power to a more receptive, relaxed, and submissive relation to reality and Reality as a Whole. One quits fighting, responds with trust, and recognizes the Power that is greater than oneself and at the same time has one's best interests at heart.

Kurt H. Wolff says that surrender is "cognitive love" in seed form. By this he means that all the fruits of love grow from cognitive love which expresses itself through the act of surrender. He says that other meanings of cognitive love spring from the acts of surrender. Several of these meanings are: *total involvement, suspension of received notions, pertinence, identifications, and the risk of being hurt.*

The person who surrenders becomes totally involved with the

object of his love, having difficulty deciding where the boundaries of the self end and the boundaries of the Loved One end.

Furthermore, in the act of surrender one starts over by suspending all previous notions, beliefs, values, and rethinks afresh the whole of life as it relates centrally to the Loved One. This is a kind of "bracketing."

In the third place, in the act of surrender, a person assumes that all that comes to his attention is pertinent and related to the approval of the Loved One.

The fourth dimension of the act of surrender is identification with rather than mastery of the Loved One. He is changed or transformed into the same likeness through the power of the Loved One in his life.

Finally, risk characterizes the act of surrender. One makes oneself vulnerable to change by the Loved One. Yet, as did Job, he says: "Though I am slain, yet will I trust." The spirit of the young Hebrew captives of a king demanding that they worship foreign gods *is* the attitude of the person who is genuinely converted, who really surrenders to God: "Our God whom we serve is able to deliver us from the burning fiery furnace; he will deliver us out of your hand, O king . . . that we will not serve your gods or worship the golden image which you have set up" (Dn 3:17-18). This is the act of surrender in face of the risk of being hurt.[12]

These five dimensions of the act of surrender are all necessary to distinguish genuine converison from specious conversion, spiritual transformation from an appeal for magical results or a bargain that is being struck with God.

Harry M. Tiebout, a psychiatrist who spent much time in the treatment of alcoholics, makes a distinction between the act of surrender and mere compliance to external demands. Surrender implies admission of powerlessness. Admission of the truth of one's finiteness and limitedness is "the blood brother of acceptance." One is able to incorporate a truth as part of oneself, not merely capitulate to a theoretical idea. Surrender produces the wholehearted acceptance of the self as one is. Compliance, on the other hand, "means agreeing, going along but in no way implies enthusiastic, wholehearted assent and approval."[13] This deep-running surrender is embodied in the first two steps of the Alcoholics Anonymous *Twelve Steps to Recovery:*

1. We admitted we were powerless over alcohol—that our lives had become unmanageable.
2. We came to believe that a Power greater than ourselves could restore us to sanity.

In increasing numbers, these persons mark these two affirmations as the turning point in their road to recovery.

In a careful study of the results of conversion in the treatment of alcoholism, C. Roy Woodruff says that there are four categories of conversion among the alcoholics who remained sober as a result of conversion. The first category is *psychosocial conversion* in which the person is changed in self-concept and relation to others. This is a horizontal conversion based on the love of people and enlightened self-interest. The second category is *restrictive conversion* which is similar to Salzman's regressive conversion but is different in that the person changes from drunkenness to sobriety but stabilizes at a level of arrogance, ambition-riddenness, and intolerance of others. A third category is called *limited Christian conversion*—the person remains dependent, indecisive about what is right and wrong. In essence, this person is inadequate, but the conversion experience removed the devastation of alcoholism. His possibility of becoming depressed or schizophrenic after his conversion should be watched closely. The fourth category Woodruff poses is the *comprehensive Christian conviction*, implying that the experience is deeply felt, total, transforming, releasing, and transcendent. The central focus is in the revelation of God in Jesus Christ. It involves a total involvement of the self in Christ.[14]

The perspective of conversion that presumes an act of surrender presupposes varying degrees of ability to commit oneself. In the studies of Bowlby, Erikson, Kenniston, and others, it was shown that this capacity varies from individual to individual in terms of the person's emotional deprivation. Some people, from a theological point of view, obviously "enter into life," as Jesus said, but they also "enter into life maimed," as Jesus also said. It is better to do the latter than to languish in hopelessness waiting for perfection or to assume that handicaps are not real at all. The psychologist of religion can identify emotional maiming or crippling in the lives of individuals and groups. He would ask: "Is there not room for these crippled-ones-in-the spirit as well as the lame, the halt, and the blind in body?" As a theologian, my answer would be: "Yes!"

Programmed Conversion

No discussion of conversion is complete when separated from the institutionalization of conversion in the programs of the churches. The realist today cannot take the position of William James in considering religious experience from a purely personal, noninstitutional point of view. This is especially true of the phenomenon of conversion, because whole religious movements have been escalated on the presupposition that conversion is *the* via par excellence into the kingdom of God. The Great Awakening was a very vital frontier movement that drew its strength from the agreed upon expectation that *all* people must be converted. They were called "converts." Furthermore, the churches of the Great Awakening—Baptists, Disciples of Christ, the Church of God, the Assembly of God, and to a great extent Methodists, and so on—were established as denominations upon a doctrine of repentance, expectation of conversion, and the ritual of the revival as *the* model for becoming a Christian and a church member. This is still true in considerable force in all these denominations, regardless of the gradual slide downward of the age level of converts toward childhood and even infancy and regardless of the subtle shifts in church programming of great numbers of these churches.

Furthermore, in the 1950s and 1960s the resurgence of piety in America and to some extent in other parts of the world has been heralded by the mass evangelism of Billy Graham, Oral Roberts, and other less well-known persons. These evangelists use the institutionalized interpretation of conversion as *the* operating hypothesis of their appeal to large numbers of people.

Now in the 1970s, the nonrational aspects of the counter-revolution have grasped at the revival model of programming conversion experiences. Explo '72 in Dallas, Texas, for example, was a mass festival of the less radical youth of middle-class America in response to the programming ability of Campus Crusade. The packaging of conversion persuasion was the pattern of the approach of this movement as well as the less well-organized Jesus Movement.

The programming of conversion introduces several new factors into the basic nature of conversion. First, the revival creates a social expectation that persons will behave in a pattern of conversion. The possibility, though not the necessity, is that the conversion will be artificially induced due to external pressure. Second, the amount of external pressure may stimulate the person's need to be obedient and compliant or rebellious and nonconformed. Both phenomena have been observed. Third, other extraneous factors may take precedence over the need of the individual to be converted to a faith in God—the need to demonstrate the charisma of the evangelist; the need to maintain the public image and financial solvency of the revival team, the local church, or the denomination; and the need to recruit membership in mass movements and organizations. As in any mass production, the redirection of time with any individual person or thing tends to increase the amounts of impersonal authority for individual attention.

Secular Conversion

As one reads the works of Abraham Maslow as he describes "peak-experiences" in the lives of productive, healthy, and creative persons, one sees the psychological equivalents of the classical meanings of conversion discussed in this chapter. Maslow speaks of the resistance to being "rubricized," by which he means a "cheap form of cognizing . . . to place a person in a system takes less energy than to know him in his own right."[15] The following description by Maslow of the aspects of a peak-experience as an acute identity experience is an empirical description of what an earlier generation called conversion and a compact summary of the contents of this chapter. Note that at no point does he call peak-experiences conversion, but also note how similar the descriptions are:

> The person in the peak-experiences feels more integrated (unified, whole, all-of-a-piece), than at other times. He also looks (to the observer) more integrated in various ways (described below), e.g., less split or dissociated, less fighting against himself, more at peace with himself, less split between an experiencing-self and an observing-self, more one-pointed, more harmoniously organized, more efficiently organized with all his parts functioning very nicely with each other, more synergic with less internal friction, etc.
>
> As he gets to be more purely and singly himself he is more able to fuse with the world.
>
> The person in the peak-experiences usually feels himself to be at the peak of his powers, using all his capacities at the best and fullest.
>
> A slightly different aspect of fully-functioning is effortlessness and ease of functioning when one is at one's best.
>
> He is now most free of blocks, inhibitions, cautions, fears, doubts, controls, reservations, self-criticisms, brakes. These may be the negative aspects of the feeling of worth, of self-acceptance, of self-love-respect.
>
> He is therefore more spontaneous, more expressive, more innocently behaving (guiless, naïve, honest, candid, ingenu-

ous, child-like, artless, unguarded, defenseless), more natural (simple, relaxed, unhesitant, plain, sincere, unaffected, primitive in a particular sense. immediate), more uncontrolled and freely flowing outward (automatic, impulsive, reflexlike, 'instinctive,' unrestrained, unself-conscious, thoughtless, unaware).

In the peak-experiences, the individual is most here-now, most free of the past and of the future in various senses, most "all there" in the experience.

The person now becomes more a pure psyche and less a thing-of-the-world living under the laws of the world.

Expression and communication in the peak-experiences tend often to become poetic, mythical and rhapsodic, as if this were the natural kind of language to express such states of being.

All peak-experiences may be fruitfully understood.

People during and after peak-experiences characteristically feel lucky, fortunate, graced. A not uncommon reaction is "I don't deserve this." Peaks are not planned or brought about by design; they happen. We are "surprised by joy." The reaction of surprise, of unexpectedness, of the sweet "shock of recognition" are very frequent.

A common consequence is a feeling of gratitude, in religious persons to their God, in others to Fate, to Nature, to people, to the past, to parents, to the world, to everything and anything that helped to make this wonder possible. This can go over into worship, giving thanks, adoring, giving praise, oblation and other reactions which fit very easily into a religious framework. Clearly any psychology of religion, either supernatural or natural, must take account of these happenings, as also must any naturalistic theory of the origins of religion.[16]

Maslow says that a person "needs a religion or religion surrogate to live by, in about the same sense he needs sunlight, calcium, or love." He calls this the "cognitive need to understand." Life has to have some meaningful framework for a person to survive. The seemingly meaningless aberrations of the most acutely psychotic person serve to provide him with a shred of understanding with which to hold on tenuously to life. As Maslow says, "What man needs but doesn't have, he seeks for unceasingly, and he becomes dangerously ready to jump at *any* hope, good or bad. ... We need a validated, usable system of human values that we can believe in and devote ourselves to (be willing to die for), because they are true rather than because we are exhorted to 'believe and have faith.' "[17]

However, the choice between a religion that exhorts and a surrogate religion that provides a freshly stated set of propositions is a hard choice for a person in the formative years of late adolescence and early maturity to make. He may be caught in a struggle—a storm and stress—between the religious tradition of his parents and the surrogate religion of a psychological system. In responding warmly to the latter, he may be simply establishing independence of mother, father, home, church, and the past. He may be on a pilgrimage to a fresh restatement of his faith which he can understand and use. This is the best possible hope. The worst possible solution may be that he does not see that the psychological systems of today are in essence surrogate religions. Thus, his teeth will be set on edge against the religion of parents that has indeed lost its power and become a "grapes of wrath" kind of bitterness rather than love, joy, peace, long suffering, and kindness which are the fruits of the spirit.

1. John Marsh, "Conversion," *The Interpreter's Dictionary of the Bible* (Nashville: Abingdon, 1962), 1:678.

2. William James, *Varieties of Religious Experience* (New York: New American Library, 1958), p. 41.

3. *Ibid.,* p. 157.

4. Clark Moustakas, *The Self: Explorations in Personal Growth* (New York: Harper & Bros., 1956).

5. Augustine *Confessions* 7. 6, 7, 11.

6. James, *Varieties of Religious Experience,* p. 144.

7. Edward D. Starbuck, *The Psychology of Religion,* pp. 224, 262.

8. Leon Salzman, "Psychology of Religious Ideological Conversion," *Psychiatry,* vol. 16, no. 2 (May, 1953).

9. Andras Angyal, *Neurosis and Treatment* (New York: John Wiley, 1965), pp. 8, 29.

10. Plato *Republic* 7.

11. Prescott Lecky, *Self-Consistency*, pp. 245-56.

12. Kurt H. Wolff, "Surrender and Religion," *Journal for the Scientific Study of Religion,* vol. 2, no. 1 (Fall 1962).

13. Harry M. Tiebout, "Surrender vs. Compliance in Therapy," *Pastoral Psychology,* vol. 9, no. 83 (April 1958), p. 30.

14. C. Roy Woodruff, *Alcoholism and Christian Experience* (Philadelphia: Westminster Press, 1968), pp. 23-48.

15. Abraham Maslow, *Toward a Psychology of Being,* 2nd ed. (Princeton, N. J.: D. Van Nostrand, 1968), p. 126.

16. *Ibid.,* pp. 104-14.

17. *Ibid.,* p. 206.

[Major deletions have been made in this edited version.]

Conversion

PAUL E. JOHNSON

Human personality is at once the best known and the least understood of all forms of existence. Each person knows himself best from inside information of his own experience and what it means to him to live through it. He can feel his own shadings of mood from moment to moment, the ebb and flow of his emotions, and the cross-currents which are almost but not quite ready to do or decide. Yet there are shadowy unknowns in the unconscious depths of his nature that impel or restrain him in a baffling interplay of conflicting tendencies. From his dream and fantasy life come intimations of surprising wishes and fears that imply the ongoing of secret plots and counter-plots in his life drama.

As he wrestles with this mystery, every person becomes a problem to himself. "Man has always been his most vexing problem," as Reinhold Niebuhr says. He is the only animal who is able to perceive himself as an object and by so doing to transcend the life of momentary experience to judge his own behavior in larger perspective. This self-consciousness which sets him apart so complicates his behavior that he is divided against himself and unable to act on pure impulse. He looks at himself and questions his own impulses, whether to follow or resist them. He may start to act, then hesitate and come to a standstill while he ponders the situation and asks himself if it is better to do this or that. So he checks and contradicts himself by the inner separation of self-consciousness.

Out of these contradictions come the possibility of freedom and the necessity of making choices. Human life is a series of forked-road situations, in which choices are inescapable. If a person is stubborn and refuses to go either way, that too is a choice. The more conscious he is, the more alternatives he confronts and the more decisions he has to make. "The more consciousness, the more self," as Kierkegaard says. And the more self-awareness, the more alive a person is. Becoming a person means this heightened awareness of "I-ness," in the experience that I am acting in response to the events of my world.

Yet for this new dimension of self-awareness man must pay a considerable price. Out of the very contradictions that provide his freedom come the distresses of conflict. Life can never be simple or easy for a conscious person. He must forever contend with the competing demands of a complicated world and the clashing desires of a complex inner life that give him no rest. Like Adam, the prototype of every man, he is lured by the unknown, tempted by untasted possibilities, seduced by the one he loves, forbidden by highest authority, caught in conflicts of desire, overcome with guilty remorse, and driven forth to wrestle and sweat in a world of contradiction and uncertainty.

In these struggles who will not suffer anxiety and dread? Through such experiences every person must pass in the process of his self-realization. Anxiety is the psychological climate of conflict and uncertainty, in which alternative possibilities clamor for attention and choice in either-or situations. "Dread is the first reflex of possibility," says Kierkegaard, "a glimmer and yet a terrible spell." It is the "dizziness of freedom" in the tempting-forbidding stress of diversified options and alluring contradictions. Out of such anxiety a person comes to heightened awareness and passionate intensity of unique individuality. In this way he discovers his finitude and sin; he knows that he is incomplete, and yet he knows that he is not alone. He confronts Thou in the depth of his anguish and the height of his aspiration.

Freud also finds basic conflicts in every personality. From

a "seething cauldron" of excitement known as the id, primitive desires press impulsively and persistently for gratification. So irrational are they that if they have their way unrestrained, they will come to destruction. In so far as these primitive impulses conflict with the standards of conduct established by society, they are met by a restraining 'No' from persons in authority, such as parents who speak from the urgency of their own conflictual struggles.

As the growing child admires and fears his parents, he will identify with them and model his behavior after theirs. To the young child his parents seem omnipotent in the ability to gratify their desires, and he seeks to be like them in such traits as will gain him his desires. Also he needs their approval, for they are so close to him from day to day that he cannot tolerate the anxiety of their disapproval. A two-way relationship develops in which the child reaches out to identify with the parent and then to introject or take into himself their most insistent demands. So he will internalize their moralistic demands and regulate his conduct by the introjected authority they represent.

This internal authority, which Freud named the superego, is set against the impulsive id from which it derives its energy. There are two ways in which the superego operates. The conscious incorporates the punishments from the parents and continues to bring the punitive force against the impulsive life. In this eternal warfare the person suffers incessant guilt and moral anxiety which intensifies the distress, and punishes himself for trivial and unrealistic guilt feelings.

Another response of the growing person is to incorporate the approvals of the parents as the ego-ideal. This is the positive and rewarding effect of identification that motivates the person to strive for perfection at any cost to his contrary impulses. In his drama of urging and checking forces the drive for perfection collides with the drive for id pleasure, and the outcome is a civil war of interminable psychic struggle and intolerable feelings of guilt. In the lure of pleasure he is forever guilty, and in the light of the ideal he is forever condemned. He becomes his own accuser, and as the conflict is internal and largely unconscious, it is inescapable.

At the center of the conflict is the ego, aware of the demands of society and serving as the executive function that seeks to adjust to this reality principle. But its energy is derived from the impulsive life of the id, and the demands of the pleasure-seeking id are constantly upon the ego. The person is again in conflict which is inescapable, and he requires the utmost ingenuity to work out compromises between the conflicting demands. In this three-way conflict the moralistic demands of the superego operate against the reality seeking of the ego as much as against the pleasure seeking of the id. And the insistent demands of the id are striving against the restraints of the ego as well as the superego. To manage these recalcitrant forces the ego activates a series of defenses to repress the painful conflicts. But these defenses only drive the conflicts into the unconscious, where they continue their underground warfare in explosive dynamics that disturb the whole personality.

Neo-Freudians like Horney and Sullivan give priority to interpersonal relations over instinctual drives. Impulses of love, anger, and fear are responses to other persons who are perceived as approving or disapproving. These relations to other persons, which Freud also emphasized in his later years, are introjected to constitute the dynamic character of personality. Disturbing relations set up anxieties and neurotic defenses that react in perpetual conflicts. The neurotic person is not free to make realistic choices, for he is locked in conflicts of equally compelling forces driving in opposite directions, neither of which he wants. A person so blocked is stranded with no way out unless a radical change in him is accomplished affecting his relations with other persons.

Likewise William James recognized the sick soul as a divided self caught in basic conflict. Even when he may prosper and appear happy, he is haunted by a feeling coming from a deeper region of the precarious uncertainty of every good. A vigorous mind like Goethe can look back on his life from seventy-five years and say, "It has been nothing but pain and burden." Luther, when he had grown old, confessed, "I am utterly weary of life." This sense of failure and futility may vitiate all gains and infect any happiness with contradiction. Confronted with evil and loss as a finite person whose days are numbered, it is easy to fall prey to despair and melancholy. "I must first pass a sentence of death," said Bunyan, "upon everything of this life." The vitality of feeling that was once heightened to the anguish of acute distress may then turn to numbness and apathy. Again the cloud of anxiety may come to a storm of panic fear or settle down into obsessive compulsions to perform strange rituals in vain efforts to cope with fear.

Boisen from his own experience and research is able to give an inside view of mental illness. He finds the focus to be an intolerable sense of personal failure and guilt. Three different reactions have been noted: (1) drifting, withdrawing, and giving up the struggle; (2) delusion, self-deception, and projecting blame elsewhere; (3) a desperate attempt at reorganization. The first two are not conducive to recovery. They result in social isolation and progressive disintegration of personality with no fighting spirit or will to get well. But in the third reaction a person is willing to acknowledge the seriousness of illness and take radical steps to reconstruct his whole life. The more acute the crisis, the better is the prognosis, as there is less opportunity for drifting or deception when the distress is all-engrossing.

In this acute crisis he discovers healing power at work in psychotic illness, when it is a desperate attempt at reorganization of a way of life that had become intolerable. It may issue in a dramatic religious experience akin to conversion. In profound distress there is ultimate concern for the whole destiny of life. There may be honest confession of failure and guilt with earnest desire to enter upon a new life. In the study of historical religious leaders like Jeremiah, Ezekiel, Paul, Luther, George Fox, John

Wesley, Bunyan, and Swendenborg he traces conflicts similar
to mental illness but emerging into religious conversion. In a
religious crisis a person feels that he is confronting Thou, while
his fate hangs in the balance. In these periods of ultimate concern
creative forces are exceptionally active, as are forces of destruction also in the heat of seething emotions that intensify the
struggle. In such eruptive and decisive experiences the person
may have a religious conversion to change the whole course of
his life.

Crisis is inevitable for man. Conflicts are inherent in the
dynamic structure of his personality and emerge to acute distress
in his self-conscious awareness. Human growth undergoes critical
periods in birth, puberty, marriage, parenthood, climacteric,
aging, grief, and dying. There will be frustrating situations to
confront and intrapsychic conflicts to suffer. Minor hurts and
problems may be healed and adjusted, but underlying them is
the deeper wound of perpetual conflict at the center of his being.
It would be superficial to deny this basic disturbance and gloss
it over with optimistic rationalizations. There is nothing to be
gained in hiding or belittling the seriousness of man's predicament.

Is there no way out of this unyielding conflict in which every
person wars against himself as his own worst enemy? Freud saw
the psychic conflict as interminable, and while he did much to
understand and heal the sufferings of his patients, he remained
pessimistic about ultimate solutions. Kierkegaard, who took an
equally serious view of man's predicament, believed there was
a way of salvation open to man by renunciation and singleness
of devotion to God in Faith that only God can give. James and
Boisen agree that the crisis of conflict and despair is of fatal pro-
portions and that there will be no easy way out. The solution
is to be found in religious conversion, which is a revolution
decisive enough to transform the whole personality.

If such a conversion is possible, the crisis may not be alto-

gether evil. It may be an unusual opportunity to deal with life
in a new and creative way. Until problems confront us, we
do little serious thinking at all, and only then do we engage in
active search for solutions. A crisis arouses heightened awareness
and acute perceptions to sense danger and cope with the situation. It causes a desperate search for resources by which to
meet the need so vividly experienced. It brings into sharp focus
a person's role in the situation, his relationships and his responsibility to do what is best at such a time. Actions are to be weighed
more seriously, and questions are asked as to why this is so,
what it means, and what is required.

Not only does a crisis serve to awaken and mobilize resources
for the individual; it has the same effect upon a social group.
Boisen has shown by extensive research that times of crisis are
the most creative periods in the history of religious movements.
What the crisis of mental illness may do for an individual personality as a religious conversion, so the acute distress of economic depression may do in launching and augmenting a religious revival as in the Pentecostal movements around 1930.

Where there is little awarenss of need, there is little concern
for anything. But where the need is great, human concern rises
with the sense of urgency to ultimate pitch. Religion as ultimate
concern is a quest for the greatest value and destiny of life.
When local values are lost and the familiar props of complacency
fall, then our little securities are broken and we know they are
helpless to save us. Desperate need calls for greater resources
than our customary defenses and feeble futilities. When the
half-gods go, we turn to the ultimate Thou, realizing as never
before that no other will be relevant to our ultimate concern.

Every person is insufficient in his own isolation. This we
learned at an early age and found answers, if we were so fortunate, in the sustaining love of our family relationships. But
then we clamored for independence and gained a certain pose of
self-sufficiency by relying just enough on faithful relations to

keep our balance in an unsteady existence. We might do so well for a while as to forget that we are finite and gain a deceptive illusion that we are sufficient and secure.

But when the crisis strikes, we learn again what had been so easily forgotten. Now we know our needs, and after vain efforts to regain the self-sufficient pose, we must turn one way or the other. Either we hide behind defenses that cannot save but only foil us, or else we must honestly confess our folly and seek with ultimate concern for Thou. If we turn in that direction, the outcome may be a religious conversion. . . .

A genuine religious conversion is the outcome of a crisis. Though it may occur to persons in a variety of circumstances and forms, and though we may find many preparatory steps and long-range consequences, the event of conversion comes to focus in a crisis of ultimate concern. There is in such conversion a sense of desperate conflict in which one is so involved that his whole meaning and destiny are at stake in a life-or-death, all-or-none significance. Unless a person is aware of conflict serious enough to defeat him, and unless he is concerned ultimately enough to put his life in the balance, he is not ready for conversion. If in such a crisis a person reaches out to Thou, willing to give all of himself to this relationship, and out of mingling despair and hope decides to enter a new way of life, he may be radically changed in a religious conversion.

William James put it this way:

> To be converted [is] the process, gradual or sudden, by which a self hitherto divided, and consciously wrong, inferior and unhappy, becomes unified and consciously right, superior and happy, in consequence of its firmer hold upon religious realities. . . .

If religious conversion can do this, it is not to be shrugged off as wishful thinking or mere illusion. Where the results are inconsequential, there is reason to infer that the conversion was not genuine. But, you may be asking, is conversion necessary for everyone? Why trouble the contented persons who face no crisis or see no need for a new life? We may hear various replies to this question, and they are entitled to honest consideration. When we put this question, however, in the ultimate sense of the nature of man, we perceive that life for every finite person is a crisis. For no person is self-sufficient or able to fulfill his needs from within himself alone. He is incomplete, and to live at all he must depend upon resources beyond his own. Consequently, the very existence of man from moment to moment is a crisis. He may evade or deny the issue of his finitude. He may even claim that he is content to be what he is for the limits of time he can stand his ground, and then let him die without regrets and no questions asked. But in this defiant pose he deceives no one more than himself, who is too stubborn to acknowledge the infinite possibilities that might enlarge and enrich the meaning of his life. There is no crisis more serious than the pride that refuses to face the crisis. There are none so blind or so much in danger of defeat as those who will not see. The crisis is here whether we assent or not, as deep as our finite need and as great as our infinite potentialities by which to realize the meaning and integrating purpose of life.

There are those who scoff at religious revivals or quarrel with the methods by which religious groups may conduct evangelistic meetings. This is to be expected in a culture of such diversity as ours, in which there is freedom to differ in religious beliefs and practices. Some prefer the gigantic mass meeting, others the individual work of personal evangelism, and others the face-to-face interaction of the small group. Others will prefer none of these and ask only to be let alone. But when it becomes clear that the crisis confronting us will not pass, that it is inherent in our finite tendency to court defeat by cutting ourselves off from larger potentialities, then our concern may be ultimate. Then we may see that life is forever a crisis by the very terms of our finite existence, that our human aspirations will defeat us until we reach out for a response from beyond ourselves. Revival is necessary for the survival of all that we hold most ultimate in this restless search of human life.

Toward a Theology of Conversion in the Light of Psychology

SEWARD HILTNER

It will be the contention of this discussion that conversion to Christian faith, in our present western and heterogeneous society: (1) is to be seen as a direction of movement rather than as a once-for-all completed fact; (2) is most important, most likely, and most cultivatable in the thirties, rather than being regarded primarily as an adolescent phenomenon; (3) is most likely to be stimulated, in perdurable fashion, by an approach that begins from the genuine phenomenological concerns of pastoral care, proceeds without apology through processes of education, is attentive at every point to the Church's task of saving the world; (4) and is finally understood as the decisive joining of a fellowship of those who, though sinners yet saved, reach out in evangelism, in missions, and in social service and reform to share the treasure that God's grace in Jesus Christ has brought to them.

Styles of Turning Around

The subjects of the first psychological studies of conversion to Christian faith, by G. Stanley Hall and then, in more detail by one of his students, Edwin D. Starbuck, were teen-agers. Sometimes they were converted from immorality; sometimes, from confusion or apathy or meaninglessness. But always, there was a turning around and a constructive focusing of values. William James, anticipating nearly anything we can say today, drew heavily upon Starbuck's material; but he also used, anonymously, his own "case," his severe depression and its "conversion" into creative energy. And he was not a teen-ager when it happened.

In *Huckleberry Finn*, Mark Twain was not, with all his tongue-in-cheek, far behind William James. His revival meeting makes us shudder, and laugh, and then reflect. By the literary device of Huck Finn's being not quite up to teen-age, and hence not obligated to act and feel like an approaching adult, we are given perspective on the revival meeting. Through Huck, we are outside it. And yet, with all of Mark Twain's spoofing, we are in it too. Contentless though it mostly seems to be, it lures us, even after we have shuddered and laughed, and it lures us regardless of age. At our peril do we omit Mark Twain from our gallery of contributors to the psychology and theology of conversion.

In a conservative religious environment that was more moralistic and pietistic than it knew, I was "nudged" in the direction of "conversion," from the age of about eight. The special pressures came when we had a special preacher and a special series of meetings and sermons. I recall one occasion, when I was about eleven, when the pressure was very strong. Had I been appropriately moved, I would have stood up, gone up to shake the special preacher's hand, bowed rather obtrusively in prayer, and perhaps have been "converted" within. Then, as now, I seem to have had some kind of resistance to social pressure, and I would not stand up. When I "joined the church," a year or so later, the one thing I can recall is that the clerk had misplaced my name, had to be prodded by some one, and that I rode into church membership on the wings of the clerk's guilt feelings about having forgotten or misplaced "Seward." Anyhow, I made it.

Recently I got out my Latin dictionary and looked up "converto." I was not surprised to find "turn around," even though

I got a slight jar from the synonym, "whirl around." In Cicero, I found, it meant "to turn in the opposite direction," which is not so surprising if you get a proper definition of what "opposite" means. But I was truly startled to find that "conversio" meant, in Cicero, "a periodical return." No once and for allness here! And I was even more astonished to think of the relationship between "conversio" and "conversatio," the root of our modern "conversation," which routinely meant "frequent use," but which, in Seneca, meant "dealings with persons." A classical education, even with the help of a pony, is illuminating. Conversion, it seems, is a real turning around, even in the opposite direction (if you can figure out just what opposite means). Like a weather-vane, it may be periodic; and, like the related conversation, it may have a truly social reference. Perhaps the Latins were more penetrating than they realized.

Surely the most celebrated turnings-around of our day are to be found in Alcoholics Anonymous. I have heard many testimonies, including that of Bill the co-founder. In them all there is the long-continued, "I felt I could lick it myself," and then the final spree or stupor in which one began to think he was beaten for sure. At that point enter the colleagues, who interpret his being beaten as not bad but good. With their help, he joins a group. He hears of their defeatedness, and tells of his own. He acknowledges a "power greater than himself" that exists and is interested in him. He also quits drinking. He subjects himself to the social and moral discipline of Alcoholics Anonymous, which has the great merit of combining individual and self-therapy with group support and group challenge. He has been converted—above all, converted from drinking; but no less important, converted to acknowledgement of the fact that, whatever may be true for other people, *he* can not drink with impunity. What he is converted *to* may be theologically vague, even if disciplinarily precise. But anyhow, he quits drinking, attends A.A. meetings, and starts paying his bills and kissing his wife again. If he stays dry, he may learn, in due course, how to evade his wife and dodge his bills. But let us leave him at this point of his conversion. And it really is, quite literally, a conversion, a turning in the opposite direction. He lets alcohol alone.

As its wise leadership makes crystal clear, A.A. cannot reach all alcoholics, nor can it "convert" all those with whom it has contact. Nevertheless, its record, even statistically, is quite astonishing. And A.A. members, if they stay members and remain dry, become more mature. They work out the implications of their "conversion," first in A.A. itself but then to larger arenas including the work of the church. Happy the minister with a dry A.A. member on his board. He was "converted"—in his thirties, mind you, from degradation to usefulness, from self-contempt to social concern, from one kind of "reach" to another. Like Harold Begbie's "Twice-Born Men," he knows how depraved life can become; and now, freed from depravity, he can invest himself—even though, as A.A. wisely keeps pointing out, he is licked unless he remembers that he is "still an alcoholic."

A.A. is important in itself, but it is equally important beyond itself. For one thing it deals with adults, mostly in their thirties or so. Teen-agers may have drinking problems, but very few have become true alcoholics before they are twenty-one. For another, it shows how real conversions may be helped and how they may be hindered. Here is a typical illustration. Drunk, whose wife previously compelled his contact with A.A., and who told the boys that, unlike them, he was not a real alcoholic, begins to come out of the stupor, sees his A.A. friends, and begins to apologize. He was wrong, he says. He thought he had it under control but he hadn't. Will they, he asks, forgive him? But why the devil are they here, he asks himself? They were right and he was wrong. At that point an A.A. member may say to him, "Gratitude, my friend, will get you nowhere. This is *your* problem, not ours. But we have been there too."

The sobering drunk, his friends realize, could very well evade his own problem by attributing all kinds of Christian love to the A.A.'s who persist in helping him despite his smug self-sufficiency, now proved unstable. They will not permit his thanks to them to take the place of his reconsideration of his own situation. And that is the paradoxical dynamic of A.A. They *are* concerned. But no one can simply deal with their concern by thanking them for it. Either he gets on to his own problem or he is faking. The Twelfth Step of Alcoholics Anonymous makes the point crystal clear. One helps others not because he has some large altruistic quotient but, at least initially, because therein lies his own continuing salvation.

As the A.A.'s realized from the start, they have one advantage, whatever their disadvantages; they know precisely who and what their devil is, from which they need "conversion." It may, indeed, be a similar fact, although less obvious, that Starbuck was studying at the turn of the century, whether he knew it or not. For the most part, the devil of his teen-agers was sex in general and masturbation in particular. True, there were both euphemisms and complications. Still, those teen-agers knew their devils; and, whether indulging or not, called them by name.

Various writers have shown that "turning around" may be a political, or economic, or other, as well as a religious kind of event. Like James, they have shown that no real turning around is without antecedents, dissatisfactions with the *status quo* psychic, or lures from an ideal. With the insights of Freud, the actual conflicts may be traced. The "conversion" may be seen as a conflict-resolution, in one sphere or many—not precluding future conflicts but giving direction to the concern, which just might have turned the other way. You may be converted to communism, to the John Birch society, or to many other things besides Christian faith. You may even be converted to democracy. In no instance does the turning around, in itself, attest to the soundness of what you now espouse. For that, other criteria than your personal experience are required.

There are, therefore, many styles and modes and meanings of "turning around," of conversion. Even if the object is Christian faith, the same statement remains. One may pledge tonight

allegiance to the Flag or the Bible, or against the Demons Rum
or Sexiness. As the A.A. experience clearly shows, what happens
from then on is likely to depend, in a complexly interrelated
way, upon: (1) accurate understanding of the immediate enemy
from which deliverance has been won; (2) social support that
transcends one's natural psychological defenses (3) a discipline
which is not prevented by pride from looking ever and again
at the source of deliverance, and which is aware that it has been
saved in "principle" rather than "all over." This is, in truth,
a spelling out of what Martin Luther meant by saying that the
redeemed man in Christ is *simul iustus et peccator.*

Conversion for the Second Half

For many years I have even memorized the page number in
Modern Man in Search of a Soul (264) where Carl G. Jung
gave vent to an important and true statement which has been,
in its interpretation, the most hashed-up quotation in Protestant
history. Jung wrote:

> Among all my patients in the second half of life—that is to
> say, over thirty-five—there has not been one whose problem
> in the last resort was not that of finding a religious outlook
> on life. It is safe to say that every one of them fell ill because
> he had lost that which the living religions of every age have
> given to their followers, and none of them has been really
> healed who did not regain his religious outlook.

In this important statement, Jung was doing two things. In the
first place, he was implying what he considered to be the true
function of religion in any age; namely, helping men to encounter, deal with, and be related to the depths of life including
those that emerge from within; and, at the same time, to give
them social and patterned support in the encounter with depths
so that they are not thereby overwhelmed. When religion, regardless of its content, is performing its proper function in
human life, it is this twin service, Jung believed, that it per-

forms. Men are not permitted to become "flat," by reason of detachment from depth. But on the other hand, they are not, thanks to religion, fated to be helpless pawns when the powers of depth ("principalities and powers") rise up to overwhelm them. Thus religion provides both depth and dignity.

Jung was also, in his statement, rendering a judgment on our own western culture. Our rationalism, he felt, had divorced us from even wanting contact with the depths. We had become, in his words, "one-sided" about trying to handle all of life through our minds, even when feeling and intuition and sensation should have some proper attention, and be recognized as having integrity. When a man has lost the twin guarantees of earlier religion—encounter with depth, but protection from it— then he is adrift, Jung felt, not only with the individuality of his problems, whatever they might be, but also without the rudder his religion would otherwise have provided. Let him, by all means, get squared away about his Oedipus Complex, his passive-dependent or some other kind of tendencies, and all the idiosyncrasies of his own characterological defense system. All this, to Jung as well as to Freud, was important. But with that done in fair shape, what then? There still remain, Jung believed, the "depths." He who insulates himself from them impoverishes himself. He who approaches them naively and without protection invites disaster. Hence the statement about "regaining" a religious outlook. Too few of the quoters have noted the Jung sentence immediately following, "This of course has nothing whatever to do with a particular creed or membership of a church." Jung's words, on analysis, bring no more comfort to the smugly faithful than did those of Samuel Butler when he noted how many would be equally shocked to hear Christianity doubted or to see it practiced.

But there is another angle to what Jung is saying. There is "the second half of life." Still dealing exegetically with Jung, there is no implied opprobrium of younger people including young adults. Suppose that they have not been able to "regain" a "religious outlook"? Between heavy commuting hours, keeping the gadgets working, doing-it-yourself, and above all, making the children socialize properly, young adults may be forgiven for seeing very little beyond the next diaper or week-end. But come the disappearance of 2:00 a.m. feedings, distraction over the mortgage, re-mastering of the binomial theorem, or the push toward music or ballet lessons, what then? The excuse for extra-verted inattention to meaning is gone. Some kind of existential confrontation is finally in order. What, *then*, is it all about? In his own way, that is what Jung means. Before, you could be, excusably, too busy to reflect. Now, you either reflect or regress!

Conversion or catastrophe? By this age it is, according to Jung, one or the other. If you have succeeded in your early-set goals (two cars in the mortgage-free garage, from two to six children launched and in space, social relations bringing clear-cut identification, etc.), then you either consider the long-term goals of life in deeper terms or you keep beating old bushes for scraps of outworn meaning. If you have not succeeded in the same goals (whether you have hit the Bowery or not), then, equally, do you need fundamental reconsideration of life's meaning. To what, *now*, are you committed? What, *from here on*, are to be your emotional investments? Success or failure, by your own standards, what you simply cannot have is business as usual, i.e., the pattern of young adulthood. If there is trauma, it is not produced, as commonly reported, by the departure of the last child from the home. If that event seems to produce an "empty nest," the nest was in a precarious fork all along. Now, the precariousness has to be faced; or there will be catastrophe, not ordinarily in a "blow-up" fashion, but mostly by descent into either nostalgic mediocrity or compensatory denial.

Without necessarily underwriting every detail of Jung's reasoning, I think he is brilliantly right on the main point. The age when conversion means life or death—the eleventh hour, in biblical language—is the entrance to the middle years. Before that, one's value system is probably sufficiently affected by the general culture that he is mostly not in jail, not a traitor to his country, not a Don Juan or a lush; and, for a time, those negative virtues may be sufficient when allied with their positive counterparts. For the long pull, however, they are not enough. At this point the "depths" (either in Jung's sense or some other) must, whether one knows it or not, either be faced or, by some cultural legerdemain, avoided.

When Lowell G. Colston and I did our special study of pastoral counseling (with the modern scientific apparatus of electronically recorded interviews, pre-test and post-test and all the rest, published in *The Context of Pastoral Counseling*), we realized only in retrospect and reflection that the vast majority of our counselees were just beginning the "second half of life." None of them consulted us just because they were growing older. All of them had specific life problems. In so far as we were able to help them, or to get them to other sources of help, we finally concluded that these people were fortunate. They were troubled by specific circumstances (including divorces, for instance). But in the counseling, they had of necessity to consider not merely and solely the presenting problem (divorce, etc.) but also what life might mean from then on. Consequently the counseling dealt with both the immediate problem and the long-term meanings and values. Had they not had the immediate and individual problems, they might never have got to the value reconsiderations. Hence the ascription of "fortunate." Unless purely individual problems rear their ugly heads, most persons entering the middle years do not revalue their values. And here I am with Jung: brother, things have changed, whether you know it or not!

Guiding Conversions

As it happened, no one of the persons reported in the Hiltner-Colston study came to us and said, "Please, I want to be converted; show me the way." Some people, because of their way of life, their previous disbelief, or their new insight, do say this. And if so, the minister needs to be attentive, and not (as are most of my students) thrown off base and rendered speechless at this evidence of the Holy Spirit's perpetual work.

Most persons, in a culture that is still evidential of Christianity even if it has lost the words allied to the tune, approach a potential conversion more indirectly. They begin from a personal problem whatever its nature. They move to extrapolation about "the universe." This occasion is, if I may say so to pastors, not a retreat but an opportunity. Never mind that the immediate frame of reference of the person bears little overt resemblance to the "anxious inquirer" of previous ages. He may nevertheless be a very "anxious inquirer" indeed, even if his sole immediate communications are about the flatness of his marriage, the invasion of his income tax, the ingratitude of his children, or the oddness of sexuality. Can we grasp the nettle, and helping him with it, nevertheless not be fobbed into believing the problem area is the real problem? In every such pastoral encounter, there is the chance for conversion. The mode may vary. The parishioner may gripe or yearn or despair. The discourse may be about God in Jesus Christ, or about the general hellishness of life. All modes are of equal concern to God, we may be assured, if they are serious and not flippant.

It is thoroughly appropriate that some Christian conversions should be social before they are articulately theological. Reared in a Christian culture, and absorbing more of it than he knows, one may indeed "come alive" only with Selma, Alabama, or some such; and only then realize that, whatever the performance of the churches at Selma, or especially before, Christian faith must be at Selma, and indeed is behind Selma. Only then may he begin seriously to think of why this is so. He may be impressed with hypocrisy, delay, stagnation—and who could say these are absent in the actual churches? But he may—through Selma or other critical incidents—be able to recognize that which lies behind, the power of the Lord Jesus Christ in relation to every dimension of life. Any guide to conversion should be prepared to have his conversions come either head-first or hind-end first. It makes no difference. If he thinks it does, he is not *en rapport* with the Holy Spirit.

Conversion and the Church

According to one proper definition of conversion, a man is converted when he stops thinking of the church as it or they, and thinks of it as "we." Let us suppose that a man, upon the threshold of middle years, has pastoral counseling, has got some competent help on the individuality of his problems, and has, thereby, turned to reconsider the meanings and values of his life from then on. In these days, the chances are that he has been a church member since his children reached nursery school age, that he and his family have been "church related" for years, he is not in jail or a mental hospital, that he supports his community chest. But he has probably thought of the church as "it" or "the" or "she." He may or may not have been active in the actual programs of the church. But suppose that now, he feels, with a new insight into himself, that the "church" is no longer "over there," but something in which *he* is involved, on the vocation of God himself. This does not bless his particular ideas about program. But it does indicate a radical conversion, however unobtrusive it may seem from surface perspectives.

He may, especially in his new "converted-to-the-church" condition, raise questions about the "church." Why haven't we conquered poverty, juvenile delinquency, mental illness, war, and much else? he may well ask. And his asking may be sharp and bitter. For, the fact is, we have not conquered any of them. But if his asking leans toward a "we," an involvement, then, whatever the situation, he has had some kind of conversion. For him it is no longer just "it" or "they" or "the churches," as if he were detached, but something to which he too, with whatever reluctance, is committed.

In my judgment, conversion is all around us, not only as potentiality but very often as actuality. Can we recognize it when we see it? I am not so sure. We may foster it, and indeed we should. Let us not be confused by some particular mode of change so that we are blind to real conversion when it occurs. It is, after all, the Holy Spirit that produces all Christian conversions. Can we be attentive to his work?

Conclusion

A theology of conversion is a theology of change in the direction of what Christ calls us to heed and to do. It may begin with a quintessential acknowledgement of what Jesus Christ has done for us, sufficient for all eternity; or it may begin from grousings and gripings about how bad things are. The Holy Spirit, which comes from Christ too, may be in both modes of movement.

What does in fact produce real change? This may occur, in teen or any other years, whenever there is serious reflection upon our human condition in the light of God and his justice and grace. My argument has been that some kind of conversion, while desirable at any age, is a must upon entrance to the middle years, that this is the great "conversion frontier," and that much of our previous thinking about "conversion" must be altered to heed the work of the Spirit in the thirties and forties.

Experience and Conversion

JACQUES PASQUIER

The title of this article could be misleading—or, at least be interpreted in several ways. At one time we spoke of a conversion-experience. Biographies of saints, or even more recently the charismatic movement, seem to view conversion as if it was something instantaneous, happening once for all, and reflected in the total transformation of the personality. However, my own experience, and the experience of those to whom I minister, have taught me that instantaneous conversion is not the norm. Conversion is rather a long process, a spiritual journey made up of failures and falls and, also, made of new beginnings, new discoveries, the experience at every moment of the fidelity of a God who calls us back to him, who changes our hearts of stone "into hearts of flesh."[1]

Instead of talking about "conversion-experience," it seems more appropriate to say that there is in every human experience a call to conversion which involves a double movement of self-acceptance and a reaching beyond what we are now. These seemingly contradictory movements are in fact the center of our faith conversion. I would like in the limits of this article to address myself to the nature and the process of this conversion, which could be looked at logically. But in fact conversion has neither harmony nor order. "Unless you die ... unless you are reborn." Life and death have in fact no proportion in them; and it is the same with conversion.

The nature of conversion

Denis Vasse defines prayer as the passage from need to desire.[2] I suggest that it is the same with conversion. Need has to do with a taking hold of the object, and when the object is possessed, there is still a desire that can never be fully satisfied. In fact, the "object" becomes a "subject"; it is the other, which cannot be reduced to an object.

At the basis of any religious experience, as in any relationship, there is the strong desire to possess, to reduce the other to an object which the person can assimilate to his own identity. Psychoanalysts tend to talk about the refusal to accept the trauma of the birth-separation, the refusal to accept the other as other. At the center of conversion is the destruction of our own image of God, in order to allow God to be God for us: a God who not only is other than what we are, but is also other than what we want him to be. It is in the acceptance lived at the daily level of our experience that "My ways are not your ways,"[3] that a person begins the long process of conversion.

Psychoanalysis shows that all our representations and images can be used as "security blankets," which refuse to allow us to be in touch with reality, blocking it in a static vision. And our image of God is no exception to this. In fact the most difficult image to get rid of is our image of God; this is our last refuge. Our whole life needs to be submitted to this constant critical attitude which is not only the destruction of our own images but an openness to the reality, to the truth.

Faith is the readiness to enter into this long process of the destruction of our false images of God, in order to allow God to be God. The history of Israel, like the history of the Church, can be understood as a continual process of destroying one idol after the other, in order that his people might grow in the knowledge and the experience of who God is. At the center of conversion is the experience that no tabernacle can ever be built, no image of God can ever be possessed; but that God is always working at the limit, at the edges, stretching us beyond the today and leading us to learn how to trust and how to love, opening us to a constantly new reality, a new truth.

The passage from one image to another (unfortunately we always need an image—be it of ourselves or of God) and the constant call to leave behind the present image is the process of death and rebirth of which Jesus speaks to Nicodemus. In death, life is not taken away; it is radically transformed. In our experiences of powerlessness, of being stripped of our masks, we come to realize that new life is given, a new call, a new reality: "No one can see the reign of God unless he is begotten from above."[4]

This conversion can be concisely exemplified in an area which is central to our life: the area of self-acceptance. Spiritual events take place in our psychic life, not outside of it; and the movement of conversion begins and ends in the acceptance of who we are. A few weeks ago *Time Magazine* had an article on some of the narcissistic trends of modern psychotherapy in the United States.[5] It dealt with this need for self-knowledge which very often leads to self-centeredness. But self-knowledge is not for self-centeredness, it is for self-love; and this is not the same.

Genuine love and self-giving are impossible for someone who has not learned—sometimes through painful experience—that he can love himself without being threatened by the self he is discovering. Self-acceptance—this being at ease with the totality of oneself—is neither solely nor primarily a question of self-knowledge, a psychological process of clarification and self-understanding. At the basis of this self-acceptance is faith.

We would easily draw a picture which would give us the perfect image of what the person should do in order to become perfectly mature. It would be enough simply to make a list of all the "I shoulds" or "you shoulds" that we have heard since our childhood. But in fact when we begin to travel the long path of self-knowledge two things happen. First we become aware that there are many aspects of the self which cannot be understood or possessed. Wanting to answer all the questions about ourselves, being over-concerned about the meaning of our lives, can lead us to many compromises: into looking for self-worth in what we can achieve, into justifying our existence in the categories of material success, efficient techniques, and somehow identifying the building of the Kingdom with the building of our own image.

The second thing we discover is that we are not as good as we thought we were. We slowly come into contact with some of our needs, and our neurotic tendencies; we discover or unveil our need for security which makes us use God and others for our own satisfaction. We discover that we are too exclusive or possessive of others. We get in touch with all our fears: fear of loneliness, fear of loving or being loved, fear of our own sexuality. Yes, we are not the perfect person we thought we were or that we would like to be or that others think or expect us to be. Little by little our tiny store of self-confidence evaporates. No big games are possible; and even little games begin to appear too difficult for us. We begin to be honest with ourselves; and nothing is more painful than this honesty.

Maybe conversion takes place at this point: being able to say "yes" to who we are, to our limitations, to our possessiveness, to our selfishness, to our fears. A "yes" which does not mean "I will remain what I am"; but rather a "yes" which means "I recognize what I am now, I accept it, I am not other than what I am."

In a certain sense, if holiness is a gift of God, we are asked to be opened to this gift. Can we see ourselves as being the gift of God to us? Or are we saying—in very subtle ways—that God has done a bad job with us? Can we see ourselves as being lovable and therefore loved by God and by others, not in spite of what we are, but because of what we are?

The movement of conversion which is a movement of faith —begins with one's acceptance of one's being. Mary Magdalen, the Prodigal Son "who came to his senses,"[6] were first able to accept their limitations without any self-pity or any sense of despair.

The movement of self-acceptance is a movement of faith. Without faith man does not know how to sustain the weight of his existence. If the gift of being is a given, a gift becomes a gift only when it is freely received. It is in faith that we are called to respond in freedom to the gift of being. It is in faith that we say "yes" to who we are: a self which we do not fully understand, a self limited and yet open to possibilities hardly dreamed of. We become free, free to make choices, not knowing where they will lead us. We are ready to abandon a static self-image in order to allow the self to become.

Because faith is openness, openness to a gift which is constantly being realized, we cannot rest at the level of the answers which we have or want to possess. Faith is to live not only with what we are today, but also with what we are called to be tomorrow. Self-acceptance is not static: it is not only acceptance of who we are, but also of what we are called to be. and, like any horizon of reality. it is always beyond the grasp of any apprehending capacity.

The Process of Conversion

It is always difficult to schematize a phenomenon which is not and cannot be described in logical terms. And yet in every conversion there is a pattern which cannot be avoided. I would describe it as the passage from one certitude (or set of values) to an openness to another reality. The key word is "passage." It evokes the breaking through a wall of resistances in a free act. Two aspects in this process of conversion need further reflection: the aspect of resistance and the aspect of freedom.

Resistance

The process of conversion begins with a crisis point which can reach different depths of affectivity. But it is basically a sense of dissatisfaction, the feeling that whatever value-system we have at a given point is in contradiction with other tendencies in our own being: tendencies which are not clear, and yet which are deeply experienced at the level of our own being. Carl Rogers would talk of a certain sense of incongruency. It could be in the area of moral behavior, religious behavior or any other area of one's own life. This feeling of incongruency can come out of an experience: the experience of the death of a loved one, or of a long process of self-searching. But conversion, if it is to be true, will affect the totality of one's behavior: one's relationship with God, with others and with oneself.

But conversion is possible only if, at the same time that we experience dissatisfaction or incongruency, we can also see alternatives or at least the possibilities for new ways: the crisis point without these alternatives leads to depression and, in the last analysis, to suicide.

The first resistance one experiences is in accepting the "crisis point" or the dissatisfaction. The temptation is to deny it either through repression or sublimation. The refusal to deal with one's own depression, one's own sense of incongruency, through work, alcohol or any other form of escape-mechanism, is the refusal to accept the call to "go beyond" the experience. It can immediately take many different forms—and for the sake of clarity I would like to underline different ways of expressing this refusal.

i) *Resistance to the reality of the present by living*
either in the past or in the future

I am not referring to a chronological factor, but to a scheme of interpretation we use as we look at reality. How do we interpret the "here and now" experience? We can look at it either in terms of the past—as we saw it and understood it in the past which allows us to know which responses should be given—or in terms of the future, as we would like to see it. Both past or futurist schemes of interpretation are a means of escape, of self-protection, a refusal to listen to the newness of the here and now.

ii) *A refusal to accept the mystery of one's own existence*

I believe that one of our greatest temptations is wanting to understand all our tendencies, all our behavior in the constant effort of trying to control and predict them. If the phenomenon of conversion is the passage from a known situation or value-system to an unknown value-system, such a passage is possible only as far as we are ready to accept the dimension of mystery in ourselves. Rudolf Otto speaks of the twofold aspect of the Sacred—and therefore of the mystery—in terms of *tremendum et fascinans*. The *tremendum* is so much part of this experience of the mystery that the fear makes us run away from the mystery we are to ourselves.

Maybe the best way to understand the process of conversion is by looking at the process of death and dying. Conversion is nothing else than that: death to a certain image of oneself, of God, death to a known reality: experiencing—much more than knowing—that somehow in the acceptance of this death a new life is emerging.

In her book *Death and dying*,[7] Kübler-Ross talks about different stages which take place in the process of dying. Maybe we could apply these different stages to the process of conversion. The first stage is the stage of *denial*. We have already spoken of the different forms this denial could take. Following denial is the stage of *anger*. It is one of the most difficult stages to recognize and accept. Somehow we have not learned how to express our anger. Having a confused feeling that dying is part of the process of any spiritual journey we tend to rebel against it: "Why me? Why is God doing that to me?" And yet we find ourselves extremely uncomfortable in trying to verbalize or articulate this anger. It creates a lot of guilt; anger—or the expression of it—is always seen as something bad. Maybe it could be helpful to look at the psalmist struggling and wrestling with God, articulating in very powerful language the feeling of having been abandoned, and resenting it.

This leads to the third stage: the *bargaining* stage: our bargaining with God can take many different forms, but somehow it is like entering into a dialogue with a God reduced to our own image. We sit together at the same table to see how many compromises we can find: "If you give me this ... I will give you that." And yet in spite of all this bargaining one becomes more and more aware of one's own helplessness: that God is not a God you bargain with, that God is God and beyond that nothing can be said. One comes into touch with one's own powerlessness and sinfulness. We come into touch with our finitude and limitedness or brokenness. I think it is when we come to this point that, in the experience of *helplessness,* we begin to realize that running from place to place, knocking on all the doors, is leading us nowhere. Maybe we can enter into the act of *acceptance,* ready for the act of surrender: the point where words are no longer necessary. In the experience of silence, the Word begins to speak to us. In the experience of darkness, the light begins to shine: very uncertain, very weak, yet becoming more and more real. What is left is not loneliness, but an emptiness, a vulnerability which is the beginning of conversion. We can let go because new life, which is no more greatness, but more littleness, is coming through, in the experience of dying. One has grown to understand the real Beatitude ... "Happy the poor," happy the one who has nothing, who can lay naked on the earth and taste it. Accepting our own powerlessness, we experience the power of God's love and life.

Maybe we can understand better now how the process of conversion is nothing else than the constant living out of the Paschal Mystery, lived at the level of the daily experience: the death to a part of oneself, that the real self—the "God self" part in us—may grow. Paul's prayer for the Ephesians expresses this constant call: "That your hidden selves may grow strong, that through faith Christ may dwell in your hearts."[8]

Freedom

Somehow at the center of the process of conversion is the experience of freedom. The act of surrender has to be a free act: God does not force himself upon us. The lying down, face in the dust, being able to utter "your will be done" is not the result of a lost battle against an invisible and invincible God. Sometimes, listening to people describing their experience of conversion, one has the impression that the experience does not give too much room for personal choice, and is more an acting out of a compulsion than the result of a free choice.

And yet freedom is at the center of this surrender. Maybe the aspect of freedom is clearer at certain stages than others. The breakdown of resistance is the first free act. We can deny and protect ourselves behind roles and façades, we can conform to all the expectations that others put on us and that we ourselves too willingly put on ourselves. To break down this resistance is the choice that one makes to stop "running away," in order to look at the reality of one's experience is the *locus* in which God reveals himself, talks to us as individuals. We can accept or refuse this challenge. But more central to the process of conversion is the readiness to accept the consequences of our conversion and surrender. We all experience having uttered the words "your will be done," but spend a great deal of energy denying these words in our daily behavior.

A conversion is not only surrender: it is a choice for life. Acceptance of death does not make sense if it is not the choice for a new life: one made of challenges, of unknown and of possible and real failures, of rejections and communions. Can we own the consequences of our choices? Can I own the suffering which is part of life? A lot of suffering in our life has been and is unproductive for the simple reason that it is received passively—imposed on us. The choice for life—for new life—is the choice for suffering, trying to be authentic in our choices.

In a culture where everything is "instant" we obviously look for the instant result; we find it difficult to accept that the spiritual journey in which each one of us is involved cannot be instantaneous. The temptation is to give up. Thomas Merton wrote in one of his letters about this temptation:

> We are not converted only once in our lives, but many times; and this endless series of large and small conversions, inner revolutions, leads to our transformation in Christ. But while we may have the generosity to undergo one or two such upheavals, we cannot face the necessity of further and greater rendings of our inner self, without which we cannot finally become free.[9]

It is only "in the fullness of time that God has spoken to us in his Son."[10] God reveals himself not only in the fullness of time but also in the slowness of time, in our sinfulness and forgiveness, in our struggles and our defeats, in our deserts and in our land of milk and honey. He reveals himself as a God of Covenant, a God who cannot be known or possessed, but a God who can be trusted because he is Father: he allows each one of us to experience him as a Father of love.

Conversion is the abandonment of our own securities. To allow God to be God for us is accepting that we cannot be "the man with all the answers," but that we are ready to become "the pilgrim with questions."[11]

1. Ezk 36:26.
2. Vasse, Denis: *Le temps du désir* (Paris, 1973) pp. 19-20.
3. Is 55:9.
4. Jn 3:4.
5. *Time Magazine* (October 23, 1976), p. 57.
6. Lk 15:17.
7. Kübler-Ross, Elizabeth: *On Death and dying* (New York, 1969), pp. 39-137.
8. Ep 3:17.
9. Merton, Thomas: letter published in *Information Catholiques Internationales* (April, 1973, back cover).
10. Heb 1:2.
11. Sheehy, Gail: *Passages* (New York, 1976).

Part Four

THEOLOGICAL PERSPECTIVES

Conversion

KARL RAHNER

A. Theology

1. *Methodology*

a) The content of the theologically important and indeed central concept of conversion will be presented here from the point of view of dogmatic theology, but that of biblical theology will also be taken into account.

b) It is difficult to distinguish the concept precisely from related theological concepts: faith (as *fides qua*) and consequently hope and love, contrition, metanoia, justification (as an event), redemption. Reference must therefore be made to these terms. In accordance with the corporeal-spiritual, historical and social nature of man, conversion has always, though in very varying degrees, a liturgical and social aspect in all religions, including Christianity (rites of initiation, baptism, penitential liturgy, revivalist meetings, etc.) This can be the embodiment and social side of conversion, but if it is not performed with genuine personal conviction, it constitutes a deformation of conversion and of religion generally. This aspect cannot, however, be dealt with further here.

c) The biblical terms שוב, ἐπι -, ἀπο - στρέφειν, μετάνοια and others are specifically religious terms which denote more than an intellectual change of opinion (as in Greek). They concern the whole human being in his fundamental relation to God,

n)t merely a change of moral judgment and attitude in regard
to a particular object (and commandment).

2. *Conversion as fundamental decision.* From the point of view
of the formal nature of freedom, conversion is the religiously and
morally good fundamental decision in regard to God, a basic
choice intended to commit the whole of life to God inasmuch
as this takes place with some definite, if only relatively higher,
degree of reflection and consequently can be located at a more or
less definite point in a lifetime. For the freedom which finds realization in one individual life as a whole is not a mere sum of moral
or immoral free actions, simply following one another in time.
It involves one act of freedom as fundamental decision. Nevertheless, this fundamental decision is not wholly accessible to ana-
lytical reflection. It cannot, therefore, be fixed with certainty by
such reflection at a quite definite moment in the course of life.
This must always be borne in mind in the theological interpretation of conversion.

3. *Conversion as response to God's call.* From the biblical and
dogmatic point of view, man's free turning to God has always
to be seen as a response, made possible by God's grace, to a call
from God. And he himself in the summons gives what he asks.
This call of God is both Jesus Christ himself, as the presence of
the Kingdom of God in person, with the demands this involves,
and his Spirit which, as God's self-communication, offers freedom and forgiveness to overcome the narrow limits and sinfulness of man. It also comprises the actual situation of the person
to whom the call is addressed. This is the precise particular embodiment of the call of Christ and the Spirit.

4. *The content of the call,* which cannot be separated from
its utterance, is a summons, imposing an obligation and making
obedience to it possible, to receive God, who communicates himself, liberates man from enslaving "idols" (principalities and powers), and makes it possible to have courage to hope for final liberation and freedom in the direct possession of God as our absolute
future. The call therefore summons us from mere finitude (since

grace is participation in the divine life itself) and from sinfulness, in which man in mistrust and despair makes an idol of himself and of certain dimensions of his own existence in the fundamental decision of his life (since grace is forgiveness). The call is not simply a command to fulfill particular moral obligations, to "amend one's life."

The content of the call can, of course, also be described the other way round. Where a man is detached from self ("denies himself"), loves his neighbor unselfishly, trustingly accepts his existence in its incomprehensibility and ultimate unmanageableness as incomprehensibly meaningful, without claiming to determine this ultimate meaning himself or to have it under his control; where he succeeds in renouncing the idols of his mortal fear and hunger for life, there the Kingdom of God, God himself (as the ultimate ground of such acts) is accepted and known, even if this occurs quite unreflectingly. In this way the conversion remains implicit and "anonymous" and in certain circumstances Christ is not expressly known (though attained in his "Spirit") as the concrete historical expression of God's definitive self-utterance to man. Ultimately the intention is the same, whether Jesus calls for conversion (*metanoia*) to the *basileia* of God present here and now in himself and confronting the whole man with its radical demands, whether Paul calls us to faith in God who justifies without works through the Cross of Christ, or John admonishes us to pass from the darkness to light in faith in the Son who has appeared in the flesh. All continue the preaching of penance by the prophets of the OT and give it a radical character through the faith that in Jesus Crucified and Risen the call of God, which makes conversion possible, is definitively present and invincibly established, but precisely for that reason imposes the gravest obligation.

5. *The "today" of conversion.* Conversion itself is experienced as the gift of God's grace (as preparation) and as radical, fundamental decision which concerns a human life in its entirety, even when it it realized in a particular concrete decision in every-

day life. It is faith as concrete concern about the call, which in each instance uniquely concerns a particular individual, and as the obedient reception of its "content." Conversion is hope as trusting oneself to the unexpected, uncharted way into the open and incalculable future in which God comes (which is predestination). It is a turning from one's past life (freely performed yet experienced as a gift), ending the repression by which the past was detained in sin. It is love for the neighbor, because only in conjunction with this can God really be loved, and without that love no one really knows with genuine personal knowledge who God is. It means standing firm and grasping the unique situation which is only found at this particular moment "today," not soothing oneself with the idea that it will come again, that the chance of salvation is "always" available. It is the sober realization that every conversion is only a beginning and that the rest of daily fidelity, the conversion which can only be carried out in a whole lifetime, has still to come.

6. *Conversion in non-Christian religions* (and even the secular analogies in psycho-therapeutic practice) has to be judged by the same general criteria as are used to interpret theologically non-Christian religions and perhaps even "implicit Christianity."

B. Pastoral Aspects

1. In ordinary Catholic pastoral practice the occurrence of conversion as a central event in the history of an individual's salvation is very often masked. The reasons are easy to see. Baptism, which was *the* event of conversion in the early Church with its baptismal devotion, is in most cases administered to infants. Confirmation also for the most part does not in practice figure as the ritual expression of a conversion. The same applies to our practice of First Communions in early childhood. Furthermore, our pastoral practice treats as the normal case a Christianity lived in a relatively homogeneous Christian society, where the ultimate Christian attitudes and decisions are taken as a matter of course (even if it is questionable whether this is really the case).

Practice in the confessional, frequent confession and preaching on morals, which deals chiefly with the particular demands of Christian daily life, also tend to a perpetually repeated rectification and improvement of Christian everyday life on its average level rather than to a fundamental, unique "new birth."

2. Pastoral practice and theology, however, ought not to overlook the phenomenon of conversion as a decisive function of pastoral care of the individual. Not only because freedom in the sense of man's unique, historical self-realization intended to be final in regard to God, implies a fundamental decision (*option fondamentale*), but also because a decision of this kind ought to be carried out as consciously and explicitly as possible, since reflection and history are constitutive of man's very essence. From this point of view, conversion is not so much or always a turning away from definite particular sins of the past, as a resolute, radical and radically conscious, personal and in each instance unique adoption of Christian life. And in this, freedom, decision as absolutely final, and grace are really experienced (cf., e.g., Gal 3:5). Furthermore, in a society which in philosophical outlook is extremely heterogeneous and anti-Christian, Christianity in the individual, deprived of support from the milieu, cannot survive in the long run without a conversion of this kind, i.e., personal fundamental choice of faith and Christian life.

3. Pastoral theology and practice should therefore cultivate more the art of spiritual initiation into this kind of personal experience of conversion. Not that a genuine conversion can simply be produced at will by psycho-technical methods. But as clear and conscious as possible an accomplishment of the fundamental Christian decision can be considerably furthered by really wise and skilled spiritual guidance on the part of an individual pastor (as the preambles of faith demand). In an age of atheism which declares it cannot discern any meaning in the question of God even as a question, or discover any religious experience whatsoever, this spiritual initiation into conversion has not primarily a moral decision as its immediate goal, but the bringing about and

voluntary acceptance of a fundamental religious experience of the inescapable orientation of man towards the mystery which we call God.

Catholic pastoral practice was and is mistrustful of any deliberate production of conversion phenomena ("methodism," "revivalist campaigns"), and with good reason (regard for "objectivity," fear of pseudo-mysticism, fanaticism, will to preserve the ecclesiastical character and sobriety of Christian everyday life, etc.). Nevertheless, there have also been in existence for a long time in Catholic pastoral practice all kinds of ways of methodically promoting conversion, adapted to the general human and cultural level of Christians, e.g., popular missions, retreats, days of recollection, novitiates, etc. All such pastoral methods directed towards conversion ought, however, to be examined to see whether they are precise enough and correctly adapted to the dispositions of men today which make possible for them a genuine religious experience and conversion. Catholic pastoral practice should realize its own particular dangers and obviate them by a determined effort to provide genuine spiritual guidance towards really personal conversion. The dangers are those of the merely liturgical and sacramental, of legalism, of the practice of comfortable church-going and mere conventionalism, of conforming to the average level in the Church.

4. Since the fundamental decision has perpetually to be maintained or renewed in quite novel situations, the fundamental phases of life constitute so many situations and specific forms of conversion. Puberty, marriage, entry into a profession, beginning of old age, etc. ought to be regarded as situations offering the opportunity for conversion, and pastoral practice ought to know how its spiritual initiation into religious experience and conversion must be specially adapted to fit these situations.

5. From the very nature of freedom, the fundamental decision of which has to be concretely realized and maintained in the multiplicity of particular voluntary choices in daily life, and because of the connection between conversion and the limits of

human life, its individual differences and phases of growth, it is understandable that a Christian life may run its course like a slow uninterrupted process of maturation, without very clearly marked breaks (though these are never wholly lacking). On the other hand it may appear as a dramatic event with one or more apparently almost revolutionary conversions which can be dated with considerable precision (as, e.g., with Paul, Augustine, Luther, Ignatius Loyola, Pascal, Kierkegaard, etc.). But even a sudden conversion can be the result of a long but imperceptible development.

C. Conversion from Another Christian Community to the Catholic Church

1. Special problems arise on the "conversion" of a Lutheran or Orthodox Christian to the Catholic Church. What is in question here is not solely (or not even necessarily in all cases) an interior change in the ultimate fundamental attitude concerning the whole of life. It is a change in the ecclesiastical situation of the convert. On the one hand it is conceivable, for example, that in such a case a "saint" may be converted, and then only the external ecclesiastical status would be altered. It is possible for someone merely to change his denominational membership without special inward change of heart, although this is really needed, and to become a Catholic, even for reasons which have no religious significance at all. The normal case, however, will be one in which conversion to the Catholic Church also involves something in the nature of an inward religious conversion.

2. "It is clear that the preparation and reception of those individuals who desire full ecclesiastical communion is in essence different from ecumenical work; the two, however, are not incompatible, for both derive from God's wonderful design" (Vatican II, Decree on Ecumenism, no. 4). In practice this conciliar declaration means that the ecumenical work of Catholics as such must take care not to aim at individual conversions to the Catholic Church, for this would bring that work into disrepute and make

it impossible. On the other hand, even in the age of ecumenism such individual conversion is legitimate and indeed a duty, the necessary conditions being presupposed. The same applies, therefore, to the endeavors of Catholics and of the Catholic clergy to promote such individual conversions. At all events, however, in case of actual conflict in practice, ecumenical work must take precedence in importance and urgency over individual conversion.

3. The following principles might perhaps be indicated as important in the endeavour to promote individual conversions.

a) If such work is not to degenerate into a false proselytism, the pastoral missionary work at the present day in the countries which are called Christian but are largely de-Christianized ought to be concerned with the re-Christianization of contemporary atheists, of people who belong to no denomination and of the unbaptized, rather than with promoting individual conversions of the kind mentioned. Winning the former to the Catholic Church then represents simply the final stage of a conversion in the genuine religious sense of the term.

b) In view of the limited pastoral resources in personnel of the Catholic Church, non-Catholic Christians are not in practice suitable "subjects" for the work of conversion, even if this gave promise of success, if they are pursuing a Christian life in the genuine Christian spirit in their own Church and if they would not be much changed or advanced in the central and essential concern of Christianity, which they are of course in a position to live in accordance with their concrete religious possibilities and needs. Consequently, for them a denominational conversion could scarcely mean in practice a conversion in the real sense. It is different with those who denominationally belong to a non-Catholic Church or community but do not practice and religiously speaking are homeless.

c) Anyone who wishes to become a Catholic on genuinely religious grounds may not be turned away but must be afforded most attentive pastoral care.

d) If ecumenical or personal grounds suggest it, the interval of time between recognition of the Catholic Church as the true Church of Jesus Christ and official conversion to it need not be restricted to a very short period.

4. The pastoral care of converts involves more than instruction in Catholic dogmatics and moral theology. As far as may be, it ought to aim, in preparing for the act of entering the Catholic Church, at making this a conversion in the full religious sense of the word. This presupposes a good knowledge of non-Catholic theology and an understanding of ecumenical work. It must endeavor to counter rather than to strengthen a purely negative attitude of protest in the convert against his former ecclesiastical community. It must encourage the convert not to lose any element of his positive Christian heritage by his move, and assist him to cope in faith and patience with the often very imperfect life of the Catholic parish. The pastoral care of converts cannot, therefore, simply be regarded as ended by their conversion.

The Characteristics of Conversion

BERNARD HÄRING

The biblical message of conversion does not consist in an abstract human figure confronting a literal law (Judaism) or an ideal of virtue (Stoicism). According to the Bible, two camps, the dominion of God and Satan with his following, confront one another in reality. Two forces struggle for our heart, the old Adamite man and the redeemed man created anew in Christ and through his Spirit. The teaching of conversion gives the answer to the question of how the two camps and the two ways of existing oppose one another in the world and in the heart of every man.

Conversion and the Ultimate Experience

Conversion is simply the work of separation, at the end of which Christ, the victor in the great confrontation, will hand over those on the left to the pool of fire and lead those at his right hand into his kingdom. We understand the biblical assertions on the incomprehensible change, on the violent revolution which fulfills itself in conversion in the light of the last things, in the light of the judgment that begins on Christ's cross and will be made manifest to all on the last day. It is the passage from death to life, from darkness to light, from lies to truth, from damnation to salvation. It means a rebirth in God (Jn 1:11, 13; 3:35), a birth from above, "in the Spirit" (Jn 3:5), adoption by God in a true "new creation": "If any one is in Christ, he is a

new creation; the old has passed away, behold, the new has come"
(2 Cor 5:17).

From the urgent brevity of the saving fullness of the end
of time, conversion receives the character of radical decision.
On the cross the fearfulness of the final battle (Rv 8:20) and
the seriousness of God is made visible, in the resurrection of
Christ we see his victory: already the outlines of the last judgment and of the final triumph of God are painted before our
eyes. Who could wish to settle down complacently between
the two camps? Who could play with death when the life of
the world has already won its victory?

The end of time is the time of separation and of a holy radicalism. But it is still the interim, a phase between the resurrection
and Parousia of the Lord, in which the New which has broken
upon us, the divine dominion constantly in process, is still veiled.
The fronts of the battle are drawn very clearly, of course, in the
cross and in the resurrection of Christ. But the separation of
men into the two camps is still in progress. For humanity it will
be concluded only with the Parousia, for the individual man
with death. *This entire time is under the sign of conversion.* The
knowledge of this truth guards the individual and the entire
Church from that dangerous triumphalism which was again and
again indicted and deplored at the Second Vatican Council and
which had formed a largely incredible "style."

The reconciliation of the radicalism of the already begun
last age and the veiling of the interim period—the violent upheaval in conversion and its still unfinished character—presents
difficult questions. They have found their false expression in the
Lutheran expression *peccator simul et justus.* In this view the
"convert" retains in this temporal world essentially the inner
form of existence of the "sarxist." Adamite man. His justification,
his new form of existence, is reserved for him in the gracious
judgment of God; it remains beyond this life. In accordance with
an inevitable automatism the old trunk puts forth its bitter fruits;
in the same way the fruits of conversion grow in the manner of

an automatism—by the power of the irresistible act of the gracious God—out of fiducial belief which is put on from without and which alone merely covers over the conversion.

In Catholic teaching, after the first and basic conversion—after justification—a virulence does indeed still persist from the Old, but the New takes its stand beside it. This battle does not run on one-sidedly between the "wicked world" outside and the angel in one's own breast. These forces struggle with one another in one's heart as well as in the world. But it is not a battle on the same plane of existence. In the heart of this interim God's dominion has already established itself. Perhaps the devils conquered by Christ in the judgment battle may still pursue their work in this world. But already the Church succeeds in restraining them. How forceful her word and sacrament would be if our culpable failure did not obtrude and retard them! The same holds true of the individual who has been justified: the victorious powers of Christ at the end of time are in him; he is a new creature. If he gives the powers of the age to come (Heb 6:5) no place, it is free and genuine guilt, not merely an external addition.

Thus in Catholic teaching conversion is treated with bright optimism, but an optimism which does not permit one to wait idly for the kingdom of God to break in from heaven. The last things are effective signs as much of the hope of the soul converting—for conversion proceeds only from a forceful hope—as of the judgment on the lazy servant.

Conversion and the Kingdom of God

The *eschata* are simply the kingdom of God which some day will be manifest and even now is always beginning, veiled. *The powerful and urgent invitation to conversion proceeds from the coming of the kingdom of God.* "Jesus came into Galilee, preaching the gospel of God, and saying, 'The time is fulfilled and the kingdom of God is at hand; repent, and believe in the gospel' "

(Mk 1:14f.). The establishment of the dominion of God in this world by the incarnation, the death, and the resurrection of Christ and by the sending of the Holy Spirit creates for the sinful world the gracious possibility of a return home. The single stipulation is the humble acceptance of this loving dominion in Christ. For this reason Christ's preaching on conversion constantly repeats the demand for the childlikeness which gratefully lets itself be endowed (see Mt 18:3; Mk 10:15).

Conversion is a grateful and joyous acceptance of the kingdom of God as God wishes to establish it between the day of Pentecost and the Parousia. Therefore, the question of how the kingdom of God is present in the interim is most important for a theology of conversion. If it is an affair of "pure subjectivity," then conversion means a mere change of disposition, to which little or nothing in the affairs of this world matter or can matter, because the kingdom of God would not have yet begun for them.

If the kingdom of God is a power which will come from heaven unexpectedly only at the end of time, then conversion can limit itself to mere fiducial belief and in pure subjectivity give the course of the world over to the devils.

Scripture and tradition make other assertions about the kingdom of God: the Lord himself is "the light of the world" (Jn 8:12; 9:5), so too his kingdom is comparable to a city on the mountain, a light on a stand (Mt 5:14f.). "The kingdom of heaven is like leaven which a woman took and hid in three measures of meal, till it was all leavened" (Mt 13:33). "You are the salt of the earth; but if salt has lost its taste, how shall its saltiness be restored?" (Mt 5:13). Thus the acceptance of the kingdom of God and with it also conversion in the strict sense means entering into the intentions of God towards the world and the earthly community. Through the converted, through those who have opened themselves to the dominion of God, the world and the community should feel something of the "first fruits of redemption," of the already proclaimed loving dominion of God (see Rm 8:19ff.).

It is true that the turning to the kingdom of God does not happen primarily with a view to the world and earthly affairs, but as a response to the saving invitation and saving works of God. And yet the complete turning of man to the kingdom of God would renew the face of the earth: for one cannot give himself to Christ and his kingdom and then stand indifferent to the great work of his redemption, which is valid for all creation. Though the Christian knows that the final consummation of the world lies in the eschatological future and will be effected by God alone, he is nevertheless also conscious that the future kingdom has already begun with Easter and Pentecost and that the converted have the privileged task of manifesting to all areas of life God's claims to dominion and the saving intentions of the redeemer.[1]

Certainly, conversion in the sense of the gospel is primarily transformation of the heart, the happy turning to a new conviction, a life hidden in Christ. There is no doubt that the "rebirth in God" must show itself first in the disposition, in a new basic relation to God and to one's neighbor and to the good. But conversion is no partial act alongside our life, but an incident of indivisible totality.

As the coming of the loving dominion and of the kingdom of God also means the redemption of the cosmos, of all things—which means the establishment of the saving dominion of God in Christ over everything that is created—so genuine conversion of the individual and of the community always also demands and signifies a change in the milieu.

We are still the world even after we are transplanted into the kingdom of God. Indeed, the transition from the "wicked world" into the kingdom of the delivering love of God can be accomplished in us only if we let the "first fruits of the blessed freedom of the children of God" come to the world which hungers for redemption—to our own milieu, especially. If I wish to make a genuine and effective conversion, I must at least will to convert myself together with my milieu. I cannot honestly say *yes* to God's dominion in my heart if I do not affirm God's dominion in the sphere of my life with the contribution of my entire heart and all my powers. It is indeed the entire Christ, the savior of the world, who wishes me to transform completely.

The kingdom of God which has begun in Christ is a "*kingdom of love*" especially concerned with the salvation of all men. Acceptance of the kingdom of God—and that means conversion —is, therefore, a solemn obligation to the law of love and to its vital center, the apostolic zeal for the salvation of one's neighbor. The entrance of God's right of dominion in the world, the fulfillment of the commission to be "leaven and salt of the earth," and the fulfillment of the kingdom's great commandment of love form an inseparable unity. If one hands over the world to the devil and withdraws into pure subjectivity, not only is the recognition of the divine dominion lessened, but the achievement of salvation in the midst of a corrupted environment is made more difficult for a great number of people.[2]

The Church of this interim is not to be equated simply with the kingdom of God, but she is the beginning, the sign, and the instrument of the gracious dominion of God. For this reason she can be called "the quasi-sacrament of the kingdom of God." Conversion thus has an ecclesiastical aspect. Acceptance of the kingdom of God means a *yes* to the Church as the community of salvation in which we are delivered and in which and together with which we may and must act for the salvation of the world and for the honor of God.

"The kingdom of God is like a grain of mustard seed" (Lk 13:19). The law of growth is suited to the kingdom of God as a whole. The same is therefore also true of conversion. Not only the conversion of the full number of the chosen, but also the complete conversion of the individual is subject to the law of gradual growth. The great break—the transition from the kingdom of darkness and damnation to the light of the life of grace—is customarily prepared amid an entire chain of helping graces. In the same way, the newly given divine life needs a long time to develop itself fully. Usually, only the final *yes* to the loving will of God in death brings final maturity. But one thing must not be overlooked in this: the great transition from death to life with Christ does not proceed from the forces of this world but is a powerful new creation by God. From the human point of view it is a breakthrough, a violent revolution against the old condition; from God's view it is a regeneration, a rebirth in the Holy Spirit. Only God can bestow growth on the "mustard seed" of his kingdom—but not, of course, without the free cooperation of man.

Because we must understand conversion from the perspective of the kingdom of God, it is clear to us that the growth of the new life in individuals must not be isolated from the growth of the kingdom of God as a whole. The salvation of the individual stands in most intimate connection with the fulfillment of salvation of the kingdom of God. Each man opens himself to the growth given from above particularly by praying and working for the coming of the kingdom.

Thus all statements about the relation of the kingdom of God and conversion point to one thing: to the active solidarity with the concerns of the kingdom of God. The summons of the Christian to the apostolate does not stand only as an inevitable addition at the end of his conversion. At all his steps the man becoming and struggling should in gratitude and co-responsibility be conscious of his unity with the concerns of Christ and of immortal souls.

The Good News of the Return Home

The Vulgate's translation of Christ's first call to conversion has also contributed in obscuring one essential characteristic of the sermon on conversion. It gives the Greek word μετανοεῖτε as either *poenitemini* (Mk 1:15) or *poenitentiam agite* (Mt 4: 17). This could give the impression that the sermon on conversion was in essence concerned primarily and perhaps completely with the summons to works of penance. The Greek word in the original text means in its direct philological sense the radical "thinking around." It has, however, still another tone if one knows that the word in the Septuagint was the rendering for *schub*, or returning home. So the sermon of Jesus, preached in Aramaic, was not a direct summons to "penance in sackcloth and ashes," but the good news of the already begun era of the great return home, of renewed hearts, of the kingdom of heaven which has come very close.

In order that the message of the possibility of returning home can be thus correctly accepted as good news, the consciousness of the wretchedness of sin and the need of redemption must of course, be alive. Only the person who understands the homesick longing of the exiled people can suspect the jubilation which is released by the call of the prophet: The time of homecoming is come. This aspect of the penitential sermons of the prophets and the penitential rites of the old covenant has had such a great significance that the call to conversion can be understood rightly as good news. Papini in an overstated poetic fiction presents a hell growing ever more hellish and devils growing ever more devilish, who finally, having arrived at the extreme abyss of evil and torment, say to themselves: "Our defiance has gone far enough; we must humble ourselves and convert." It doesn't happen that way. Man does not approach conversion through increasing evil, but through growing insight into his sin and into the misery of being cut off from God. Our world today is truly sinful enough to say, "This has gone too far; we must convert!" What is needed today is a serious effort to bring the humanity cut off from God, the open or concealed neopagans, the entire misery and injustice of sin, to consciousness so that the preaching on conversion, preaching on offered salvation, can really be understood and accepted as good news. But the sermon on sin must be very clearly oriented to the good news of the inconceivably glorious coming home to the paternal heart of God, to the unending privilege of being taken into the kingdom of God.

Just what is the idea of penance then? Is it only a concealment of the good news? By no means! Without penance, or at least the readiness to do penance, there is no true lasting and profound conversion. But it is important that the stress not be misplaced. Tediousness must not be placed in the foreground. One must not wish to call in and harvest the "fitting fruits of conversion" (Mt 3:8; Lk 3:8; Rv 23:20) before one has sown the joy over the homecoming. Of course, in further progress the one must be furthered with the other and by the other. So many conversions beginning well do not last because the seriousness of the desire for penance, the sense for expiation in the face of the just God, the *yes* to the cross of Christ was not awakened. But perhaps a still greater number of men have not set out on the way of conversion because it was not proclaimed and exemplified for them as the Easter message.

Not only the first reversal and return to God—culminating in justification, in the rebirth in God—but also the second conversion, the *conversio continua*, stands essentially under the "law of grace" and can therefore be correctly proclaimed only as good news. Certainly, we must always also hear the accusation which the law, especially the chief commandment and the sermon on the mount, raises against us; even our very contrition and humility in view of our past sins must call us to ever deeper contemplation and return, and to penance. But from the Catholic perspective this is not the primary thing. In the foreground of our consciousness and our proclamation must stand the experience of the good news: "He that is mighty has done great things in me!" The call to the intensification of conversion in the New Testament proceeds especially from the *magnalia Dei*: You are consecrated; fulfill this in your life! You are the children of light; therefore walk as children of light! You have risen with Christ; let that be visible in the way you live![3] "He who says he abides in him ought to walk in the same way in which he walked" (1 Jn 2: 6). He who is converted and is constantly called to a more profound return is not subject to a merely exterior regime of law; he is subject to the order of grace (Rm 6: 14). The life of grace given him and each new grace call him to continuous conversion and to a lasting growth in the good.

Sacramental Structure of Conversion

Christ oriented his own sacraments to conversion. The basic sacrament of homecoming is *baptism*. Already in the work of John the Baptist the preaching of conversion formed with the baptism of conversion a unity which was a type of the coming baptism of the Spirit which was to be the actual sealing of conversion.[4] Justin the apologist calls baptism "the bath of conversion which can wash only those who are converted."[5] In the bath of rebirth Christ gives assurance of his gracious meeting to those returning. He makes them like himself and takes them to himself irrevocably.[6]

After baptism, no first conversion, no conversion from death to life, should any longer be necessary. It is a great miracle of God's compassion that he offers to the baptized soul who has again turned from him the sacrament of penance as a second Easter gift. The remaining sacraments are "sacraments of the living": they are intended to bring the grace and friendship with God already present to maturity and to perfection. For this reason we might also call them sacraments of the second conversion.

All sacraments have the eucharist as their center. This makes clear that the meaning of the second as well as the first conversion is an ever more fervent meeting with Christ.

In the light of the teaching on the sacraments, which are indeed all in some way oriented to conversion, the character of conversion as taking place within the kingdom of God reveals itself still more clearly. "The sacraments designate and effect incorporation into the Church. As signs of the Church the sacraments are gifts of grace within the community and for the benefit of the community; they are appointed to build up and to deepen it."[7] Thus the effective language of the sacraments shows us that conversion is always also a gift from the fullness of grace and the apostolic spirit of the Church and signifies a gracious membership in and obligation towards the Church. The reception of the sacraments will only attain its full fruitfulness, and conversion will only then fully mature, if one tries to become a vital, solidaric-feeling, actively cooperative member of the kingdom of God, the Church.

All the sacraments are cult signs and signify the orientation of our entire life to "worship in spirit and in truth." Baptism, the basic sacrament of conversion, effects the release from sin through "consecration," through the being placed in the glory of God in order to glorify God. As consecration received in baptism is the fruit of Christ's sacrifice on the cross, so the stamp of baptism orients Christians to the valid and heartfelt participation in the glorification of the Father in Christ. The sacrament of re-conversion, the sacrament of penance, restores the cult-worthiness bestowed by the character of baptism and confirmation, or, as the *Pontificale Romanum* says in the rite of penance, it gives the sinner "back to the altar." The radical orientation of the entire life after conversion, and even the conversion itself to the glorification of God, is a powerful imperative of grace: *for those returning home are given their commission not by a mere positive commandment, but by the gracious act of God in Christ and in the Church.*

1. See B. Häring, *Macht und Ohnmacht der Religion*, pp. 51-67.
2. See *Lebendige Seelsorge*, 8, 1955, with the over-all theme "Pastoral Care in the Environment."
3. See Rm 6; 1 Cor 5:7ff.; Ep 2:1ff.; 4:20ff.; Col 1:21ff.; 2:20ff.; 3:1ff.
4. Mk 1:4; Lk 3:3,16; Ac 13:24; 19:4ff.
5. *Dialogue with Trypho*, 14, 1.
6. See Rm 6; Col 3:1 ff; 1 P 2:22 ff.
7. *Pastoral Directives of the French Episcopate*, nos. 4 and 11.

Conversion: The Central Moral Message of Jesus

CHARLES E. CURRAN

Conversion is the central moral message of Jesus. St. Mark summarizes the entire teaching and preaching of Jesus in terms of the call to conversion. Jesus came into Galilee preaching the good news of the reign of God: "The time has come . . . and the reign of God is at hand. Be converted and believe in the good news" (Mk 1:15).

This chapter will develop three points. First, the call to conversion is the joyful proclamation of God's love calling for a change of heart in the individual. The second point will consider God's role in the work of conversion, whereas the third point will discuss man's response in the process of conversion. From the different theoretical aspects of the teaching on conversion practical conclusions will be drawn for Christian life in our times and for the sacrament of penance which is the sacrament of conversion.

I. CONVERSION AS THE JOYFUL CHANGE OF HEART

Jesus is direct, straightforward, simple; and yet Christian teaching and preaching today is too often legalistic in tone. People are warned to do this, to avoid that. The emphasis falls on a particular action or mode of external conduct. The authentic Christian message, however, calls above all for a change of heart —a radical, internal change of the person; external actions will follow from the person's changed heart. The gospel reminds us that the good tree will bring forth good fruit and the evil tree will bring forth evil fruit (Mt 7:17-20). The Christian message aims to produce the good tree from which comes good fruit. If a man changes his heart, then his actions will change accordingly.

New Testament theology teaches that conversion is the joyful change of heart that comes from hearing the good news of salvation. The good news is that God, here and now, offers his love to man. The motive for conversion is the presence of the reign of God in Christ. Translations frequently employ the word *kingdom*, but *reign* perhaps better approaches the meaning of scripture. *Kingdom* tends to connote a static reality and is too often identified with a monarchical political structure. *Reign* avoids the prejorative connotations of *kingdom* and better shows the reality of the reign of God as his love made manifest to man, especially in the person of Jesus. To be converted and believe in the good news, then, means to change your heart and to accept the gift of God in Christ Jesus. This change of heart is not, however, a moment or a static state once and forever effected. Conversion is a continuous turning, a growing, a becoming. And if it is not that, then it is the opposite—a turning away from God.

The *kerygma*, or central preaching of the early Church, tries to bring about a change of heart by recalling the marvelous works that God has done for man, especially in the resurrection of Jesus. Through his resurrection Jesus has become Lord—Messiah—and eternal priest. The proper response of the hearer is conversion and baptism in the name of Jesus. The Acts of the Apostles contains many examples of calls to conversion as preached by the first disciples of Christ. The theme is constant: the good news of salvation requires a change of heart in the person who, hearing, believes.

The parable of the Prodigal Son (Lk 15:11-32), perhaps, contains the most appealing scriptural presentation of the meaning of conversion. (Some scriptural exegetes prefer to call the parable the story of the merciful Father, for the essential features of the parable stress the prodigal—lavish—mercy and forgiveness of our Father in heaven.) The son demands his inheritance and leaves his father's house to go to a far away country. There appears to be no good reason for his leaving but to be free from the parental yoke and to pursue pleasure. The delusion of sin quickly becomes evident. The son does not find what he expected. Instead of happiness, freedom and joy, he experiences only sorrow, slavery and misery.

The details of the story bring out the miserable condition of the sinner, the degradation of sin. Sin is not just a wrong action; sin is not primarily the breaking of a law. The parable poignantly portrays sin as the breaking of the intimate relationship of love with the Father. The sinner leaves the loving abundance of the Father's house to seek his happiness elsewhere.

What is the conversion of the foolish son? Conversion means the joyful return to the Father. The son has experienced his own misery and realized his error in leaving the house of his father. The return to the father's house is a joyful experience. The father does not treat his son harshly; there are no words or scenes. The father does not even remonstrate with his wayward son. Rather, the father runs to greet him and cries tears of joy because his lost son has been found. A joyful banquet celebrates the return of the son.

The parable of the Merciful Father portrays the meaning of sin and conversion. The early Church used the parable to refer to those Christians who had deserted Christ (obviously Christ could never have used the parable in that sense) but were called to experience the joyful return to the Church, the house of the Father. For the Christian who has broken his relationship of love with God through sin, the call to conversion echoes the story of the Merciful Father who is ready and waiting to receive his wayward sons with outstretched arms and a joyful celebration.

Practical Conclusions

The central notion of conversion as the joyful change of heart entails many practical consequences for those who try to teach and live the Christian life. First, the call to conversion always should echo the joyful call of Christ. Conversion is man's response to the good news of God's love—the gospel. The urgency of the call to conversion in the New Testament stems not from motives of fear but from the greatness of the gift of God and the shortness of time. Now is the great moment of history. In a sense, the countdown of all history has been leading to the coming of Jesus. Now he is here. Now is the opportunity for man to accept the great gift of God. There is no time to delay. Leave everything—father, mother, brothers, sisters—to follow the call of Christ (Lk 14:26-33).

The New Testament call to conversion differs somewhat from the call to conversion addressed to the Israelites in the Old Testament. In the Old Testament conversion frequently was motivated by fear of punishments that would be inflicted if conversion did not take place. Christian teaching and preaching has tended, unfortunately, to overemphasize this motivation of fear and punishment. The New Testament motive for conversion is always the good news of God's love made present for his people.

Popular teaching not only has overemphasized the importance of punishment but also has distorted the meaning of punishment in Christian life. Theologians today tend to see punishment as the natural consequence of sin, the refusal of God's love. Punishment is primarily intrinsic and not extrinsic; that is, punishment is the logical consequence of the action performed.

A second practical consequence of conversion as the joyful change of heart concerns the sacrament of penance. The primary role of the confessor is to proclaim the good news of conversion and to celebrate the joyful reconciliation of the wayward son to the Father. The confessor is above all the herald of God's loving mercy and the representative of the community in the joy of reconciliation with a wayward member of the community.

A third practical consequence for Christian life also follows from the notion of conversion as the joyful change of heart. Too often in the past Catholic teaching has insisted on particular, individual actions in and of themselves. External conformity received the foremost emphasis. However, the primary aim of Christian teaching is to change the heart of the hearer. Again, the circumstances of our own age reinforce the need for Christian teaching to center primarily on the change of heart and not on external actions as such. In the complexity of modern living, Christianity demands much more than just conformity to a comparatively few norms of conduct. Christian education should aim at forming the new heart through which the Christian can sensitively respond to the call of God and neighbor in the intricate situations of modern life. Actions spring from the heart; hence, the heart first must be renewed.

Conversion is the change of heart by which a person becomes a friend of God and a recipient of his love. Mortal sin is the opposite of conversion. Mortal sin is the change of heart by which a person turns away from his relationship of love with God. Mortal sin marks the refusal of life, the refusal of light, the refusal of Christ. Sin, like conversion, involves a profound change of heart. Although theology has taught always that sin is a turning away from God, popular teaching too often has identified sin with a particular, individual, external action. We say that lying is a sin, or we ask if war is a sin. The action, however, becomes sinful only if the action involves a change of heart. The external act alone can never express with certitude the fact that the person has had a change of heart. The wrong action might be the sign of ignorance or passion or an honest mistake —or a change of heart. Every wrong action does not involve necessarily a change of heart. Theology and catechetics should carefully distinguish between wrong actions and sin. . . . The ex-

ternal action is grossly sinful only to the extent that it is the
expression of the fundamental change of heart which is sin.

   The realization that conversion and sin involve a change of
heart again has important consequences for the sacrament of
penance. Penance is not a "magical" rite. Penance does not merely
cancel out a few bad actions or "wipe away" some mortal sins.
The sacrament of penance calls for a profound change of heart
that involves the core of human existence. The so-called "devo-
tional confession" or "confession of venial sins" involves a
strengthening of the new heart of the Christian. The actions required of the Christian illustrate the profound change which penance brings about. The penitent Christian now is willing to love
and forgive others in the same way that Jesus has loved and forgiven him. This is the central biblical message of conversion.
It has to have important consequences for the teaching and living
of the Christian life.

II. CONVERSION AND THE REIGN OF GOD AS HIS GIFT

   Conversion to the reign of God in Christ is the central moral
message of the New Testament. However, conversion and the
reign of God are primarily God's work and not ours. The primary truth of Christianity is the fact that God saves us. Too often
Catholic theology and catechetics have emphasized the role of
man in salvation. Too often people think that man saves himself
by his own actions. Salvation is frequently pictured as an agree-
ment between God and man. If man does these things and fulfills
these conditions, then God will give him the reward of salvation.
Theology has always tried to wrestle with the God-man relationship, but a danger of emphasizing the role of one at the expense
of the other is always present. Ultimately, the work of theology
is to explain the relative roles of God and man, faith and works,
gospel and law. Both aspects are essential. In the past, Roman
Catholic theology has not always stressed the primacy of God's
love. In many ways the scriptures recall the primary truth of

Christianity—it is God who saves. God in Christ works the transformation and brings man from darkness to light, from death to life, from slavery to the freedom of the children of God.

The scriptures show that salvation is primarily God's gift by the emphasis on the privileged members of the reign of God. One might naturally expect that the privileged members of the reign of God would be the rich, the powerful, and the influential. But according to the scriptures the privileged members of the reign of God are the poor, children, and sinners. The privileged position of the poor, children, and sinners indicates that man does nothing to deserve or earn the gift of salvation. The non-value of the recipients of the gift of God shows the divine good pleasure in loving man and establishing his reign. This insistence on the poor, sinners, and children also illustrates the necessary disposition on the part of men who are to receive the gift of God's love.

The privileged position of the sinner in the reign of God also illustrates the fundamental truth that salvation is primarily God's gift to man. Obviously, the sinner has nothing to offer God in return for his love. The sinner has no claim whatsoever on the love and mercy of God. The privileged position of the sinner merely highlights the divine mercy and forgiveness. At first glance, the sinner would seem to be the person furthest from the reign of God. How can one ever dare to say that the sinner has a privileged position in the reign of God? The goodness and mercy of God know no bounds. There is no better illustration than the privileged position of the sinner to show that salvation depends primarily on God's loving mercy and forgiveness. Man does nothing to earn salvation. His good works or merits do not count. The determining factor is the love of God, who allows his sun to shine on the just and the unjust and extends his mercy to all men.

The privilege of children also emphasizes that salvation is God's gift to man. The child is the perennial symbol of help-lessness. The child has nothing to offer but needs the love and protection of others. Luke the evangelist puts on the lips of Jesus a prayer thanking his Father who has chosen to reveal these things to the little ones: "Yes, Father, for such was thy good pleasure" (Lk 10:22). God has revealed his love and his works to man not because of man's actions or merits, but simply because of his own benevolence, because of his own good pleasure. Salvation, conversion, the reign of God, is his gift to man. The privileged position of the child merely highlights the gratuitousness of God's reign.

The parable of the Merciful Father (Lk 15) has already been mentioned as providing excellent illustrations both of sin as the breaking of a relationship of love and of conversion as the joyful return to the house of the father. Perhaps the story of the merciful Father makes an even greater impression if one sees the story in modern dress. After his parents have raised and educated him, a son abruptly takes all that he has and leaves home. The parents never hear from him again. Years later the son returns—poor, in debt, and in need of help. What might a modern father say to that son? Perhaps it would go something like this: "You really hurt your mother and me by going away. We were growing older, and I wanted you to stay and help with the business. Now that you have spent all our hard-earned money and are miserable, you want us to bail you out and welcome you again into our home. I am afraid that it would not be fair for us to bring you back into our home. It would not be fair to your brother who has spent these many years working in my business and looking after your mother and me. And really it would not be fair to you. You have to prove yourself before we can take you back. This might sound hard-hearted to you, but it will be the best thing for you in the long run. You will be grateful in the future for what I am doing for you because it will make a man out of you."[1]

How different is the attitude of the merciful Father! He does not demand any proof on our part. God's love is such a gift that man could never do anything to prove worthy of receiving it. Our worthiness or merits do not influence the attitude of the merciful Father.

Meditate for a moment on the attitude of the elder brother in the parable. When the elder brother discovered what occurred, he was angry and would not participate in the joyful celebration of his brother's homecoming. The elder son rebuked his father. The older son had served his father for many years and obeyed all his commands, but his father had never celebrated a feast for him. The action of the father is not fair or just. The younger son who left home and spent all his money on harlots and false friends now receives a joyful reception and a banquet in his honor. Notice that the elder son cannot even refer to the prodigal as "my brother" but rather speaks of "your son." The attitude of the elder son is typical of so many Christians who think only in terms of justice and obedience and commandments. The elder son cannot understand mercy and love and forgiveness. One who knows only justice does not know the real meaning of God's love and mercy.

The gospel narratives frequently teach that the first shall be last and the last first (e.g., Mt 19:20; Mk 10:31; Lk 13:30). The parable of the laborers in the vineyard dramatically illustrates that man's approach is not the same as God's (Mt 20:1-16). Salvation is not primarily a recompense due in justice for the actions man has performed. The householder went out at various times in the day and brought in men to work in his vineyard. Some had begun work early in the morning, whereas others were hired late in the afternoon. At the end of the day, all were paid the same amount. However, those who had worked for the whole day and bore the brunt of the day's heat murmured against their employer. "It is not fair to give those who have worked but one hour in the cool of the evening the same wage given to us who have been working all day." At first sight, the complaint seems legitimate. The owner replies that he has done them no injustice. As owner he can choose to give to the latecomers the same wage given to the others. The owner defends

his own freedom and generosity. The owner of the vineyard
serves as a constant reminder that God is free in distributing
his love as he wills. No one has any claim in justice on God's
generosity. The parables of mercy repeat in a dramatic way the
primary teaching of Christianity—it is God who saves.

Practical Conclusions

The emphasis on the primacy of God's love shows the importance of worship in the life of the Christian. Man is always
a worshiper before God's loving gift. With grateful and rever-
ent attitude men received everything from their God. The eucha-
ristic motive in the Christian life is summarized in the prayer
of the psalmist: "What shall I return to the Lord for all that
he has done for me." The liturgical renewal in the Roman Catholic Church will achieve its fullest meaning only when men
realize that their whole life is a eucharist—a continual and grateful response to the call of God. The entire life of the Christian
manifests the gift and goodness of God's love. Our every action
is in praise of God's loving mercy.

A second practical conclusion from the reign of God as his
gift concerns the place of justice in the God-man relationship.
Too often Catholic theology has seen the God-man relationship
exclusively in terms of justice and rewards. But the divine love
does not depend on the works and dispositions of man. Justice,
or *quid pro quo*, does not adequately explain the relationship
between God and man. Some Catholics have opposed any change
in the teaching on contraception or divorce on the grounds that
any change would be unfair to the people who lived according
to the present norms. Such people think they have earned their
salvation by obeying these difficult norms and that others must
do the same thing. The person who thinks in terms of justice
frequently is very narrow and lacks the openness of heart which
can understand mercy and forgiveness. The example of the elder
son in the parable of the prodigal son could apply to many people
today.

An overly exclusive emphasis on man's actions has produced a Pelagian mentality. Man forgets that everything he has comes as a gift from God and tends to think that he saves himself by his own works. Such an attitude easily leads to pharisaism. The pharisaical attitude describes the smug and content approach of those who believe they are justified by their own works. My observance of the law or my good works do not mean that I can look down my nose at others. The temptation to pharisaism is frequently pressing when the primacy of God's love and mercy is forgotten. Pharisaism implies a self-sufficiency and self-righteousness which is incompatible with the notion of the Christian as the poor of Yahweh who is constantly extending his hands to receive the gift of God's love. Emphasis on the primacy of God's love precludes the possibility of falling into the temptation of pharisaism.

An overemphasis on man's actions also leads to seeking a false sense of security. Man believes that his good actions give him the security of God's love. However, the hope of the Christian rests only in God's mercy and in nothing else. Too often Christians try to find security in created, human things; when in reality our only security comes from faith and trust in God.

III. CONVERSION AND THE REIGN OF GOD AS MAN'S RESPONSE

Christian theology has always known the tension between the role of God and the response of man in salvation. Too often in the past, debate has become sterile because the opposite sides really were not listening to one another. The present chapter does not intend to solve the theoretical problem of the respective place of God and man, faith and works, gospel and law. However, the scriptures seem to emphasize both elements—the primacy of God's loving gift and the need for man's response to the gift. Perhaps the solution ultimately lies in seeing the whole of salvation as completely dependent upon God's acting in his way and also dependent on man's acting in his way. What does a contemporary Christian understanding of the scriptures tell about man's response to the gift of God's love and man's part in the coming of the final stage of the reign of God?

The primary disposition on the part of man is openness to receive the gift of God's love. The fundamental human disposition is in accord with the primacy of God's love. The poor of Yahweh is always ready with outstretched arms to receive the mercy and love of God. In the New Testament the writers recall that Jesus became angry with only two groups of people. The attitude of Jesus to sinners and publicans shows no trace of wrath or anger. Jesus' anger is reserved for those who are not open to receive the gift of salvation—the Pharisees and the rich. Jesus cursed those who were hypocrites and smugly self-sufficient. The rich man who was content with what he owned and thought only about how he could store all his goods for the future was also condemned. He too was not open to receive the good news of God's love. Both the Pharisee and the rich man are content with their present lot; they believe they are doing all that is necessary. The sinner or publican who strikes his breast and asks for forgiveness is closer to the reign of God.

The Christian is ever open to the call of God in whatever form the call might come to him. Thus the necessity for the contemporary Christian to read the signs of the times. Openness characterizes the entire life of the follower of Jesus. The responsibility of the Christian is to hear the saving call of God and to respond to it. The scriptures constantly call for vigilance. The Christian is ever alert for the coming of the Lord whether it be in the form of the neighbor in poverty or hunger or in any kind of human need. The frequent call to vigilance in the New Testament is in accord with the basic disposition of openness to receive the saving mercy of God.

However, man's response to the gift of the reign of God involves more than just an openness to receive the gift. Man's response is to be total and complete. The follower of Jesus is called to leave all things to follow the Master. The true disciple cannot even try to serve two masters. A total giving to God and the neighbor in need points out the fullness of the response of the Christian to the call of God in Jesus. The very totality of the claim in general and the particular aspects of that claim in concrete circumstances indicate the radicalness of man's response. Conversion truly demands a change of heart in the Christian. Now the primary concern of the Christian becomes the neighbor in need. The Christian who has experienced the mercy and forgiveness of God must exhibit the same mercy and forgiveness to others. To be forgiven by God is not just a juridical fact. To be forgiven means that man has completely changed his own heart. The scriptures frequently stress the fact that true forgiveness from God means that the individual is now willing to forgive others the same way that Jesus has shown God's mercy to us.

Continual Conversion

Conversion is not a once-for-all action. Continual growth and conversion mark the entire life of the Christian. The dynamism of the Christian life results from a number of factors. The openness which is the fundamental attitude of the Christian serves as the basis for continual growth and development. A continual openness means that the Christian can never be content with what he now does. The Christian is always looking for further development. No matter how long or well he lives, the Christian must always remain open for the call of God and neighbor. No static norms can ever express the fundamental vitality and dynamism of the Christian life.

The eschatological nature of the reign of God also calls for a continual growth on the part of those who are sharing in the work of bringing about the final stage of the reign. The majority of Christian theologians today accept some type of inaugurated eschatology. The messianic or eschatological era has begun with the coming of Jesus. Men are now living in the "times in between the two comings of Jesus." The reign of Jesus is now present and pushing toward its final completion and perfection. The individual Christian is now called to participate in the work of bringing about the final stage of the reign of God. The follower of Jesus is caught up in the urgency of the reign of God which is inexorably pushing forward towards its final stage.

Conversion calls for a continual growth because man in this world is never totally converted. The Christian always remains, in the expression of Martin Luther, *simul justus et peccator*—at the same time just and sinful. Christian experience constantly reminds us that we are spiritual schizophrenics. There are still the remains of sin in all of us, and we are called to share in the redeeming work of overcoming sin through love.

The documents of Vatican II have spoken eloquently about the pilgrim Church. Like the Church, the individual Christian is also a pilgrim. The pilgrim Church is in constant need of reformation, like the individual who is in need of continual conversion. Sin still exists to some extent in the pilgrim Church and in the pilgrim Christian. Roman Catholic theology speaks of the four marks of the Church: one, holy, Catholic, and apostolic. Perhaps we could add a fifth mark to the Church. The Church is one, holy, Catholic, apostolic, and sinful. Yes, the Church is the bride of Christ and the People of God; but the Church embraces us sinful people. The Church is never perfectly faithful to its spouse. The sinful Church is in constant need of reformation and change. However, the individual Christian can never look with disdain on the sinful Church because he himself also experiences his own sinfulness. The pilgrim Christian continually strives to grow closer to his goal of perfect union with God and neighbor. The sinfulness of the Christian is a constant reminder of the gift of salvation from God and the need for an ever greater cooperation and growth in the love of God.

Cosmic Dimension of the Reign of God

Perhaps the most important characteristic of conversion and

the reign of God today is the social and cosmic dimension. The Christian attitude in the past has been too often unilaterally individualistic and personal.

There are a number of factors which have influenced the lack of a social and cosmic dimension to conversion in the past. One factor prominent in the Catholic tradition has been an attitude which does not attribute much importance to the material and this-worldly aspect of human life. An important influence that underrated the value of life in this world was the *fuga mundi* (flight from the world) spirituality which developed in early Christianity with the rise of monasticism. Such a spirituality in itself is not wrong, for it does point out one aspect of the reign of God. The problem arose from the fact that such a spirituality became identified with the only true way of striving for Christian perfection. The world was considered incompatible with the fullness of the Christian vocation. At best, the world was neutral and man's daily life did not contribute anything to the reign of God.

A Greek philosophical prejudice against materiality also affected the Christian's understanding of the material world and man's existence on this earth. According to the Platonic concepts, the body is the prison of the soul. Happiness obviously consists in freeing oneself from the body and returning to the world of ideas and contemplation. Material things are looked down upon as hindrances and obstacles to the higher part of man—his soul. The material universe was really an obstacle to the full development of man's higher life. Such a pejorative attitude towards materiality definitely colored the Christian outlook. Many remnants of the Greek mentality have continued to exist in Christian thought.

A third factor influencing the negative attitude of Christian thinking towards the importance of human life in the present world was the overly spiritualistic heresies which have constantly plagued the Church throughout its history. The historical recurrence of such thinking shows the fascination which such an approach has for the human mind. A dualism which in some ways looks down upon the material part of man has frequently appeared in the history of the Church. From the earliest influences of Manicheanism down to the Jansenism of the last few centuries Christianity has not been able to retain a balanced understanding of man's corporality and materiality.

Catholic theology also favored a negative attitude towards the world and existence in the world by developing a notion of two classes of Christians. Those Christians who were called to perfection embraced the vows and the religious life to unite themselves more closely to God. However, the vast majority of Christians were not called to such perfection and holiness but were only called to live in the world and obey the commandments. The Ten Commandments obliged all Christians, but those who embraced the religious life were vowed to perfection through the following of the evangelical counsels. Life in the world was not a way of seeking Christian perfection. All that was required of the ordinary Christian living in the world was the observation of the Commandments. However, the far greater part of the ordinary life of the Christian in the world was outside the pale of his Christian faith and had nothing to do with his faith.

The Christian Attitude toward this World

Man's relationship to the world is not merely that of renunciation or flight from the world. The Christian is called to transform the world and to cooperate in bringing about the final stage of the reign of God. The relationship between this world and the final stage of the reign of God is not merely a relationship of discontinuity. There is some continuity between this world and the next. What man does for the betterment of the world and human society is a promotion of the reign of God in Christ. The attitude of the Christian toward the present is not totally negative or pessimistic. There is a positive orientation of human reality here and now towards the final stage of the reign of God in Christ.

There are many theological arguments supporting the more positive view of man's life in this world as contributing towards the final stage of the reign of God. Man in his daily efforts cooperates with God in bringing about the new heaven and the new earth. Life in the world is not just a matter of busy work to while away the hours but rather a positive cooperation in working for the reign of God. The mystery of the Incarnation furnishes the cornerstone for the basis of an incarnational spirituality. Material things do belong to the mystery of God's loving reign. The world is intimately joined to the mystery of salvation. Jesus himself took the world and the human enterprise seriously by becoming man.

The entire mystery of salvation shows the cosmic and social aspect of the reign of God. Sin itself has an effect on the world. Sin, according to the Genesis account, not only affected man in his relationship with God; but sin also affected man in his relationship with his fellow man and with the whole world. The social and cosmic aspects of sin in Genesis are dynamic. Sin grows as a force in the world so that other people are easily brought under its sway. Sin pollutes the air men breathe and becomes incarnate in the very structures of human life and society so that men are unable to avoid sin. We know from our own experience how difficult it is for an honest Christian witness in some aspects of life because of the corruption and dishonesty which seem to be taken for granted. So strong is the cosmic and social aspect of sin that theologians are now considering original sin and its passage from one generation to another in terms of the sin of the world.

Since sin has a cosmic effect, redemption too embraces the whole world. The first chapter of Colossians speaks about Christ as the image of all creation and the head of the Church. In him all things are tied together. "Through him God chose to reconcile the whole universe to himself, making peace through the shedding of his blood upon the cross—to reconcile all things, whether on earth or in heaven, through him alone" (Col 1:20). The letter to the Ephesians also stresses that through Christ

the whole universe, all in heaven and on earth, is brought into
a unity (Ep 1:9-10). The letter to the Romans affirms that all
creation is awaiting the fullness of its redemption. The universe
was subject to frustration in sin, but the universe too is to share
in redemption and enter into the joyous liberty of the children
of God (Rm 8:18-25). Redemption thus has a cosmic dimension which cannot be forgotten in the Christian life. The Christian is called not only to change his own heart but also to change
the social, political, economic, and cultural structures of human
existence. Conversion is not addressed to the heart alone.

The sacramental celebration of redemption also indicates the
cosmic dimension of the reign of God. The sacramental principle
follows from the incarnation. God's favor and love come to man
in a visible and historical form. The incarnation brought material things into the plan of redemption. The sacramental celebration points to the same cosmic dimension. Basic human elements
such as bread, wine, water, and oil are brought into the celebration. The sacraments themselves are signs not only of the historical redemptive work of Jesus but also of the future perfection
of the work of salvation. The sacraments point to the future.
There is a connection and also a continuity between the historical event of the past, the present celebration of redemption, and
the final stage of the reign of God. The incarnation and the
sacramental principle dovetail very well with the psychosomatic
nature of man. Man is not just a pure spirit. Man is intimately
connected with his environment and the cosmos.

The insistence on the immanence of God and the theology
of secularity also are indications of the cosmic dimensions of
salvation. A change in the emphasis in ecclesiology likewise
manifests a greater appreciation of worldly and secular values.
An older theology tended to identify the Church and the Kingdom of God. In such a world view, the world itself had little
or no value. Now theology speaks of the Church as the servant
of the world. The world does not exist to serve the Church and
keep the Church going; rather, the Church exists to serve the
world and promote the true values of the world. In a certain

sense, the Church belongs to the times in between and will cease to exist when the fullness of time arrives. However, then the world will not only continue to exist; the world will exist in all its fullness and splendor in the new creation.

Thus the cosmic dimension of the reign of God and conversion illustrates the importance of man's cooperation in building the new heaven and the new earth. Man's human activities are not mere basket weaving or whiling away the hours with busy work waiting for the kingdom to descend from above. However, there is also the danger of falling into a naive optimism and progressivism. Christian theology has definite safeguards against such a naive and simplistic approach to human existence. In general, the theological limitations to a complete continuity between this world and the next stem from the limitations and sinfulness of man and also from an eschatology which definitely holds for some discontinuity between man's efforts and the final state of the reign of God.

The sense of progress and growth towards the new heaven and the new earth is not always readily perceptible. There will be frustrations and obstacles precisely because of limitations and sin. In any Christian life there is always room for the cross and the Paschal Mystery. Suffering and frustration will confront the Christian as he tries to make human life more human. The transformation of the world involves man's participation in the Paschal Mystery of dying and rising. Hope in the saving word and work of God gives the Christian the strength to continue despite opposition, frustrations, and frequent setbacks. The cross of Christ casts its shadow and its light over every human endeavor.

Not everything that arises in the world is good. There is a danger for the Christian in becoming too conformed to the social, cultural, political, and economic structures of a given nation or a given period of history. The greatest idolatry is to absolutize what is merely a very historically limited reality. The prophetic aspect of Christian eschatology calls for the

Christian to continually criticize and perfect the structures of human existence. "Perfect" might even be too weak a word. At times, the revolution of structures is asked of the Christian. An article has recently appeared entitled: "Metanoia: The Moral Principle of the Christian Revolution."[2] The world can set up its own idols. The Christian going towards the new heaven and the new earth always has to judge the earthly structures critically and try to transform them into more human dimensions. The prophetic Christian life in the world cannot merely accept uncritically the moods or structures which appear in human culture and life.

Man's cooperation in the coming of the new heaven and the new earth is essential and necessary but not sufficient. There will still be some discontinuity between man's efforts and the final state of the kingdom. There are always two aspects of the reign of God—his gift and man's cooperation. There is at times a danger of forgetting that the reign is his gift. The true Christian in the world can never develop the Messiah complex that so often characterizes persons and movements in history.

Conversion has many aspects and dimensions. As the central moral message of the New Testament, the Christian message of conversion must be properly understood in all its manifold dimensions. This section has emphasized especially the dynamic aspect of continual conversion and the social and cosmic dimensions of such conversion. The entire chapter has not really tried to solve theoretically the problem of bringing together the role of God and the role of man in the work of conversion. It has maintained the need for both. However, existentially in his own life each Christian must bring the two together. The radical ethical demands of Jesus actually help the Christian to bring together the aspect of the reign of God as God's gift and its aspect of man's cooperation. The Christian always tries to achieve the goal outlined in the ethics of Jesus. Although constantly falling short, the Christian thus realizes his own need for continual forgiveness and receives the hope that is necessary in continuing his own efforts despite the frustrations and oppositions he experiences in himself and in the world of people and things around him. Thus the radical ethics of Jesus are both gospel and law, gift and demand. In continually striving to come closer to the ideal proposed by Jesus, the Christian experiences both the reality of God's merciful love and man's own cooperation in bringing about the new heaven and the new earth. The gospel call to conversion is in all its dimensions the central moral teaching of Jesus.

1. A somewhat similar modern parable is found in Paul Ramsey, *Basic Christian Ethics* (Charles Scribner's Sons, 1950), 70.
2. Oswald Dijkstra, "Metanoia: The Moral Principle of the Christian Revolution," *The Clergy Monthly*, 30 (1966), 457-467.

[Major deletions have been made in this edited version.]

Sin and Conversion

JOSEPH FUCHS

The topic to which I address myself is a consideration of sin and conversion. In dealing with these issues I propose to discuss the more fundamental, existential and personal dimensions of the moral Christian life. Sin and conversion are only two examples: namely, what is going on in the human person as sinner and in the human person as convert? In this consideration we shall delineate four points: First, the moral and the theological relevancy of sin; secondly, the theological aspect of sin; thirdly, the existential aspect of sin; and fourthly, conversion itself in its moral, theological, existential aspects.

Now to the first point: the moral and theological relevancy of sin. We know what the nature of sin is. Sin, morally considered, is a violation of a supposed material moral order. Violation of this order has as one of its constituent parts a certain "matter"; and this matter can be more or less important. As human beings we are obliged to bring order into our own lives, and through such activity to bring order into human society and the entire world. In a very real sense the entire world belongs to us; it is an extension of what we are as human beings.

A sin is precisely a defect; by sin we refuse to put order into this world. Therefore a sin, objectively considered, is against the Creator of this world and the order of this world, against the Creator of the human person and the order of the human person. Sin is a violation and this violation is brought about by a free choice, a psychologically free act. In this psychologically free act we make a choice of this or that reality out of all the realities of the world (*liberum arbitrium*). Here we find the *moral* relevancy of sin.

The *theological* relevance of sin affects the personal relation of a human person to God; so we speak of theological relevancy. A sin is not so much an individual act about a particular object. It is much more a disposition of myself as a person, not merely one single act. True, sin involves an individual act about a particular object, but far more important is the realization that in sin I bring about a certain self-realization. Here we find the central reality in sin; it is much deeper than simply introducing moral disorder into this world.

In every moral act a person tries much more to realize himself as a whole, as a person, than to realize a particular act. Even if he is thinking explicitly only about this particular act with its supposed good for him, still through the particular act he is much more engaged in realizing himself as a person. A person, however, is not without his own purpose, his own ultimate end, as we say in scholastic terminology. He is not without a relationship to his God, for without that he does not exist. Therefore, if in a sinful moral act a person is realizing not only one particular act but himself as a person, then in this moral-act this person is realizing his personal relationship to his ultimate end, and therefore to God. Here we find the theological relevancy of sin.

We must note that this realization of myself in personal relationship to God will not be achieved by the same psychological liberty as the realization of the particular act itself. To dispose of myself *as a whole* I need another liberty; today we call it fundamental liberty. It is a liberty that makes it possible for me precisely to *actualize myself*, not merely an *act* of mine. There is a major distinction between these two liberties: the particular liberty to make a choice between one good or another and the fundamental liberty that makes it possible for me to dispose of myself as a whole, as a person. With this fundamental liberty I am not only committing a sin, an act, but I am also making myself a sinner. By this act, by this liberty of the sinful act, I am actualizing my own person with my own will. In this act my will is actualized as the will of a sinner, permanently refusing to God my own self-donation, denying to God my love. For love is not only giving something, not only giving this or that particular good. Love is giving oneself as a whole with a whole future insofar as this is possible. The sinner by one act refuses this self-giving love to God. From this moment a sinner is really a sinner: a *person* refusing himself to God. Surely there is much more here than a simple act of moral disorder.

Autonomy is withdrawal

For what I say now, perhaps we may turn for some help to the New Testament. For instance, let us take Luke's narrative of the prodigal son (5:11-32). The prodigal son withdraws himself as a whole from the charity and the love of his father. Why? He wishes to be perfectly autonomous before his father and to be independent of his charity. Likewise sin is not only an act refusing *something* to my Father; rather it is the basic withdrawing of *myself* from my Father, God, and from his charity. I do not want to depend on his charity. I desire to be *autonomous*. Here we have the true character of sin.

St. John in his first letter (3:4), according to the recent interpretation of biblical scholars, points to the essential nature of sin: iniquity. In John iniquity means the autonomy, the hostility of a man against God, and precisely against God as the Savior from whom we could have salvation. Every sin is that. All the variations of particular sin culminate in as well as originate from precisely this hostility. The only distinction between different sins consists in the fact that they are different expressions of what sin is—an autonomy, an hostility, against God our Savior.

I now turn to my second point, the theological aspect of sin. First of all, sin is a personal self-realization apart from and against God. Objectively, I think there is no difficulty in understanding this point. Sin is against the order created and established by God our Creator and Savior. Sin is against the natural as well as the Christian order. This is to consider sin objectively, but our precise problem is not located in the objective order at all. The problem is that sin is always a personal matter, a subjective reality, a sin against God. Or is it? That is the question. Is a sinner always aware of the theological aspect of what he is doing? Is he always aware that he is acting against his God and Savior. Sometimes a sinner is aware of his sin as sin. Often he knows it explicitly; he knows what he is doing and he does it. Much more commonly, however, a sinner in doing what in some sense appears good to him does not think of God—at least not explicitly. Conceptually he does not think of the personal God: he thinks of other things. Therefore the question arises: when man sins, is he really unaware of God?

Levels are distinct

We have to distinguish levels of consciousness. I can be conscious of myself and what I am doing in a conceptual way, of sinning against my God. But I can also be conscious of myself and what I am doing in a non-conceptual way. Thus in sinning I would not be aware of God in the order of conceptualization, but I would be conscious of God as the background of my whole life. In *this* way, I think, the inner person, Christian or non-Christian, can be aware of his God. I also believe that without being explicitly and conceptually conscious of God, he could act consciously against his God. The real disposition of myself in relation to God is not on the conceptual level of my consciousness. I can posit my whole personality only if, as St. Thomas says, I am present to myself as a whole, as a person. Only thus can I posit my personality as a whole. Hence the full disposition of my self is on a deeper level where I am present as a whole to myself.

But on this level complete conceptual reflection is impossible.

I can be aware of what I am doing: I am actualizing myself as a person and in this person my own relationship to God. But I am also aware of much that escapes conceptual reflection. If I could exploit in conceptual reflection what I am doing about myself as a whole, as a person, whether I am refusing or accepting God's love, then I would know with conceptual clarity and certitude whether I am in the state of grace or not. Or, on the other hand, if I am a sinner, I would know with conceptual clarity and certitude that I am not in the grace of Christ. To claim such certitude, I believe, is against the teaching of the Council of Trent.

So it follows, on the one hand, that I cannot dispose of myself as a whole without being aware of what I am freely doing. On the other hand, I cannot know myself and my actions exhausively in conceptual reflection. Therefore, I am aware of what I am doing before God, but not with complete conceptual reflection. Also from a philosophical and anthropological point of view, in any moral act made with conceptual reflection, in order to dispose of myself as a whole, I should be present to myself as a whole. But in conceptual reflection there is a distinction between the *self reflecting* and the *self as reflected;* therefore, I never possess myself in the totality of my personality in conceptual reflection. On the other hand, if I am expressing my whole person, realizing myself, for instance, by a sin, I have to know what I am doing; otherwise I am not sinning. Hence, I am aware, I am conscious of myself sinning. I am freely disposing of myself as a person but not with exhaustive conceptual reflection. Moreover, it is not possible for me to grasp fully what is going on inside of me in sinning because of my pride and the disorientation of my free will.

Sin is a personal self-realization against Christ the Redeemer. Again, the objective aspect presents no difficulty. It is clear that in a world created in Christ and redeemed by the God-man every sin in this world is objectively a sin against his world, against his order, and therefore against him.

But here again the problem manifests itself on the subjective level. Is every sin subjectively a sin against Christ? The answer is yes. But how? We have today a very sound theological principle that is accepted by all Catholic theologians. Each and every man is called by Christ. He has his vocation not only in the sense that Christ is calling the entire world, but in another sense, indicated by the Second Vatican Council. Christ is calling every man *personally*. Therefore every man, it seems to me, is aware somehow of this vocation and this call of Christ. Otherwise, how is it possible for him to be called personally by Christ? Hence, each man must have an experiential awareness, a consciousness of the call of Christ; this "I am called" belongs to me. It affects me as a person. Therefore if I am realizing myself as a person, I am not realizing myself in an abstract way. Rather I am realizing my personality as it is existentially affected by this call of Christ my Savior. Perhaps I do not have any explicit reflex knowledge of this call. It may well be true that the Christian sinner does not very often think explicitly that he is sinning against Christ. But he is always aware that in his moral actions he is realizing himself as a person called by Christ and therefore his sin is consciously, if not with conceptual reflection, a sin against Christ.

Sin is a self-oriented declaration of autonomy. On the conceptual level of consciousness a sinner indicates through his freedom of choice what has appeared to him as a good. Perhaps he knows, even explicitly, perhaps reflectively, that his action is really sin. On this conceptual level of consciousness the sinner does not accept his salvation from God and from Christ. He knows very well that what he is doing is against his own nature and that as a human being he has his salvation only from God in Christ. What happens then on the deeper level of consciousness? On this level, he is destroying himself, emasculating his own nature, because he can be saved only by God in Christ but he refuses this salvation.

Sin, therefore, is the utterly destructive affirmation of self. By so acting the sinner loses his Christian liberty, the freedom by which Christ and his Spirit enable us to love the Father, and to give ourselves totally as persons to him. By his sin the sinner has forfeited his Christian liberty, and this from the very moment that his will is actualized in sin. It is not only in the actual moment of sin, but from this initial moment on, his will is actualized in opposition to God, against Christ, and against the acceptance of his salvation in Christ. He is a sinner. He cannot go back by himself. He cannot become alive again all by himself; that would be self-redemption, which we know from revelation is not possible. Hence from the moment of a true sin the sinner has lost his Christian liberty. He is and will remain with his will set against his God. He cannot change unless Christ by his grace restores to him his freedom to come back, to make a new choice for God, and on this deeper level to love God once more.

Let us consider the existential aspect of sin. Any voluntary moral disorder is in itself objectively a *no* to God and to Christ. My question now is this: Is it possible that a human *no* to one's Creator and Redeemer would not be a mortal sin? My answer: I cannot think so.

A fully human *no* to God or to Christ is a mortal sin. The important matter in a sin is not ten cents or a million dollars; the main element in any sin is a *no* to God; if you really say *no* to God, that is mortal sin. This is true whether such a denial deals with a light matter or a million dollars. If this *no* really is a personal *no,* if this *no* is clearly self-realization, if this *no* is really a total disposition of myself in relation to God, then this *no* is always a mortal sin. Therefore whether a sin is a mortal sin or not depends on the answer to this question: In this sin am I fully engaged and really involved as a person? If my person as a whole (*tota persona*) is involved in this act, I am finished. That is mortal sin. What I am doing is refusing my personal self-donation to God and insofar as I am refusing to love God, I am in mortal sin. I refuse *some thing*—ten cents or a million dollars or whatever I might give to someone else. But in such an act where I am fully engaged as a person, I am refusing myself, closing off my whole being to God.

Venial sin differs

But what about venial sin? Why is venial sin only venial? Why is it not a mortal sin? A venial sin seems also to be a *no* to God. We argue by analogy. In venial sin, a person is not engaging himself as a whole. There are so many superficial acts in which the center of personality where the whole person is present to himself is not engaged. In these acts the center of the person, as a matter of fact, is not involved; they cannot in any true sense be called fully personal. The full engagement of personality is on another level. In venial sin a "just" man does not really dispose of himself in relation to God. He remains a person who loves God, whose fundamental liberty is still intact, but on a more superficial level, he is going in the opposite direction. However on this level, since his person as a whole is not engaged, the *no* of venial sin must be understood in some other sense than as a fully personal *no*. In such a situation I am not refusing my love or closing up my personality to God, and it is only because this objective *no* of venial sin is not realized in the center of my person that it is not a mortal sin.

A second question arises: What about the matter in the sin? It is easy to distinguish light matter, grave matter, etc., and this distinction is not without importance. But much more important is the existential engagement of the person in saying *no* to God. I think in regard to what is called light matter, such as a lie, a person normally at least will not be able to engage existentially the center of his personality. In this act, then, he will not be able to dispose of himself. This is so because a small disorder in this world is usually not so important that a person will be aware that his whole person and therefore his whole life is engaged in such an act. On the other hand, if a person is faced with a choice in some matter of importance, he will normally realize that his person as a whole is involved. Since his whole person and his whole life is engaged, he will understand without reflection that in what he is doing he is disposing of himself. Therefore, usually but not always, in any free choice involving grave matter, the action itself will most probably be a mortal sin.

Can we then say that telling a lie is a perfect human act with full freedom? We must distinguish. There is the full freedom to choose between one or another road; but this is *not* the freedom, the liberty, to dispose of oneself. Is a venial sin then a perfect human act? Yes or no? It is not a perfect act such as would be the case in mortal sin, because a mortal sin is precisely an engagement of the whole person in this action; a venial sin is not. However, in venial sin insofar as it is the choice between this or another act, there can be full conceptual freedom, and *only* in this sense is it a human act.

Thirdly, by a full disposition of self, a person takes a stance in relation to God. His will is and will remain committed to loving or refusing to love him. So sin, as a grave act (or as theologians say today, a fundamental option), becomes a permanent orientation of the will. This fundamental option brings about an abiding fundamental intention. The whole person is committed in this direction. Consequently, I believe it is not so easy to change ourselves, to change what we are. It is easy to change an act; but it is not easy to change ourselves, a sinner or a man who at the center of his being loves God.

Therefore, when we are considering venial sin, whether it be venial sin in a just man or in a sinner, we may say in both cases that it is an act that does not engage the entire person. In the just man his already actualized good will is not engaged; in the sinner his actualized hostility toward God is not fully reasserted. That is precisely what makes a venial sin venial.

What is Conversion?

Let us now consider our fourth point: the nature of conversion. It is a more interesting subject, easier to speak about after having spoken about sin. First then, what is conversion? Conversion is not any good act, such as "O my God, I am sorry," not just some other act which follows upon an act of sin. No, conversion is a change in the whole person, for the whole person is a sinner, enduringly committed to be a sinner. Conversion means to change the whole thrust of one's life. In other words, conversion means recapitulating and transforming the basic orientation of a person who has been so against God that he cannot come back to God by himself. Conversion is the total person changing himself. Once a sinner, he is now committing himself totally to the love of God, giving himself as a person to the Father. So conversion is not the sum or substance of many good acts—not, for example, the gift or gifts of a millionaire to the church. Perhaps by such acts a sinner gives something; yes, but he is not giving himself. He is taking some necessary steps with God's help to pass out of his situation as sinner, but he remains in his person as a whole against God.

Therefore conversion is not achieved by just *any single good* *act.* Conversion takes place on the deep personal level where a man is able to dispose of himself as a whole; this disposition of self is not possible through a superficial act. In principle, we may say that conversion is possible only on the same level where the fundamental possibility of sin is found. Just as a person becomes a sinner only on the deep personal level, so it is also only there that a sinner can experience conversion. Conversion therefore contains contrition for all sins committed, precisely because it is a turning away from the fundamental orientation to sin. Thus contrition for some sins and not for all mortal sins is impossible. For if the sinner would exclude one sin from his contrition, he would not be converted; he would not be changing himself on the deep personal level where he is a sinner. He would still retain in his will his fundamental option against God. He would not be giving himself as a whole to God.

Somewhat in the same way conversion also contains a promise, at least implicitly, or virtually as we say in theology; likewise a true promise involves true contrition. We might say that very often this is not the case. For instance, suppose that a sinner who is getting married tomorrow is as a matter of fact getting out of the occasion of sin; he will not be committing the sins that he has been committing. Obviously for such a man this change is very easy because he no longer will be in an occasion of sin. Is this change a conversion? Is this a true promise? He says he will not sin again. But is this promise a true promise not to sin; that is, not to do anything against the will of God? If he rejects in the depth of his person his sinful orientation, we have a promise in the true sense. In this promise we have conversion, since his promise contains contrition, at least virtually.

Self-realization

Conversion evidently is the disposition of the whole person—a self realization. This self realization is to be achieved through an explicitly conceptualized act realizing some particular good action. Through this act on its deeper level, i.e., at the center of the person, conversion is achieved. Hence, once again, conversion is always on the level where a person is present to himself, where you *cannot* fully reflect on it. Consequently, in conversion we are conscious that we are converting, that we are now moving from sin to a love of God above all else. I cannot love God without knowing it; as subject I am aware and conscious of it but this love of God is not as an object of reflection. For full reflection is impossible. It would mean that I would have to go out of myself; when that occurs I as a whole am not present to myself. I cannot go out of myself and with conceptual clarity and certainty know that I am living in grace. True conversion occurs in the subject as subject, not as object of reflection. Suppose a sinner says; "Oh my God I regret my sins." Is he really regretting his sins and his being a sinner? On the conceptual, reflex level, I cannot tell you with certainty. The sinner cannot do this himself. But in the center of his person, he is aware of whether he is really loving God or not.

But even though full reflection on this conversion is not possible, we do have signs of it just as we have signs for a mortal sin. Normally if we know we are doing wrong in a

matter of importance and if we are psychologically free in
making the choice, most probably we are committing a mortal
sin. But most likely in such an act grave matter is only *one*
sign. There are also other signs of what I am in the very inmost
being of my soul. For instance, during such acts I am aware of
the degree of my psychological freedom to make a true choice
of this or another act. So also in conversion, I have signs whether
I am really converted or not: e.g., I am sincere with myself;
I recognize the fruits of my conversion; or as St. Ignatius says,
I look for signs of true consolation, etc. We do have signs.
However, it still remains true that we cannot fully grasp in
conceptual reflection whether we are converted or not. Christian life does not have this certainty whether I am in grace and
love my God or whether I am a sinner and am refusing myself
to God. We know this only "by conjecture," as St. Thomas
says. Christian joy is not the joy of a possessor but of a man
who has hope in Christ. This state is typical for the Christian.

Secondly, how is conversion possible? This is a crucial question! If a person is a sinner with his whole person committed
to hostility against his God, how can he come back? Is it
possible? You may say, "Yes, by grace." But this working of
grace also poses the same question. How can this person who
in the self realization of his person stands against God be
changed and become a different person? Here we must observe
that although this person did dispose of himself as a whole,
he did not and could not do so *totally*. Why? A human person
lives his life successively by moments and days, by months and
years. He cannot realize himself totally in any single moment.
Hence, if a sinner disposes of himself as a whole but not totally,
and does so continuouosly during his entire life, much of his
total reality still remains to be integrated in him as a sinner,
and in this life he will never accomplish it totally. In him
other tendencies always remain—e.g., not to be a sinner. It is
at this point that the grace of Christ can help him.

The good man is in a similar situation. He too has disposed
of himself as a whole, but not totally; hence he can become a

sinner. You are familiar with St. John's phrase, *justus non peccat.*
But still it is true that the Christian does sin sometimes? How
is this possible? It is possible precisely because the justified man,
while loving God with his whole person, has not yet integrated
into this love the whole reality of his long life. As a fallen man
he has many tendencies against God, and throughout his whole
life he is called upon to integrate all that his life means and is
into his love of God. But as long as he lives in this world, there
is always the possibility that his contrary tendencies may lead
him back to a life of sin. Therefore, sin is possible in the just
man just as conversion is possible for the sinner. Conversion,
however, requires the grace of Christ; otherwise there would
be the possibility of self redemption, which is excluded.

How should we describe this always-given grace of Christ?
Can it be that Christ is *in every moment* offering the grace of
conversion? I do not think that this is possible. Why not?
Conversion is not possible in or through a superficial act. Conversion is possible only in an act which engages the entire
person. It is in such an act that the grace of conversion is
offered by Christ. In this way Christ helps the person to become free once more and to accept his grace as a son of God.

Thirdly, I wish to offer a few thoughts by way of analogy
on "conversions," as we commonly use the term. A first type
of conversion *per analogiam* can take place in the first perfect
human act of a person, whether he be baptized or not. In this
first perfect human act a person becomes involved in the entire
disposition of himself. Before this moment such a person is not
as yet a sinner in a personal way. But neither at this moment is
he totally indifferent; he is not a zero. He is a human person,
tainted by the sin of Adam and possessing all the egoistic tendencies of fallen man. Now at a single moment of time he has
to dispose of himself as a person, to set the direction of his life.
Will he accept the inclinations of his fallen nature? Or will he
resist and in this sense convert to the other side, giving himself
as a whole to his God and to Christ who is calling him by his
vocation, by grace? If he resists and decides to give himself to

God, then this first act is in a true sense an act of conversion by analogy. In such an act of conversion a person is involved as a whole in a fundamental option (*optio fundamentalis*). This is a free act, realized perhaps by choosing one or another good, but more deeply a giving of oneself to God within the center where the whole person is present to himself. Such a person could thus actualize his whole being in the direction of God, and although he would be aware of what he is doing, he could not capture it in full conceptual reflection.

There is another analogous type of conversion, the so-called continual conversion which occurs in three different forms: 1) the radical neo-conversion, 2) continuous verification of one's self-gift to God, and 3) conversion from venial sin.

Conversion can grow

What is radical neo-conversion? A man has committed himself to love God. That is his will, enduringly. But in a certain moment, for instance in a retreat, he substantially deepens the intensity of his own option for Christ and God. His subsequent life would then be an expression of this deeper self realization in relation to God. This would be a new conversion. This person really would be a new man thereafter.

The second form of *conversio continua* is the continuous verification of what we are, of our self-giving to Christ and to God. It is continuous verification because we have to verify successively throughout our lives what we are in our relationship to God. We have given ourselves to God. Depending on different situations there is a successive growth that must be realized. Some of these acts of verification will perhaps be deep enough to justify the use of the term, fundamental act; other acts will be superficial expressions of what we are. In all these acts we are integrating the whole reality of our lives into the personal disposition of ourselves. It seems to me that by this continuous verification of what we are as converted men, we will also grow in what we are and not remain merely what we were. We shall grow, develop, and mature in love.

Finally, the third form of this *conversio continua* is conversion from venial sin. This much is clear: Insofar as venial sin is not a fundamental act engaging the entire person, conversion from venial sin need not be on the level of the disposition of myself as a person, as a whole.

Let me now conclude this consideration of sin and conversion. Sin is a fundamental reality of the Christian life. It is a powerful reality, a reality full of consequence. A true sin—not venial sin which is sin only by analogy—involves the whole person. In this sin a person is constituting himself through his will in an actualized, permanent resistance against God and the grace of Christ.

Conversion is not possible without the help of the grace of Jesus Christ. Christ's grace makes the sinner once more able and free to change himself, to overcome his resistance against the Father. In converting the sinner, Christ enables him to change the orientation of his whole person and his whole will in relation to God and to Christ. Not every sinful act nor every good act is in the full sense of the word either sin or conversion, but only those acts which engage the person precisely as person, as a whole. From the moment of his first perfect human act, an adult person is always, continuously, freely, and as a whole engaged, either giving himself as a whole to God, or refusing himself as a whole to God. A morally adult man is never indifferent; he is always committed as a total person. This is true whether he has been converted from a true sin or has just made his first perfect human act in coming from his situation as fallen man. By his conversion he becomes a "spiritual man" (*homo spiritualis*); the sinner is a "carnal man" (*homo carnalis*); the fallen man is *inclined* to be a sinful man (*homo carnalis*). A convert is, by the grace of Christ, a spiritual man. Every man is either a spiritual man, in St. Paul's sense, or a carnal man. It is in the human act in which our person as a whole is engaged that we actualize ourselves fully as spiritual men or sinful men. It is a case of either/or; there is no middle ground. In other acts, superficial acts, we do not engage our personalities fully. Indeed, so many of our human acts are, as a matter of fact, not acts in this full personal sense at all. They are neither sin (in the full sense) nor conversion.

[Major deletions have been made in this edited version.]

Final Integration

The Christian concept of man, a concept which is held in common by all the religions which can be called "higher" or "mystical," is one which sees man as a spiritual, or self-transcending being. That is to say that man, unlike other animals, does not find his fulfillment or self-realization merely on the level of his own nature. Even the most satisfactory exercise of those biological functions which preserve and propagate the life of the species is not enough to fulfill man's inner capacities, even when this exercise is also psychologically mature and rewarding. As long as man acts *only* as a member of the human species, within his limits as an individual subservient to the inescapable finalities of his common "nature," he is still subject to the deepest and most radical form of spiritual alienation. He is not fully "free" because he is not able to transcend his specific individuality and function on the level of a spiritual *person* with all the perfection and autonomy implied by that concept.

In other words, it seems to me that we must remember the need to explore the full spiritual depths of such concepts as "life" and "love of life," "freedom" and so on. This will necessarily imply at the same time a deepening and in some way an apparent complicating of the notion of man's alienation. I fully accept Fromm's analysis of alienation. But I think the concept needs a great deal of further exploration, beyond the limits of sociology and psychology, even of depth psychology.

I think it has too often been forgotten that there are two

aspects of that vast, mysterious area of our being which we call the unconscious. There is the psychosomatic area which is so to speak rooted in man's biological substratum, but there is an infinitely more spiritual and metaphysical substratum in man's being, which the Rhenish mystics called the "ground" or "base" of the soul, and which the Zen Masters continually point to, but which they refuse to describe except by incomprehensible and paradoxical terms like "your original face before you were born." So, to put my point briefly, I would like to suggest the overwhelming and almost totally neglected importance of exploring this spiritual unconscious of man. There is no real love of life unless it is oriented to the discovery of one's true, spiritual self, beyond and above the level of mere empirical individuality, with its superficial enjoyments and fears.

In fact I would like to suggest what would seem to me to be perhaps the most fruitful avenue of approach, at least for one in my own field: namely, the clear recognition of the ambiguities and ambivalences generated by false personalism. I refer to the fateful error of reducing the "person" or "spirit" to the individual and empirical ego, the "self-as-object," the self which we observe as it goes about its biological business, the machine which we regulate and tune up and feed with all kinds of stimulants and sedatives, constantly trying to make it run more and more smoothly, to fit the patterns prescribed by the salesman of pleasure-giving and anxiety-allaying commodities.

When our empirical ego is taken, without further qualification, as the true "person," the true "self," as the being who is the genuine subject of life, freedom, joy and fulfillment, or indeed of religious salvation, then we arrive at the most tragic frustrations and errors, because this implies a radical alienation of our true being. While recognizing the great importance of depth psychology (we cannot get along without it today!) I would like to say—and I am sure all analysts worthy of their salt will agree—that considerable mystification is involved in the complacent and beatific sort of counseling that aims only to remove "guilt feelings" and adjust the empirical self to a society of which Fromm has questioned the basic sanity. We *ought* to feel guilty and we *ought* to experience anguish in the fabulous irresponsibilities and panics we are generating every week of the Cold War. The trouble is rather our moral obtuseness and our spiritual insensibility to fundamental human values.

It would seem that we ought to pay a great deal more attention than we do to the traditional spiritual and contemplative wisdoms which prescribe disciplines (in the deepest sense of "discipleships") to help man transcend his empirical self and find his "true self" in an emptiness that is completely "awake" because completely free of useless reflection. This is a realm of paradox and risk, because there are false and unsatisfactory spiritualities which do not go far enough, which indulge in Platonic oversimplifications, which objectify that which can only be grasped as subject, and even then is lost as soon as it is "grasped." Some spiritualities generate divisive contempts which flower in destructiveness. In other words there is great danger in facile and thoughtless verbalizations of spiritual reality. All true spiritual disciplines recognize the peril of idolatry in the irresponsible fabrication of pseudo-spiritual concepts which serve only to delude man and to subject him once again to a deeper captivity just when he seems on the point of tasting the true bliss and the perfect poverty of liberation. The supreme risk in this quest for liberation resides in the paradox of transcendence itself. For the Transcendent is also at the same time Immanent, and the mystery is that while man's spiritual liberation consists in a self-renunciation and self-recovery "beyond self," it is also at the same time a fantastic awakening to the truth and transcendent value of one's *ordinary self.*

I know that this apparent contradiction is thoroughly outrageous and I have perhaps no real excuse for introducing it in so short a piece of writing, except that even the longest and most complex explanation would not serve to clear it up. All I can say is that for those who are interested, there are documents of all kinds which say that the highest and most "biophilic" expression of man's extraordinary capacities is precisely in this *ecstasis* in which the person is at once totally empty (of separate-ness and material individuation) and totally full, realizing him-self in unity not only with all being(s) but with the very source and finality of Being. It is the paradox of D. T. Suzuki's formula that zero equals infinity, or the *todo y nada* of St. John of the Cross.

Hence I want to say that the highest form of life is this "spiritual life" in which the infinitely "fontal" (source-like) creativity of our being in Being is somehow attained, and be-comes in its turn a source of action and creativity in the world around us. The common jargon of religions tends to speak of this sometimes as "contemplation," sometimes as "liberation," sometimes as "salvation," sometimes as "divination." The words are not indifferent, because they do have definite implications, some of which can easily be unfortunate.

* * *

The idea of "rebirth" and of life as a "new man in Christ, in the Spirit," of a "risen life" in the Mystery of Christ or in the Kingdom of God, is fundamental to Christian theology and practice—it is, after all, the whole meaning of baptism.

The notion of "rebirth" is not peculiar to Christianity. In Sufism, Zen Buddhism and in many other religious or spiritual traditions, emphasis is placed on the call to fulfill certain obscure yet urgent potentialities in the ground of one's being, to "become someone" that one already (potentially) is, the person one is truly meant to be. Zen calls this awakening a recognition of "your original face before you were born."

Sometimes it may be very useful for us to discover new and unfamiliar ways in which the human task of maturation and self-discovery is defined. The book of a Persian psychoanalyst, Dr. Reza Arasteh, who practices and teaches in America, might prove very valuable in this respect.[1]

Dr. Arasteh has developed and deepened ideas suggested by the humanistic psychoanalysis of Erich Fromm, by existential psychotherapy and by the logotherapy of Viktor Frankl. But—and this is what is most interesting—he has also incorporated into his theories material from the mystical tradition of Persian Sufism. The *Final Integration* which is the object of his research is not just the "cure" of neurosis by adaptation to society. On the contrary, it presupposes that any psychoanalytic theory that is content merely with this is bound to be inadequate. Dr. Arasteh is interested not only in the partial and limited "health" which results from contented acceptance of a useful role in society, but in the final and complete maturing of the human psyche on a transcultural level. This requires a little clarification.

Contrary to the accepted theory and practice of most psychotherapy derived from Freud and popular in America today, Dr. Arasteh holds that adaptation to society at best helps a man "to live with his illness rather than cure it," particularly if the general atmosphere of the society is unhealthy because of its overemphasis on cerebral, competitive, acquisitive forms of ego-affirmation. Such an atmosphere may favor an apparently very active and productive mode of life but in reality it stifles true growth, leaves people lost, alienated, frustrated and bored without any way of knowing what is wrong with them. In fact, in many cases, psychoanalysis has become a technique for making people conform to a society that prevents them from growing and developing as they should.

Carefully distinguishing existential anxiety from the petulant self-defeating sorrows of the neurotic, Dr. Arasteh shows how this anxiety is a sign of health and generates the necessary strength for psychic rebirth into a new transcultural identity. This new being is entirely personal, original, creative, unique, and it transcends the limits imposed by social convention and prejudice. Birth on this higher level is an imperative necessity for man.

The infant who lives immersed in a symbiotic relationship with the rest of nature—immersed, that is, in his own narcissism—must be "born" out of this sensual self-centeredness and acquire an identity as a responsible member of society. Ordinary psychotherapy is fully aware of this. But once one has grown up, acquired an education, and assumed a useful role as a worker and provider, there is still another birth to be undergone.

Since his investigation is purely psychological, not theological, the question of "sanctity" or holiness does not really arise from Dr. Arasteh. But let us make clear that ordinarily a full spiritual development and a supernatural, even charismatic, maturity, evidenced in the "saint," normally includes the idea of complete psychological integration. Doubtless many saints have been neurotics, but they have used their neurosis in the interests of growth instead of capitulating and succumbing to its dubious comforts.

Final integration is a state of transcultural maturity far beyond mere social adjustment, which always implies partiality and compromise. The man who is "fully born" has an entirely "inner experience of life." He apprehends his life fully and wholly from an inner ground that is at once more universal than the empirical ego and yet entirely his own. He is in a certain sense "cosmic" and "universal man." He has attained a deeper, fuller identity than that of his limited ego-self which is only a fragment of his being. He is in a certain sense identified with everybody: or in the familiar language of the New Testament (which Arasteh evidently has not studied) he is "all things to all men." He is able to experience their joys and sufferings as his own, without however becoming dominated by them. He has attained to a deep inner freedom—the Freedom of the Spirit we read of in the New Testament. He is guided not just by will and reason, but by "spontaneous behavior subject to dynamic insight." Now, this calls to mind the theology of St. Thomas on the Gifts of the Holy Spirit which move a man to act "in a superhuman mode." Though Dr. Arasteh takes no account of specifically supernatural agencies, it is clear that such considerations might become relevant here. But of course they cannot be investigated by experimental science.

Again, the state of insight which is final integration implies an openness, an "emptiness," a "poverty" similar to those described in such detail not only by the Rhenish mystics, by St. John of the Cross, by the early Franciscans, but also by the Sufis, the early Taoist masters and Zen Buddhists. Final integration implies the void, poverty and nonaction which leave one entirely docile to the "Spirit" and hence a potential instrument for unusual creativity.

The man who has attained final integration is no longer limited by the culture in which he has grown up. "He has embraced *all of life*. . . . He has experienced qualities of every type of life": ordinary human existence, intellectual life, artistic creation, human love, religious life. He passes beyond all these limiting forms, while retaining all that is best and most universal in them, "finally giving birth to a fully comprehensive self." He accepts not only his own community, his own society, his own friends, his own culture, but all mankind. He does not remain bound to one limited set of values in such a way that he opposes them aggressively or defensively to others. He is fully "Catholic" in the best sense of the word. He has a unified vision and experience of the one truth shining out in all its various manifestations, some clearer than others, some more definite and more certain than others. He does not set these partial views up in opposition to each other, but unifies them in a dialectic or an insight of complementarity. With this view of life he is able to bring perspective, liberty and spontaneity into the lives of others. The finally integrated man is a peacemaker, and that is why there is such a desperate need for our leaders to become such men of insight.

Dr. Arasteh describes the breakthrough into final integration, in the language of Sufism. The consecrated term in Sufism is *Fana*, annihilation or disintegration, a loss of self, a real spiritual death. But mere annihilation and death are not enough: they must be followed by reintegration and new life on a totally different level. This reintegration is what the Sufis call *Baqa*. The process of disintegration and reintegration is one that involves a terrible interior solitude and an "existential moratorium," a crisis and an anguish which cannot be analyzed or intellectualized. It also requires a solitary fortitude far beyond the ordinary, "an act of courage related to the root of all existence." It would be utterly futile to try to "cure" this anguish by bringing the "patient" as quickly and as completely as possible into the warm bosom of togetherness.

For a Christian, a transcultural integration is eschatological. The rebirth of man and of society on a transcultural level is a rebirth into the transformed and redeemed time, the time of the Kingdom, the time of the Spirit, the time of "the end." It means a disintegration of the social and cultural self, the product of merely human history, and the reintegration of that self in Christ, in salvation history, in the mystery of redemption, in the Pentecostal "new creation." But this means entering into the full mystery of the eschatological Church.

Now, as Dr. Arasteh points out, whereas final psychological integration was, in the past, the privilege of a few, it is now becoming a need and aspiration of mankind as a whole. The whole world is in an existential crisis to which there are various reactions, some of them negative, tragic, destructive, demonic, others proffering a human hope which is yet not fully clear.

The destructive and tragic solutions are not solutions at all: they simply marshal the immense resources of military, economic and political power to block real development and to maintain established patterns—in the interests of those who know best how to profit from them, and at the expense of everybody else.

The humanly optimistic answers foresee radical changes of a purely secular sort which will initiate a kind of hippie kingdom of love in a cybernated and peace-loving mega-city (presumably with free LSD for everybody). Many Christians feel that the Spirit is really summoning us to renounce our sense of spiritual privilege and enter into a fully turned-on solidarity with these secular hopes. Others, of course, and perhaps the majority, have lined up on the side of the armies and the "powers" under the mistaken idea that Christ is fully identified with the capitalist Western establishment which still refers to itself (when convenient) as "Christian."

* * *

I might doubtless be expected to conclude with gestures of congratulation in the direction of popular religion. I am afraid this is impossible. Popular religion has to a great extent betrayed man's inner spirit and turned him over, like Samson, with his hair cut off and his eyes dug out, to turn the mill of a self-frustrating and self-destroying culture. The cliches of popular religion have in many cases become every bit as hollow and as false as those of soap salesmen, and far more dangerously deceptive because one cannot so easily verify the claims made about the product. The sin of religiosity is that it has turned God, peace, happiness, salvation and all that man desires into products to be marketed in a speciously attractive package deal. In this, I think, the fault lies not with the sincerity of preachers and religious writers, but with the worn-out presuppositions with which they are content to operate. The religious mind today is seldom pertinently or prophetically critical. Oh, it is critical all right; but too often of wrong or irrelevant issues. There is still such a thing as straining at gnats and swallowing camels. But I wonder if we have not settled down too comfortably to accept passively the prevarications that the Gospels or the Prophets would have us reject with all the strength of our being. I am afraid the common combination of organizational jollity, moral legalism and nuclear crusading will not pass muster as a serious religion. It certainly has little to do with "spiritual life." Needless to say, this is more generally understood by churchmen than those who resent religious institutions are perhaps likely to realize. There is no question that Pope John XXIII, in his efforts to foster a general spiritual renewal of the Catholic Church by the Second Vatican Council, was aware of where the trouble lay. But even then, I think that the more profoundly and properly *spiritual* issues still lie too deep for common observation and interest, and are certainly far too mysterious to be captured in the concise and technical terminology of an ecumenical council.

Still I would like to conclude on a note of hope. It is precisely because I believe, with Abraham Heschel and a cloud of witnesses before him, that "man is not alone," that I find hope even in this most desperate situation. Man does not have to transcend himself in the sense of pulling himself up by his own bootstraps. He has, rather, to respond to the mysterious grace of a Spirit which is at once infinitely greater than his own and yet which, at the same time, offers itself as the total plenitude of all Gifts, to be in all reality his "own Spirit."

However, the response is not automatic. It demands a great purity of devotion to truth and to life. The delusions of a fat society glutted with the profits begotten by its own death wish hardly dispose us as to respond to the *Creator Spiritus*, the *Cantor sapientissimus*, without a fundamental re-orientation of our thought and life. All have the duty to contribute whatever they can to this re-orientation. I do not think the word re-orientation is strong enough. What is required is a spiritual upheaval such as we seldom see recorded in history. But such things have happened, and let us hope we have not gone so far that they will not happen again.

1. Reza Arasteh, *Final Integration in the Adult Personality*, Leiden. E. J. Brill, 1965.

[Major deletions have been made in this edited version.]

Christian Conversion

HANS KÜNG

In view of the ultimate and definitive reality, the kingdom of God, a fundamental transformation is expected of man: something like a new birth of man himself, which can be understood only by one who actively takes part in it. It is therefore a transformation which does not come about merely through progress in right thinking for the sake of right action (as with Socrates) or through the education of man who is fundamentally good (as with Confucius). Nor is it a transformation through enlightenment, as the ascetic Siddhartha Gautama passed by way of meditation through enlightenment (*bodhi*) to become Buddha, the Enlightened, and in this way to reach an understanding of suffering and finally extinction in nirvana. According to Jesus, a fundamental transformation is achieved through man's surrender to God's will.

Jesus expects a different, a new man: a radically changed awareness, a fundamentally different attitude, a completely new orientation in thought and action.

The changed awareness

Jesus expects no more and no less than a fundamental, and *total orientation of man's life toward God*: an undivided heart, in the last resort serving not two masters but only one. Awaiting God's rule, in the midst of the world and among his fellow men, man should give his heart in the last resort simply and solely to God: not to money and possessions,[1] not to rights and honor,[2]

nor even to parents and family.[3] In this respect, according to
Jesus, we cannot simply speak of peace: here the sword rules.
Even the closest bonds must be set aside as of secondary importance beside this basic decision. Imitating Christ in this way
takes precedence even over family ties: anyone who wants to be
a disciple of Christ must "hate" father, mother, brothers and
sisters, wife and children, even himself. Even himself! I know
by experience that the real enemy of such a transformation is
my own self. It follows immediately therefore that anyone who
tries to preserve his own life will lose it and he who loses it
will gain it.[4] Is this a hard saying? It is a rich promise.

The meaning now becomes clear of a term we have already
come across and which is of central importance, and that being
metanoia,[5] "conversion," or—as it was formerly misleadingly
translated—"repentance." It is not a question of "doing penance"
externally, in sackcloth and ashes. It is not an intellectually determined or strongly emotional religious experience. It is a
decisive change of will, an awareness changed from the roots
upwards, a new basic attitude, a different scale of values. It is
therefore a radical rethinking and re-turning on the part of the
whole man, a completely new attitude to life. Nevertheless,
Jesus does not expect an acknowledgement of sin, a confession,
from the person who wants to change his ways. He is not very
interested in the latter's problematic past, which of course has
to be abandoned. All that matters is the better future, this future
which God promises and gives to man, to which the latter must
turn irrevocably and unreservedly, without looking back, now
that his hand is on the plow.[6] Man can live on forgiveness. This
is conversion based on that imperturbable, unshakable confidence
in God and in his word which even in the Old Testament was
known as *faith*.[7] It involves a believing trust and a trustful faith,
which is something very different from Buddha's insight (based
on Indian philosophy), or Socrates' dialectic of thought (as
understood in Greek philosophy), or Confucius' piety (in the
Chinese tradition).

God himself, by his Gospel and his forgiveness, makes possible a conversion inspired by faith, a new beginning. Heroism is not required of man: he can live in the trusting *gratitude* of the man who found the treasure in the field, who received the precious pearl.[8] He should not be placed under new legal pressures or forced to accomplish something new. Certainly he will do his duty and think nothing of himself merely for doing this.[9] But his model will be the child rather than the faithful servant: not because the child's supposed innocence is to be made into a romantic ideal, but because the child—helpless and small—takes it completely for granted that he is to be helped, to be given presents, that he must surrender himself single-mindedly and full of confidence.[10] What is required therefore is childlike gratitude, not looking for a reward—not even the reward of grace—not like the son who remained at home had been doing for years and yet was left out in the end.[11] Man should not act for the sake of reward or punishment. Reward and punishment should not be made the motive of moral action: Kant's reaction to primitive eudaemonism was justified. But in his actions man should certainly be aware of his responsibility: that, with all his thoughts, words, and works, he is approaching God's future, God's final decision. And whatever a person has done—even merely giving a cup of water to someone who is thirsty,[12] but also even uttering an idle word[13]—remains present to God, even though it is long past for man.

Accepting this responsibility has nothing to do with the cheerlessness of devout observers of the law. Jesus' call to conversion is a call to *joy*. It should not be assumed that the Sermon on the Mount begins with a new list of duties. It begins in fact with a list of blessings.[14] A sad saint is for Jesus just a sad saint.[15] Because God is generous, the wage earners in the vineyard are told, that is no reason for being envious.[16] The very correct brother of the prodigal son should have rejoiced and been rather happy.[17] Aversion from the sinful past and the return of the whole man to God is a joyful event for God and men. And for the person concerned it is a true liberation. For no new law is imposed on him. The weight is light and the burden easy[18] and man can bear it gladly if he submits to God's will.

Once again, however, we are thus faced by a question which has hitherto been constantly present, but which now—after so much talk about God's will as the supreme norm of human action and life—should be expressly stated and answered: just what is the will of God? What does God really want?

What God wills

God's will does not waver. Nor can it be manipulated. From all that we have said hitherto, from the concrete requirements of Jesus himself, it should already have become clear that God wills nothing for himself, nothing for his own advantage, for his greater glory. God wills nothing but man's advantage, man's true greatness and his ultimate dignity. This then is God's will: *man's well-being.*

From the first to the last page of the Bible, it is clear that God's will aims at man's well-being at all levels, aims at his definitive and comprehensive good: in biblical terms, at the salvation of man and of men. God's will is a helpful, healing, liberating, saving will. God wills life, joy, freedom, peace, salvation, the final, great happiness of man: both of the individual and of mankind as a whole. This is the meaning of God's absolute future, his victory, his kingdom, which Jesus proclaims: man's total liberation, salvation, satisfaction, bliss. And this very radical identification of God's will and man's well-being, which Jesus took up from the standpoint of God's closeness, makes it clear that there is no question of putting a new patch onto old clothing or of pouring young wine into old wineskins. Here we are actually faced with something new and it is going to be dangerous to the old.

What to some people might seem like an autocratic and arbitrary use of freedom on Jesus' part now becomes clearly its great and potent consistency. God is not yet seen apart from man, nor man apart from God. We cannot be for God and against

man. If we want to be devout, we cannot behave in an inhuman
way. Was that so obvious then? Is it obvious now?

Certainly God is not interpreted by Jesus in terms of human
fellowship, he is not reduced to fellow feeling. Idolizing man
dehumanizes him no less than enslavement. But man's friendli-
ness for man is based on God's friendship for man. That is why
the universal and final criterion must be: God wills man's
well-being.

1. Mt 6:19-21, 24-34; Mk 10:17-27.
2. Mt 5:38-42; Mk 10:42-44.
3. Lk 14:26; Mt 10:34-37.
4. Lk 17:33; Mt 10:39.
5. Mk 1:15 par. Cf. on *metanoia* in the New Testament, among the
New Testament theologies, particularly R. Bultmann, pp. 4-22.
6. Lk 9:62.
7. Cf., on faith in the New Testament, . . . E. D. O'Connor, *Faith in the
Synoptic Gospels*, Notre Dame, U.S.A., 1961.
8. Mt 13:44-46.
9. Lk 17:10.
10. Mk 10:15 par.
11. Lk 15:29.
12. Mt 10:42.
13. Mt 12:36.
14. Mt 5:3-12.
15. Cf. Mt 6:16-18.
16. Mt 20:15.
17. Lk 15:32.
18. Mt 11:30.

Part Five

PERSONAL CONVERSION AND THE TRANS-

FORMATION OF SOCIAL STRUCTURES

Critical Theology

GREGORY BAUM

Theology is the reflection of Christians, in conversation with the entire believing community, on the world to which they belong and the religious tradition in which they participate.

It is my contention that Christian theology, after the Enlightenment, assumes a new and important role in the life of the church. Learning from the social sciences and the various critiques of religion, Christian theologians are able to discern the ideological and pathogenic trends in their own religious tradition and then, by opting for a wider meaning of the promised salvation, interpret the Christian gospel as a message of deliverance and reconciliation. The sustained dialogue with the critical thought of the Late Enlightenment I wish to call "critical theology." Critical theology is the critical application of the various theories of alienation to the self-understanding in faith of the Christian Church. This critical method may lead theologians to discover elements of false consciousness in their perception of reality and thus produce a significant change of mind and heart.

Traditional, pre-critical theology studied the Christian religion in the light of its divine gifts. The Christian religion was here understood as a spiritual reality mediated by doctrine and sacraments and expressing itself in the holiness of the faithful. Traditional theologians studied the development of Christian teaching and the meaning of the church's sacramental liturgy. According to the social thinkers, however, religious practice has a profound structural effect on people's lives far beyond the range of faith, hope and love. Religious practice, as we have seen, affects people's personal and social lives in ways that often remain quite hidden from them. The intended effects of the Christian religion may be quite different from the actual consequences. The early Puritans would have been surprised, I suppose, if they had been told that their perception of the gospel mediated an inner dynamics to society that would eventually lead to the rationalization of economic, social and cultural life. We are able to distinguish between what religion intends to be and what it actually produces in people's lives, i.e., between the intention and the consequences of religion. It is the task of critical theology to discern the structural consequences of religious practice, to evaluate them in the light of the church's normative teaching, and to enable the church to restructure its concrete social presence so that its social consequences approach more closely its profession of faith. For what must be in keeping with the Christian gospel is not only the church's teaching and practice but also and especially the actual, concrete effects of this teaching and practice on human history. Critical theology enables the church to assume theological responsibility for its social reality. In this preliminary sense, then, critical theology is "reflection on praxis."

We note that critical theology does not designate a particular area of theology; it does not refer to a theology of society or a theology of human life that accompanies a dogmatic theology concerned with the great moments of divine revelation. No, critical theology refers to a mode of theological reflection that is applicable to every area of theology—moral, dogmatic, ascetical, and so forth. The doctrine of God, while dealing with a transcendent mystery, has in fact profound, unrecognized (and sometimes alienating) sturctural implications for social life and personal well-being. The traditional formulation of christology, while dealing with God's saving act in Jesus, actually had profound, unrecognized and totally unintended structural effects: it has inferiorized the Jews and prepared their social exclusion, and it has led to a church-centered understanding of history and legitimated the white man's colonial invasion of the world. It is the task of critical theology to bring to light the hidden human consequences of doctrine, to raise the consciousness of the believing community in this regard, and to find a manner of proclaiming the church's teaching that has structural consequences in keeping with the gospel. In the case of christology this means that a way of announcing God's Word in Jesus must be found which does not devour other religions but actually makes room for the multiple manifestation of God's grace. There is not a single doctrine of the church, nor a single aspect of spirituality, worship or church life that may be exempted from a critique that distinguishes between intention and structural consequences and evaluates the latter in terms of the gospel.

Critical theology, I wish to insist, is not the submission of dogma to an anthropological norm as if the human were the measure of the divine; critical theology is rather the submission of the structural consequences of dogma to the revealed norm of the gospel. Critical theology, we note, is not an exhortative theology that complains of the unwillingness of church members to live up to their moral ideals. Critical theology is not concerned with personal virtue. What are examined by critical theology are the structural consequences of doctrine or institution, i.e., the effects on consciousness and society exerted by religious language and religious forms, quite independent of the subjective intention of the believers. The sociologists have convinced us that the symbolic structure of the imagination is able to legitimate an existing social order and, under certain conditions, even to overcome the present order and help to recreate culture and society. The structural consequences of doctrine and institution belong to the objective order. It is with these that critical theology is concerned.

In this chapter we shall discuss one application of critical theology. Since a major distortion of the Christian religion in the West has been the "privatization" of the gospel,[1] i.e., the excessively individualistic interpretation of the Christian message, and since this privatized religion has legitimated and promoted the atomization of the social order and an economic system of each man for himself, it is the task of critical theology to deprivatize the inherited religion. Such an exercise reveals the hidden political implications of religious language and practice; that is why German theologians, following John Baptist Metz, refer to the deprivatization of Christianity as "political theology."

The theological starting point for the following critique is the thesis, commonly accepted by students of the Bible, that the preaching of Jesus Christ had to do with repentance and the coming of God's kingdom and that it had both *personal and social meaning*. Christ's message was addressed to people personally and collectively. Jesus proclaimed that the kingdom of God was near, that God was about to fulfill his promise made to the ancients and recorded in scripture, and that he himself was a special instrument and servant of God's ultimate victory over the powers of evil. Jesus did not present his work as the salvation of souls; rather he came to usher in a new age that would transform the very structures of human life. After the crucifixion and the Easter event, the disciples believed that in the resurrection the kingdom of God had manifested itself in an irrevocable manner, that God's victory over evil and all the enemies of life was assured, and that the final coming of Jesus as the fulfiller of the divine promises was not far away. In the "between-time," Christ was looked upon as the one in whom the kingdom had been anticipated. He communicated the Spirit to the community. He was the strength, the comfort, the guide, the divine revealer enabling the community to move forward in history, impatient with the enduring power of evil yet joyful that its days were numbered. The Christian message communicates both judgment and new life, and it is addressed to persons as well as society. The gospel has meaning for personal life and social history.

To reduce the Christian message to a truth about personal salvation is to suppress a basic dimension of this message and to transform it into an ideology sanctioning individualism. Critical theology counters the privatizing of the gospel with an effort to regain its double dimension of personal-and-social.

Let us begin with the notion of sin. There can be no doubt that the notion of sin in theological teaching and religious practice has become excessively individualistic. We have looked upon sin as a personal deed, a personal violation of a divine commandment, or an act of infidelity against God, freely committed with deliberation. What we have forgotten is the social dimension of sin, and by doing so we have lost the key for understanding the violence in our history and the collective evil in which we are involved.

In the scriptures, we find a twofold language about sin. There is personal sin knowingly and freely chosen, and there is social sin accompanied by collective blindness. There is sin as deed and sin as illness. An example of personal sin is King David's adultery with Bathsheba and the premeditated murder of her husband, Uriah, in which the king acted against his better judgment and for which he did penance after the prophet's reprimand. Yet even this story had a social message, for the prophets in Israel, accustomed to a confederate structure of authority, were suspicious of the new kingship and feared the possibility of despotism. They made the story of David's sin remind the people that the king was a sinner and that they should never abandon their critical attitude toward royal authority.

Social sin is more especially the topic of the prophetic preaching. There we hear of collective blindness, group-egotism, and the pursuit of a national life that betrays the covenant and violates the divine command. Peculiar to this collective sin is that it is accompanied by so much self-delusion and self-flattery that the people involved in it are not aware of their transgression. We remind the reader of what we have said of the biblical notion of "blindness" in a previous chapter. Here we have sin, understood as infidelity to God and destructive communal action, which is largely due to false consciousness. This sin is like an illness. It destroys us while we are unable to recognize its features

and escape its power. While personal conversion to God's voice
may make us discover the wayward direction of our collective
life, we are quite unable to halt the involvement of society unless
the new awareness is shared by the great number of people, and
especially by the leaders.

The symbol of the purely private understanding of sin in
the Catholic Church is the confessional. The confessional practice goes back to the early middle ages when the Church, in an
attempt to civilize the Germanic tribes, imposed detailed rules
of conduct on them, regarding as sin the violation of these
rules, and transformed the ancient penitential ritual into the
regime of private confession. This regime created a highly private, legal, and act-oriented understanding of sin. When the
Reformation insisted on a more attitudinal understanding of sin,
the Catholic Church defended the medieval confessional practice. This practice has created the imagination among Catholic
peoples that sin is always a conscious and free decision to violate
a divine commandment. To overcome this privatized understanding of sin and the dangerous political consequences, many
contemporary Catholic theologians have recommended that the
practice of private confession be replaced by a communal celebration of the sacrament of repentance[2] in which the people,
gathered in community, listen to God's word, reflect on their
sins, including their objective involvement in the injustices of
their institutions, repent of their past, and then receive sacramental absolution—the divine pardon and the divine help to continue their struggle against evil. If Christians are in need of special
counseling, and this happens occasionally in every person's life,
they should seek out a religious counselor. Self-discovery, important and salvational though it be, need not be linked to the
church's public sacramental celebration of conversion and forgiveness.

In the scriptures, sin is both personal and social, and the two
aspects are closely interrelated. In our theological tradition, we
have presented sin mainly as private. The biblical passages dealing with sin as illness have been too exclusively understood as

referring to the inherited sin, the so-called original sin, which expresses the wounded state of human nature into which infants are born and thanks to which they share in the common inclination toward evil. At one time theologians linked this inherited distortion to Adam's transgression in a literal sense and saw in it a quasi-ontological legacy which had no direct connection with the sins of people and the evil of their collective life. Catholics often wondered why the inherited sin, for which we are not responsible, should be called sin at all. In fact, original sin was an embarrassing doctrine for many Christians. Contemporary theologians, on the other hand, have tended to identify the inherited sin with what the Bible calls "the sin of the world"—that is, the structure of evil, built into society, which wounds people, distorts their inclinations, and prompts them to do evil things.[3] The inherited sin, then, is mediated through the unresolved conflicts of parents and families as well as through the discrepancies of the institutional life into which infants are born and in which, they grow up. Psychotherapists such as Freud and Laing have shown how the conflicts of parents are handed on as distortions to their children; and Marx and the sociological tradition have demonstrated that institutions create consciousness and that the injustices built into these institutions falsify the awareness of the children socialized into them. The contemporary understanding of original sin brings to light the connection between personal and social sin. Seen in this light, the ancient teaching on original sin contains an important message for our age; it corrects the liberal misunderstanding that we are born into a neutral environment, in which the good is available to us if we so choose. According to the church's teaching this is not so; we are born into a distorted environment, grow up with a partially falsied consciousness, and the good becomes available to us only through many conversions—only as we resist the easy inclination of our wounded nature and follow the challenging, transcendent summons addressed to us in life. In modern *Gesellschaft* in particular, infantile narcissism is reinforced by the individualism of the consumer society. Only as we enter a counter-culture, such as the *ecclesia*, are we able to move toward a less alienating and more reconciled experience of life.

What is social sin? This is an open theological question.[4] I wish to reply to it by relying on sociological considerations. . . . Some theologians define social sin in terms of its object; social sin, then, is an evil act of a person or persons that adversely affects the life of society. Social sin is a deliberate act by one or several people damaging the common good. This certainly is an aspect of social sin, but as a definition it does not situate the sinfulness of the world at a deep enough level. We are still in the realm of conscious and deliberate action and hence remain very close to personal sin. I propose to define social sin with reference to its subject. What is proper to social sin is that its subject is a collectivity. Social sin resides in a group, a community, a people. I am not attempting to revive here the issue of collective guilt which occupied theologians after the war. Can a nation as a whole be guilty of the crimes committed by its government? This is not the question I pose here. What is proper to social sin is that it is not produced by deliberation and free choice. It produces evil consequences but no guilt in the ordinary sense. According to the biblical description, social sin is committed out of blindness. People are involved in destructive action without being aware of it. I wish to recognize several levels in social sin.

The *first* level of social sin is made up of the injustices and dehumanizing trends built into the various institutions—social, political, economic, religious, and others—which embody people's collective life. As people go about doing their daily work and fulfilling their duties, the destructive trends built into their institutions will damage a growing number of persons and eventually destroy their humanity. This evil may go on without anyone being fully aware of it. For the contradictions implicit in institutions remain hidden at first; only after a long time do the negative effects appear, and when they do, they are not immediately recognized as effects of the system. It takes a long time before the discrepancies implicit in institutional life translate themselves into dehumanizing trends and are acknowledged as such.

A *second* level of social sin is made up of the cultural and religious symbols, operative in the imagination and fostered by society, that legitimate and reinforce the unjust institutions and thus intensify the harm done to a growing number of people. Here again we have total ignorance. We have called such symbolic systems "ideologies." Such an ideology would be the privatized notion of sin we are discussing in this chapter, for by persuading people that the source of evil is only in the human heart we make them blind to the destructive trends built into their institutional life.

On a *third* level, social sin refers to the false consciousness created by these institutions and ideologies through which people involve themselves collectively in destructive action as if they were doing the right thing. This false consciousness persuades us that the evil we do is in fact a good thing in keeping with the aim and purpose of our collective well-being. Examples drawn from our own society would be the achievement-orientation of the dominant culture, its individualistic and competitive spirit, and our arrogant collective self-understanding with its implicit racism. This false consciousness exists, of course, in varying degrees of intensity, from a total identification with the dominant trends of society, including all of its social effects, to a greater and greater distancing from these trends accompanied by growing awareness of the injustices implicit in them. It is on this level that the wrestling against social sin begins! For here people, open to the Spirit, are able to become aware of, and turn away from, the taken-for-granted injustices built into their society. This is the level where conversion takes place.

Finally, if my analysis is correct, we have a *fourth* level of social sin which is made up of the collective decisions, generated by the distorted consciousness, which increase the injustices in society and intensify the power of the dehumanizing trends. These collective decisions, made by councils or boards of various kinds, appear as if they are based on free choice and deliberation

while in fact they may simply be the rational consequences of
the distortions built into the institution and duplicated in consciousness. At the same time, this is the level where personal
sin clearly enters into the creation and expansion of social sin.
For here, out of conscious evil intention and greed, a person or
a group of persons can magnify the evil done by institutional
life and give a twist for the worse to human organization.

Once we deprivatize the notion of sin, we must also regain
the full, personal-and-social meaning of conversion. For the sake
of brevity, I shall only indicate the direction of this theology.
According to the biblical message, the divine reply to human sin
is judgment and the promise of new life. God's gracious and
critical word makes people recognize their sins, calls forth their
conversion, enables them to wrestle against the structures of evil,
initiates them into a new life of love and dedication, and makes
them yearn for the ultimate pacification of humankind. Conversion, therefore, can no longer be understood as the repentant
recognition of one's personal sins; included in conversion are the
critical recognition of, and the turning away from, the social
dimension of sin, present in the various collectivities to which
a person belongs. The *metanoia* to which the gospel summons
us demands that we examine our own personal lives as well as
the injustices and contradictions in the various institutions to
which we belong, be they political, economic, educational, ecclesiastical, or whatever. The raising of consciousness in regard to
institutional life is part and parcel of the conversion away from
sin.

The preaching of personal conversion to Jesus, understood
in an individualistic way, as it has been done in many Christian
churches, represses one side of the gospel and hence has strongly
defensive or even reactionary political implications. For the
stress on private conversion makes people blind to the structures
of evil in society. People are made to think that the inequities
of their society are due to personal sins and can be removed only
through the personal conversion of the sinners. What people
who stress the conversion to Jesus as their personal savior fail

to see is that the evil in society has a twofold root, in the sinful hearts of men and in institutionalized injustices, and that this evil can only be overcome by a movement that includes social change. The stress of Jesus as personal savior is always linked, therefore, to the defense of the political *status quo*. The individualistic religion of traditional evangelical and fundamentalist Christians legitimates the individualism of our economic system, and while they present their message as non-political, it has significant political consequences. The privatization of sin and conversion, fostered in Catholicism by the confessional practice, is promoted in the Protestant churches by the traditional evangelical stress on personal conversion to Jesus. Jesus saves! Today, it is worth noting, we find critical movements not only in the major Christian churches; we also witness the emergence of a left-wing evangelicalism which seeks to recover the social meaning of sin and conversion.[5]

The preceding remarks on the deprivatization of sin and conversion lead us to a better understanding of the nature and task of critical theology. At the beginning of this chapter we defined critical theology as the critical application of the various theories of alienation to the Christian self-understanding. Critical theology is reflection on the church's praxis and enables the church to assume theological responsibility for its social reality. Theologians engaged in this pursuit, we said, may discover elements of distorted consciousness in themselves and be led to a change of mind and heart. Theology is based on conversion. After deprivatizing the notion of sin and conversion, it becomes even clearer that critical theology is based on, and leads to, a critical analysis of the church's institutional context and a turning away from its destructive and sinful trends. The raising of consciousness is at the heart of critical theology. We want to examine the kind of commitment that this implies for the critical theologian and the Christian community in general.

In Latin America the critical reflection on praxis has led to the creation of liberation theology,[6] in which the raising of consciousness, or "conscientization," holds a central place. This

approach has even been adopted by the General Conference of
Latin American bishops held at Medellin in 1968. To discover
the social dimension of sin in their societies, the Latin American
Christians focus almost exclusively on economic injustices. Why
is this so? The various countries in Latin America are divided
into the vast under class of dispossesed people, without access
to education and the goods of life, and the small, visible class
of wealthy families, the owners of the land and the means of
production, who are linked, often as intermediaries, to the international capitalist system, and derive their power, in part at
least, from the nations in which the center of capitalism resides.
In Latin American countries, there is no broad middle class as
we find it in the industrialized countries of Western Europe
and North America. The Latin American countries are basically
divided into two classes, the rich and the dispossessed, and the
radical inequality between these two constitutes the overriding
fact of their national existence. The blatant economic injustice
determines every form of human association and distorts every
expression of social and cultural life. The state becomes purely
and simply the protector of the small ruling class. In these countries, then, the economic factor dominates all others—the political
order, the cultural trends, the ecclesiastical system, etc. All expressions of society are reflections of the economic order. In
this situation, the class domination becomes the key for understanding the misery in which people live and the form which
social sin has taken. The Catholic Left in Latin America holds
that the class struggle defines the reality of their countries and
that conversion, in such a social context, implies an identification
with the oppressed class and its struggle for economic justice.
The critical Catholics in these countries engage in the education
of ordinary people to raise their consciousness in regard to their
own exploitation. They want the people to understand the oppression inflicted on them by a small upper class, protected by
military and police power, which acts as an instrument of a
vast economic system, the center of which lies outside their own
continent. But they also want to become more aware how this

oppression has falsified their own perception of reality, how they have assimilated the ideological elements of culture and religion, and how they have unknowingly contributed to the stability of the exploitative system.

Liberation theology in Latin America is, in a wider sense, critical reflection on praxis. The praxis which is the object of reflection here includes the dominant social process in which the church as an element of culture participates and the new action flowing from faith and solidarity. Liberation theology is then not a new theological system alongside other such systems; it is not a new, updated body of social teachings; it is, rather, a new mode of reflection that arises from action, modifies people's perception of their world, and thus leads to greater engagement in action. Liberation theology wants to be the theoretic component of the church's identification with the dispossessed class and its active involvement in the movement of liberation.

Latin American liberation theology cannot be applied as such to the Christians in North America and Western Europe. To restrict the analysis of present social ills to class conflict and the economic factor is, in my view, quite inadequate.

It is unrealistic, in my view, to look for a single form of oppression in North America, to which all others are subordinated. What we have is a complex intermeshing of technocratic depersonalization and immobility, economic domination and exploitation, racial exclusion and inferiorization, and other forms including the subjugation of women. Americans will want to listen to their neighbors in the South to learn the effects that their own economic system has on the dependent countries and estimate the devastating influence of "the international imperialism of money."[7] Still, the analysis of social sin in North America will inevitably be complex.

The raising of consciousness in the complex situation of North America means the acknowedgment of the multiple forms of exploitation, and the turning away from the social dimension of sin implies an identification with the aims of the emancipatory movements. This commitment inevitably leads Christians to the difficult question how to relate these various movements to one another in a just and justifiable manner. This question, I wish to insist, cannot be solved prior to the commitment to be solidary with them. To remain aloof, to seek a neutral place (which does not exist), to examine these movements simply from the outside without identification with their aims, will not provide the historical standpoint from which these movements and their interrelationship can be understood. To withhold this commitment until the question of their interrelationship has been resolved means never to be able to transcend the dominant system. Conversion away from sin, personal-and-social, implies an identification with the poor, the dispossessed, the disfavored and with the movements toward their emancipation, an identification that precedes the critical reflection on policy and strategy. This is the radical element of the gospel. Faith precedes calculation, conversion to Christ precedes the mapping out of the converted life, solidarity with the least of Christ's brothers and sisters precedes the search for an adequate plan of joining them in their struggle.

Critical theology in North America is, therefore, different from the liberation theologies of Latin America. What is different is the combination of factors in the analysis of social evil, what is different is the form which the political commitment takes, and what is different is, as we shall see, the new imagination drawn from diverse historical experiences. At the same time, structurally these critical theologies are identical. They are reflections on faith-conversion, they are grounded in social commitment in favor of the oppressed, they raise consciousness, lead to social involvement, and regard themselves as the reflective or contemplative component of the liberating human action, in which God is redemptively present to the sinful world.

---

1. The language of "privatizing" and "deprivatizing" the gospel was introduced in Catholic theology by John Baptist Metz; see, for instance, "The Church's Social Function in the Light of a 'Political Theology,'" *Concilium*, Vol. 36. Paulist Press, New York, 1968, pp. 3-18. Metz defined "political theology" as "a critical corrective of contemporary theology's

tendency to concentrate on the private individual, and at the same time to formulate the eschatological message in the circumstances of our present society" (p. 2). "The reversal of this privatizing tendency is the task of political theology" (p. 5).

2. For a critical examination of the confessional practice, see the articles in *Sacramental Reconciliation,* edit. E. Schillebeeckx, *Concilium,* Vol. 61, Herder & Herder, New York, 1971.

3. Cf. Peter de Rosa, *Christ and Original Sin,* Bruce, Milwaukee, 1967; A. M. Dubarle, *The Biblical Doctrine of Original Sin,* Herder & Herder, New York, 1965; Karl Rahner, *Hominization: The Evolutionary Origin of Man as a Theological Problem,* Herder, Freiburg, 1965; Piet Schoonenberg, *Man and Sin, A Theological View,* Univ. of Notre Dame Press, Notre Dame, Ind., 1965.

4. The notion of social sin is found in recent ecclesiastical documents. In the Statement "Justice in the World," issued by the Third Synod of Bishops, 1971, we read, "We have been able to perceive the serious injustices which are building around the world a network of domination, oppression and abuses which stifle freedom." The bishops speak of those "who suffer violence and are oppressed by unjust systems and structures," and include in the church's mission "the liberation from every oppressive situation." They conclude, "Action on behalf of justice and participation in the transformation of the world fully appears to us as a constitutive dimension of the preaching of the gospel" (*The Pope Speaks,* Vol. 16, 1972, p. 377). See Patrick Kerans, *Sinful Social Structures,* Paulist Press, New York, 1974.

5. Cf. R. Pierard, *The Unequal Yoke: Evangelism, Christianity and Political Conservatism,* J. B. Lippincott, Philadelphia, 1970; D. O. Moberg, *The Great Reversal: Evangelism Versus Social Concern,* J. B. Lippincott, Philadelphia, 1972.

6. Gustavo Gutierrez, *A Theology of Liberation,* Orbis Books, Maryknoll, N. Y., 1973, pp. 25-32, and Juan Segundo, "Capitalism—Socialism: A Theological Crux," *Concilium,* Vol. 96, Herder & Herder, New York, 1974, pp. 105-123. On Latin American liberation theology, also consult Juan Segundo, *A Theology for Artisans of a New Humanity,* Orbis Books, Maryknoll, N. Y., 1973.

7. The expression, "the international imperialism of money," drawn from Pope Pius XI's encyclical *Quadragesimo Anno,* has been used several times in the documents of Pope Paul VI, e.g., *Populorum Progressio,* NCWC News Service, no. 26.

[Major deletions have been made in this edited version.]

Conscientisation

PAOLO FREIRE

What is conscientisation? I have noticed that conscientisation is frequently taken to be synonymous with the French expression *prise de conscience*, yet the two must be carefully distinguished. To show why, let me define the scope of each of them. As a matter of fact, conscientisation is possible only because *prise de conscience* is possible. If men were not able to become aware, there wouldn't be any conscientisation. What then is conscientisation?

One of the distinguishing traits of man is that only he can stand off from the world and the reality of things around him. Only man can stand at a distance from a thing and admire it. As they objectivise or admire a thing (admire is taken here in the philosophical sense of ad-miring, looking at), men are able to act consciously on the objectivised reality. That, precisely, is the human praxis, man's action-reflection on the world, on reality. And yet, in their approach to the world, men have a preliminary moment in which the world, the objective reality, doesn't yet come to them as a knowable object of their critical consciousness. In other words, in their spontaneous approach to the world, men's moral, basic attitude is not a critical, but an ingenuous one.

Not that there is no knowledge of reality at this spontaneous stage, but what we don't have yet is a critical attitude. There is one kind of perception of reality that gives us a real, if limited, knowledge of it: the Greeks called it *doxa* (mere opinion, or belief). Knowledge that stays at the level of mere *doxa* and goes no further to the level of a task (the reality's reason for being, as Mao Tse-tung would say) never becomes full knowledge; it is not a *logos* of reality.

To become aware, then, all it takes is to be a man. All it takes to be a man is to seize reality in the dialectical relations that flow between man and the world, the world and man; those relations are so intimate that we shouldn't really talk about man *and* the world, but just about man, or perhaps world-man. The first level of apprehension of reality is what the French mean by *prise de conscience*. The taking awareness of reality exists precisely because, as situated beings—closed beings in Gabriel Marcel's words—men are with and in the world, gazing at it.

This *prise de conscience* is not yet conscientisation, however. Conscientisation is a *prise de conscience* that goes deeper; it is the critical development of a *prise de conscience*. Hence, conscientisation implies going beyond the spontaneous phase of apprehension of reality to a critical phase, where reality becomes a knowable object, where man takes an epistemological stance and tries to know. Thus conscientisation is a probing of the ambience of reality. The more a person conscientises himself, the more he unveils reality and gets at the phenomenic essence of the object he stands in front of, to analyze it. For that same reason, conscientisation without a praxis, i.e., without action-reflection as two paired, dialecticized elements permanently constituting that special way of being the world (or transforming it) is peculiar to man.

Historical Commitment

Conscientisation, therefore, is commitment in time; in fact, there is no conscientisation without historical commitment. So that conscientisation is also a historical awareness. It is a critical insertion into history. It means that men take on a role as subjects making the world, remaking the world; it asks men to fashion their existence out of the material that life offers them. The more they are conscientised, the more they exist.

The mere fact of finding oneself oppressed will move a step ahead and become a process of liberation only if this discovery leads to a historical commitment that means an involvement. For involvement is more than commitment: it is a critical insertion into history in order to create, to mold it. And so when an oppressed individual sees he is oppressed, if he does not set out to do something to transform the concrete oppressing reality, he is not historically committed, and thus he is not really conscientised.

Conscientisation implies then that when I realize that I am oppressed, I also know I can liberate myself if I transform the concrete situation where I find myself oppressed. Obviously, I can't transform it in my head: that would be to fall into the philosophical error of thinking that awareness 'creates' reality. I would be decreeing that I am free, by my mind. And yet the structures would continue to be the same as ever—so that I wouldn't be free. No, conscientisation implies a critical insertion into a process, it implies a historical commitment to make changes. That is why conscientisation bids us to adopt a utopian attitude towards the world, an attitude that turns the one conscientised into a utopian agent. Before going any further, let me explain what I mean by the word utopian.

Denouncing, Announcing

For me utopian does not mean something unrealizable, nor is it idealism. Utopia is the dialectization in the acts of denouncing and announcing—denouncing the dehumanizing structure and announcing the structure that will humanize. Hence it is also a historical commitment. A utopia supposes that we know critically. It is an act of knowledge. For I cannot denounce the dehumanizing structure unless I get at it and know it. Nor can I announce, either, unless I know. But—this is important—

between the moment of an announcement and the accomplishment of it there is a great difference: the announcement is not
the announcement of a project, but of an ante-project. Because
the ante-project becomes a project only through a historical
praxis. Besides, between the ante-project and the moment of accomplishing or concretizing the project, a period intervenes that
we call historical commitment. For this reason, only utopians—and
revolutionaries too, to the extent that they are utopians (what
was Marx but a utopian?)—can be prophetic and hopeful.

Only those who announce and denounce, who are permanently committed to a radical process of transforming the world
so that men can be more, only they can be prophetic. Reactionary
people, oppressors cannot be utopian, they cannot be prophetic,
and because they cannot be prophetic they cannot have hope.

What future has the oppressor but to preserve his present
status as oppressor? What scope for denouncing can oppressors
have, other than the denunciation of those who denounce them?
What do oppressors have to announce but the announcment of
their myths? And what can be the hope of those who have no
future?

I see a great possibility here for a theology, the utopian theology of hope. The utopian posture of the denouncing, announcing historically committed Christians who are convinced that
the historical vocation of men is not to adapt, not to bend pressures, not to spend 90 per cent of their time making concessions
in order to salvage what we call the historical vocation of the
Church. We humans have an unbelievable vocation, and we cannot jeopardize it for any one fact, nor can we compromise it for
any single, isolated problem, because the Church has the whole
world. Why then risk one's entire historical task over any single
fact? That would be, not to be utopian, but to be Machiavellian.
It would be to concede, and to forfeit one's soul in the con-
cession.

Conscientisation clearly has to do with utopia. The more we
are conscientised, the more we become, by the commitment that
we assume to change things, announcers and denouncers. This

commitment ought to be permanent, though, because if after denouncing a dehumanizing structure and announcing a more human one, after committing ourselves to the reality (after all, the project is going to be accomplished only if we work at it), after understanding the project and being convinced of its importance (being conscientised about it), if we were then to stop being utopian, we would simply bureaucratize ourselves. This is the danger inherent in any revolution, once it ceases to be permanent. One masterly way to avoid that danger is by a cultural revolution, that dialecticalization which has no yesterday, today or tomorrow and which avoids becoming static because it is an ongoing effort for change.

That's what conscientisation is: a seizing of reality; and for that very reason, for the very utopian strain that permeates it, we can call it a reshaping of reality. Conscientisation demythologizes. Obvious and impressive as the fact may be, an oppressor can never conscientise for liberation. (How would I possibly demythologize if I am an oppressor?) A humanizing endeavor can only be an endeavor to demythify. Conscientisation then is the most critical approach to reality, stripping it down so as to get to know the myths that deceive and perpetuate the dominating structure.

One might protest: "But how can we ever find the process, the how of conscientisation?" The how of it brings up an important point, one that seems to me to be the essential difference between education as a means of domination and education as a means of liberation. An education that is used to domesticate merely transfers knowledge, as the educator passes on his thirst for knowing to his pupils, who passively, receive that knowledge. In that sort of relationship, conscientisation is impossible. We can see a certain incipient conscientisation in it, though, despite that education, in the way the students react, because the natural intentionality of human awareness cannot be thwarted by any educator's domesticating process.

A conscientising—and therefore liberating—education is not that transfer of neatly wrapped knowledge; it is the true act of knowing. Through it, both teacher and pupils simultaneously become knowing subjects, brought together by the object they are knowing. There is no longer one who thinks, who knows, standing in front of others who admit they don't know, that they have to be taught. Rather, all of them are inquisitive learners, avid to learn.

Education and Freedom

Those who propagate the superstructure's myths are, equivalently, supporting the superstructure itself. Even if there is a serious changeover, such as a revolution, the myths from the previous structure will carry over and continue to influence the new governmental structure. Unless we critically grasp this fact, we will never understand how, even after an infrastructure has been changed, people will continue to think as they did before.

An understanding of this dialectic and this sort of subdetermination (which Marx certainly had) will persuade us that a mechanistic view of social changes is no good. Someone with a mechanistic approach would expect that if the infrastructure were changed, the superstructure would then automatically be changed too—but that is not what happens. That was the problem that baffled Lenin after the Soviet Revolution: Stalin wrestled with it—and solved it finally by shooting down the peasants. It is the dilemma facing Fidel Castro today with his peasants, though it is not so crucial for him. It is also the problem that Mao Tse-tung had, but he came up with the most genial solution of the century: China's cultural revolution.

What is cultural action? What is a cultural revolution? In generic terms, but in the good sense of the phrase, it is the way we culturally attack culture. It means that we see culture always as a problem and do not let it become static, becoming a myth and mystifying us.

Whereas education, in practice, too often merely inverts the praxis and domesticates students by pumping myths into them, education for freedom, on the other hand, strives to expose that

Paolo Freire 303

inversion of praxis at the moment it occurs, so that it will not take place. A noble objective, indeed. But how do we do it? As we turn our attention to see our misdirected praxis, we fix our eyes on, as the object of our knowledge, that domesticating capability of an inversion of praxis, the very prostituting of our transforming action. At that moment our act of knowing illuminates the action that is the source of our knowing. And right there we have the permanent, constant, dynamic of our attitude toward culture itself.

Otherwise we risk falling into an elitist position, hence one that is neither liberating nor human, nor humanizing. But even supposing that we avoid that pitfall, how are we to undertake a program of cultural action, or of education for freedom, when we know that people are all the while being dominated through the so-called mass media—which are really means for sending messages rather than communicating, for propagandizing and domesticating rather than for liberating? We must save that word from the distortion being made to cover a wholesale invasion by slogans. But communications is not sloganizing. It is something completely different. As all of us recognize, cultural action for freedom is ultimately a kind of action.

Let's turn for a moment to the desperate situation of the peasants in north-east Brazil. Their awareness of what is going on is so primitive that they are wholly unable to get a structural view of the reality. They are incapable of envisaging their plight as a result of the world they live in. Yet even a peasant is a man, and any man wants to explain the reality around him. What reasons can he find? How does his dulled brain conceive his wretched lot? Normally, he will try to size up the situation. He will look for the causes, the reasons for his condition, in things higher and more powerful than man. One such thing is God, whom he sees as the maker, the cause of his condition. Ah, but if God is responsible, man can do nothing. Many Christians today, thanks be to God, are vigorously reacting against that attitude, especially in Brazil. But as a child, I knew many priests who went out to the peasants saying: "Be patient. This is God's will. And anyway, it will earn heaven for you." Yet the truth of the matter is that we have to earn our heaven here and now. We have to build our heaven, to fashion it during our lifetime, right now. Salvation is something to achieve, not just to hope for. This latter sort of theology is a very passive one that I cannot stomach.

How could we make God responsible for this calamity? As if Absolute Love could abandon man to constant victimization and total destitution. That would be a God as described by Marx.

Whenever men make God responsible for intolerable situations, or for oppression, then the dominating structures help to popularize that myth. If God is not the cause, they whisper, then destiny must be. Human reason at this level easily becomes fatalistic: it sits back and sighs: "Nothing can be done about it." Sometimes another scapegoat is found, and it too is a myth spread by the dominating structure: the helplessness of the oppressed. The dominated mind looks inward and decides that it is totally unable to cope with its misery: it concludes that it is impotent. A Presbyterian clergyman from the United States once told me that the whites in his country say God made the blacks inferior. It was a fine example of what the author of the book *Picture of the Colonised Contrasted with the Picture of the Coloniser* meant as he wrote: "The oppressor always draws a picture of the oppressed." For the oppressed mind in its desperate plight, I repeat, there seems to be nothing that can be done.

For the critical mind that conscientises itself, beyond this situation there is the future, what we must do, the thing we must create, the historical futurity we have to bring into being; and to do that, we must change whatever it is that prevents the humanization of our fellow men.

As we examine the structures and the reasons why they are so intolerable, as we expose the oppressive situation, we are forced to a decision: we either commit ourselves or we don't— but we will have to answer to our consciences for our choice.

The process of conscientisation leaves no one with his arms folded. It makes some unfold their arms. It leaves others with a guilt feeling, because conscientisation shows us that God wants us to act.

As I conscientise myself, I realize that my brothers who don't eat, who don't laugh, who don't sing, who don't love, who live oppressed, crushed and despised lives, are suffering because of some reality that is causing all this. And at that point I join in the action historically by loving genuinely, by having the courage to commit myself (which is no easy thing!) or I end up with a sense of guilt because I am not doing what I know I should. That guilt feeling rankles in me, it demands rationalizations to 'gratify' myself (the term is used here in the psychological sense). A North American theologian has called those rationalizations "fake generosities" because to escape my guilt feelings I go in for philanthrophy. I seek compensation by almsgiving, I send a check to build a church, I make contributions: land for a chapel or a priory for nuns, hoping in that way to buy peace. But peace cannot be purchased, it is not for sale; peace has to be lived. And I can't live my peace without commitment to men, and my commitment to men can't exist without their liberation, and their liberation can't exist without the final transformation of the structures that are dehumanizing them.

Fear of Freedom

In the seminars that I have given in various countries it is very interesting to observe how two attitudes are produced. Often I am violently assailed because many people, when they hear me, start to despise themselves—and their almost immediate second reaction is to strike back at whoever made them do that. Observing this process can be extremely interesting.

A similar process takes place with very simple people, too. Many of them run away from freedom. Oppression is so potent a thing that it produces fear of freedom. That fear crops up whenever any discussion or even mention of freedom makes them already feel it as a threat. But freedom isn't something that is given. It is something that is very arduous, because nobody gives freedom to anyone else, no one frees another, nobody can even free himself; men free themselves only by mutual planning, by collaborating on something wrong that they want to correct. There is an interesting theological parallel to this: no one saves another, no one saves himself all alone, because only in communion can we save ourselves—or not save ourselves. You don't save me, because my soul, my being, my conscious body is not something that A or B can save. We work out our salvation in communion. Each one of us must set out in quest of his salvation, we must do it ourselves. I don't mean that God hasn't saved us by His presence in history: I'm talking now on the human level.

Conscientisation demands an Easter. That is, it demands that we die to be born again. Every Christian must live his Easter, and that too is utopia. The man who doesn't make his Easter, in the sense of dying in order to be reborn, is no real Christian. That is why Christianity is, for me, such a marvelous doctrine. People have accused me of being a communist, but no communist could say what I have just said. I never had any temptation to cease being, to cease existing. The reason is that I am not yet completely a Catholic, I just keep on trying to be one more completely, day after day. The condition of being is to go on being.

Each of us has to give his witness, and conscientisation is a summons to do that: to be new each day. Hence it is peace, and it enables us to understand others.

Conscientisation could never be an imposition on others or a manipulation of them. I cannot impose my opinions on someone else. I can only invite them to share, to discuss. To impose on others my way of not being would be a real contradiction. For loving is not only a free act, it is an act for freedom. And love that cannot produce more freedom is not love.

A Spirituality of Liberation

GUSTAVO GUTIERREZ

To place oneself in the perspective of the Kingdom means to participate in the struggle for the liberation of those oppressed by others. This is what many Christians who have committed themselves to the Latin American revolutionary process have begun to experience. If this option seems to separate them from the Christian community, it is because many Christians, intent on domesticating the Good News, see them as wayward and perhaps even dangerous. If they are not always able to express in appropriate terms the profound reasons for their commitment, it is because the theology in which they were formed—and which they share with other Christians—has not produced the categories necessary to express this option, which seeks to respond creatively to the new demands of the Gospel and of the oppressed and exploited peoples of this continent. But in their commitments, and even in their attempts to explain them, there is a greater understanding of the faith, greater faith, greater fidelity to the Lord than in the "orthodox" doctrine (some prefer to call it by this name) of reputable Christian circles.[1] This doctrine is supported by authority and much publicized because of access to social communications media, but it is so static and devitalized that it is not even strong enough to abandon the Gospel. It is the Gospel which is disowning it.

But theological categories are not enough. We need a vital attitude, all-embracing and synthesizing, informing the totality as well as every detail of our lives; we need a "spirituality."[2]

Spirituality, in the strict and profound sense of the word is the dominion of the Spirit. If "the truth will set you free" (Jn 8:32), the Spirit "will guide you into all the truth" (Jn 16:13) and will lead us to complete freedom, the freedom from everything that hinders us from fulfilling ourselves as men and sons of God and the freedom to love and to enter into communion with God and with others. It will lead us along the path of liberation because "where the Spirit of the Lord is, there is liberty" (2 Cor 3:17).

A spirituality is a concrete manner, inspired by the Spirit, of living the Gospel; it is a definite way of living "before the Lord," in solidarity with all men, "with the Lord," and before men. It arises from an intense spiritual experience, which is later explicated and witnessed to. Some Christians are beginning to live this experience as a result of their commitment to the process of liberation. The experiences of previous generations are there to support it, but above all, to remind them that they must discover their own way. Not only is there a contemporary history and a contemporary Gospel; there is also a contemporary spiritual experience which cannot be overlooked. A spirituality means a reordering of the great axes of the Christian life in terms of this contemporary experience. What is new is the synthesis that this reordering brings about, in stimulating a deepened understanding of various ideas, in bringing to the surface unknown or forgotten aspects of the Christian life, and above all, in the way in which these things are converted into life, prayer, commitment, and action.

The truth is that a Christianity lived in commitment to the process of liberation presents its own problems which cannot be ignored and meets obstacles which must be overcome. For many, the encounter with the Lord under these conditions can disappear by giving way to what he himself brings forth and nourishes: love for man. This love, however, does not know the fullness of its potential. This is a real difficulty, but the solution must come from the heart of the problem itself. Otherwise, it would be just one more patchwork remedy, a new impasse. This is the challenge confronting a spirituality of liberation. Where oppression and the liberation of man seem to make God irrelevant—a God filtered by our longtime indifference to these problems—there must blossom faith and hope in him who comes to root out injustice and to offer, in an unforeseen way, total liberation. This is a spirituality which dares to sink roots in the soil of oppression-liberation.

A spirituality of liberation will center on a *conversion* to the neighbor, the oppressed person, the exploited social class, the despised race, the dominated country. Our conversion to the Lord implies this conversion to the neighbor. Evangelical conversion is indeed the touchstone of all spirituality. Conversion means a radical transformation of ourselves; it means thinking, feeling, and living as Christ—present in exploited and alienated man. To be converted is to commit oneself to the process of the liberation of the poor and oppressed, to commit oneself lucidly, realistically, and concretely. It means to commit oneself not only generously, but also with an analysis of the situation and a strategy of action. To be converted is to know and experience the fact that, contrary to the laws of physics, we can stand straight, according to the Gospel, only when our center of gravity is outside ourselves.

Conversion is a permanent process in which very often the obstacles we meet make us lose all we had gained and start anew. The fruitfulness of our conversion depends on our openness to doing this, our spiritual childhood. All conversion implies a break. To wish to accomplish it without conflct is to deceive oneself and others: "No man is worthy of me who cares more for father or mother than for me." But it is not a question of a withdrawn and pious attitude. Our conversion process is affected by the socio-economic, political, cultural, and human environment in which it occurs. Without a change in these structures, there is no authentic conversion. We have to break with our mental categories, with the way we relate to others, with our way of identifying with the Lord, with our cultural milieu, with our social class, in other words, with all that can stand in the way of a real, profound solidarity with those who suffer, in the first place, from misery and injustice. Only thus, and not through purely interior and spiritual attitudes, will the "new man" arise from the ashes of the "old."

The Christian has not done enough in this area of conversion to the neighbor, to social justice, to history. He has not perceived clearly enough yet that to know God *is* to do justice. He still does not live *in one sole action* with both God and all men. He still does not situate himself in Christ without attempting to avoid concrete human history. He has yet to tread the path which will lead him to seek effectively the peace of the Lord in the heart of the social struggle.

A spirituality of liberation must be filled with a living sense of *gratuitousness*. Communion with the Lord and with all men is more than anything else a gift. Hence the universality and the radicalness of the liberation which it affords. This gift, far from being a call to passivity, demands a vigilant attitude. This is one of the most constant Biblical themes: the encounter with the Lord presupposes attention, active disposition, work, fidelity to his will, the good use of talents received. But the knowledge that at the root of our personal and community existence lies the gift of the self-communication of God, the grace of his friendship, fills our life with gratitude. It allows us to see our encounters with men, our loves, everything that happens in our life as a gift. There is a real love only when there is free giving—without conditions or coercion. Only gratuitous love goes to our very roots and elicits true love.

Prayer is an experience of gratuitousness. This "leisure" action, this "wasted" time, reminds us that the Lord is beyond the categories of useful and useless.[3] God is not of this world. The gratuitousness of his gift, creating profound needs, frees us from all religious alienation and, in the last instance, from all alienation. The Christian committed to the Latin American revolutionary process has to find the way to real prayer, not evasion. It cannot be denied that a crisis exists in this area and that we can easily slide into dead ends.[4] There are many who—nostagically and in "exile," recalling earlier years of their life—can say with the psalmist: "As I pour out my soul in distress, I call to mind how I marched in the ranks of the great to the house of God, among exultant shouts of praise, the clamor of the pilgrims" (Ps 42:4). But the point is not to backtrack; new experiences, new demands have made heretofore familiar and comfortable paths impassable and have made us undertake new itineraries on which we hope it might be possible to say with Job to the Lord, "I knew of thee then only by report, but now I see thee with my own eyes" (42:5). Bonhoeffer was right when he said that the only credible God is the God of the mystics. But this is not a God unrelated to human history. On the contrary, if it is true, as we recalled above, that one must go through man to reach God, it is equally certain that the "passing through" to that gratuitous God strips me, leaves me naked, universalizes my love for others, and makes it gratuitous. Both movements need each other dialectically and move toward a synthesis. This synthesis is found in Christ; in the God-Man we encounter God and man. In Christ man gives God a human countenance and God gives man a divine countenance.[5] Only in this perspective will we be able to understand that the "union with the Lord," which all spirituality proclaims, is not a separation from man; to attain this union, I must go through man, and the union, in turn, enables me to encounter man more fully. Our purpose here is not to "balance" what has been said before, but rather to deepen it and see it in all of its meaning.

The conversion to the neighbor, and in him to the Lord, the gratuitousness which allows me to encounter others fully, the unique encounter which is the foundation of communion of men among themselves and of men with God, these are the source of Christian *joy*. This joy is born of the gift already received yet still awaited and is expressed in the present despite the difficulties and tensions of the struggle for the construction of a just society. Every prophetic proclamation of total liberation is accompanied by an invitation to participate in eschatological joy: "I will take delight in Jerusalem and rejoice in my people" (Is 65:19). This

joy ought to fill our entire existence, making us attentive both to
the gift of integral liberation of man and history as well as to the
detail of our life and the lives of others. This joy ought not to
lessen our commitment to man who lives in an unjust world, nor
should it lead us to a facile, low-cost conciliation. On the contrary, our joy is paschal, guaranteed by the Spirit (Gal 5:22;
1 Tm 1:6; Rm 14:17); it passes through the conflict with the
great ones of this world and through the cross in order to enter
into life. This is why we celebrate our joy in the present by recalling the passover of the Lord. To recall Christ is to believe
in him. And this celebration is a feast (Rv 19:7),[6] a feast of the
Christian community, those who explicitly confess Christ to be
the Lord of history, the liberator of the oppressed. This community has been referred to as the small temple in contradistinction to the large temple of human history.[7] Without community
support neither the emergence nor the continued existence of
a new spirituality is possible.

The Magnificat expresses well this spirituality of liberation.
A song of thanksgiving for the gifts of the Lord, it expresses
humbly the joy of being loved by him: "Rejoice, my spirit, in
God my Savior; so tenderly has he looked upon his servant,
humble as she is.... So wonderfully has he dealt with me, the
Lord, the Mighty One" (Lk 1:47-49). But at the same time it is
one of the New Testament texts which contains great implications both as regards liberation and the political sphere. This
thanksgiving and joy are closely linked to the action of God
who liberates the oppressed and humbles the powerful. "The
hungry he has satisfied with good things, the rich sent empty
away" (52-53). The future of history belongs to the poor and
exploited. True liberation will be the work of the oppressed
themselves; in them, the Lord saves history. The spirituality of
liberation will have as its basis the spirituality of the *anawim*.[8]

Living witnesses rather than theological speculation will
point out, are already pointing out, the direction of a spirituality
of liberation. This is the task which has been undertaken in

Latin America by those referred to above as a "first Christian generation."

1. We need only read Camilo Torres or Nestor Paz Zamora—to mention two who have left something in writing—to be convinced of this. It would be a mistake for theologians who might be offended by certain deficiencies of expression to ignore these efforts to penetrate what the Word of the Lord is saying to man in the Latin American context.

2. Arturo Gaete observed a short time ago the need for a "spirituality of liberation" ("Definición e indefinición de la Iglesia en política," *Mensaje* 19, no. 191 [August, 1970]:375). . . .

3. See José María González Ruiz, *Dios es gratuito, pero no superfluo* (Madrid: Ediciones Marova, 1970).

4. This has been clearly pointed out in "Pastoral Concern for the Elites," no. 13, in *Medellin*.

5. If Vallejo was correct when he said, "My God, if you had been a man, today you would know how to be God," it could also be said, "If you had been God, today you would know how to be man."

6. See the excellent considerations of Harvey Cox in *The Feast of Fools* (Cambridge: Harvard University Press, 1969).

7. Conrad Eggers Lan, *Cristianismo y nueva ideología* (Buenos Aires, 1968), pp. 47-48, quoted by Juan Luis Segundo, "Desarrollo y subdesarrollo: polos teológicos," p. 79.

8. "Christians and their pastors should recognize the hand of the Almighty in those events that occur sporadically—when the powerful are dethroned and the lowly are exalted, when the rich are sent away empty-handed and the needy are filled" ("Letter to Peoples of the Third World," in *Between Honesty and Hope*, p. 6).

Social Sin and Conversion: A Theology of the Church's Social Involvement

PETER J. HENRIOT

Certainly there are few topics as exhaustively worked over as the topic of Christian social involvement. Pontifical pronouncements and theological treatises, sociological surveys and political polemics: all seem to have said already whatever could—or should —possibly be said on the topic. Why do I so boldly dare to take up this topic anew?

My daring comes in response to an emphasis found in the work of the 1971 Synod of Bishops. The Synod produced the document, "Justice in the World," a stirring call for the Church's active social involvement. What makes the Synod document uniquely important, and worth more than the usual passing notice, is its emphasis upon the theme of *social sin*. That emphasis is the key to what I argue can be considered a "new" theology of the Church's social involvement—"new" at least in the sense that it has never before been so clearly explicated in an authoritative Roman document. Theologically, it helps us to understand more completely and adequately both (1) *why* the Church is socially involved, and (2) *how* the Church is socially involved. We will consider these two questions in detail here.

I. WHY IS THE CHURCH SOCIALLY INVOLVED?

"Gathered from the whole world, in communion with all who believe in Christ and with the entire human family, and opening our hearts to the Spirit who is making the whole of creation new, we have questioned ourselves about the mission of the People of God to further justice in the world." In these introductory words, the Bishops of the Synod expressed their effort to discern anew the social implications of the Gospel which the Church is mandated to preach to all nations. Since the days of Leo XIII, the Church's social doctrine has developed along fairly consistent lines. Basic human rights have been emphasized, traditional scholastic teachings on social justice explained, and—more recently—biblical theology brought to bear on Church ministry.

It is the element of biblical theology which has made significant impact in recent development of the social doctrine of the Church. This is particularly evident in *Gaudium et Spes*, Vatican II's Constitution on the Church in the Modern World, and in Paul VI's *Populorum Progressio*. The first part of the Vatican II document (nos. 11-45) spells out the social implications of the biblical themes of the dignity of the human person, the community of mankind, the value of human activity in the world, and the role of the Church in the world. The encyclical of Pope Paul—rejected by the *Wall Street Journal* as "warmed-over Marxism"—treated the topic of worldwide development and its demands on the rich nations within a framework of explicit biblical lessons.

Key to this new biblical emphasis has been a healthy stress upon the importance of serious engagement with the things of this world. I say "healthy" because all too often there has been a stated or unstated presumption that the really deeply spiritual person, the truly religious individual, did not become mixed up with social issues. Somehow it came to be accepted by many Christians that it was possible to respond to the Gospel and yet be unconcerned with social responsibilities. Although love of neighbor was always seen as basic to Christian life, effective social action and involvement to implement that love through the works of justice was not considered a necessary requisite. *Gaudium et Spes* rejected this view out of hand: "They are mistaken who, knowing that we have here no abiding city but seek one which is to come (Heb 13:14), think that they may therefore shirk their earthly responsibilities. For they are forgetting that by the faith itself they are more than ever obliged to measure up to these duties, each according to his proper vocation (2 Th 3:6-13; Ep 4:28)."

But as strong as was this teaching by Vatican II for social involvement, it needs to be moved still further. The theological topic which provides impetus for this further movement is the topic of *social sin*. This became an explicit topic of the Second Roman Synod, mentioned again and again in the debates, and referred to three times by the Bishops in the final document: 1) After reviewing the serious gap between the rich and the poor of the world and the consequent injustices which are structured into global society: "In the face of the present-day situation of the world, marked as it is by *the grave sin of injustice*, we recognize both our responsibility and our inability to overcome it by our own strength" (Part II). 2) In urging a genuine reform of educational approach in order to promote a vital education to justice: "But education demands a renewal of heart, a renewal based on the recognition of *sin in its individual and social manifestations*" (Part III). 3) In emphasizing the role of the liturgy in educating Christian people to the demands of justice: "The practice of penance should emphasize *the social dimension of sin* and of the sacrament" (Part III).

Sin and redemption are, of course, major biblical themes. The Old and New Testaments are filled with accounts of man's infidelities and God's mercies. For the Christian community the sin-redemption theme is central. Gathered in the Eucharist, we proclaim a redemptive mystery of faith which has particular meaning because we "all have sinned, and have need of the glory of God" (Rm 3:23). The Gospel which the Church joyfully proclaims is a "Gospel for the remission of sins."

If we are honest with ourselves, however, we must admit that by and large we have tended to restrict the category of sin to a very narrow *personal* sense. Evidence of this can be easily obtained from a quick glance at the standard forms for the examination of conscience available in catechisms and prayer books: "Have I missed my morning and night prayers? ... Have I failed in my Sunday obligation ... Did I lie? ... Did I steal? ... Did I entertain impure thoughts? ... Did I swear?" We might object that such forms of examination are very passé in the Post-Vatican II Church of the 1970s. Yet for the overwhelming majority of adult Roman Catholics, these truly did serve as "forms"—profoundly formative of moral sensitivities.

The Bishops of the Synod appeared keenly aware of this fact and voiced their concern that such a narrow focus on sin in a personal sense was the major reason for the failure of Catholics to see the situation of the modern world as truly a "sinful situation." The official synthesis of the Synod debates noted: "Here, indeed, there emerged a major preoccupation of the Synod. How is it, after eighty years of modern social teaching and two thousand years of the Gospel of love, that the Church has to admit Her inability to make more impact upon the conscience of Her people? But it was stressed again and again that the faithful, particularly the more wealthy and comfortable among them, simply do not see *structural social injustice as a sin*, simply feel no personal responsibility for it and simply feel no obligation to do anything about it. Sunday observance, the Church's rules on sex and marriage tend to enter the Catholic conscience profoundly as *sin*. To live like Dives with Lazarus at the gate is not even preceived as *sinful*. It was this very strong reaction of the Synod that the whole social teaching of the Church has to be removed from the high level of doctrinal pronouncements and forced into the consciences of the People of God" (no. 7).

The theme of social sin was well focused for emphasis at the Synod by the opening section of the pre-synodal working paper. Men of our times, the paper states, "demand profound changes in the very structures of society, structures which often constitute in themselves an embodiment of the sin of injustice" (no. 2). That sin is somehow related to social structures is the very essence of "social sin," and to understand this we need to look at some recent developments both in theology and in sociology.

Examples of Social Sin

It will be helpful to look at three examples of social sin.

1. A social structure which oppresses human dignity and stifles freedom is a sinful structure. For example, a welfare system based on the premise that the poor are somehow bad and therefore not to be trusted or given a say in what happens to them is a structure which oppresses the dignity of the poor. It is a structure which victimizes those obliged to follow its patterns and customs: minimal payments, excessive surveillance, demeaning interviews, the ever-present fear of a cut-off of necessary funds. As we would refer to personal action of such an oppressive nature as sinful, so we must refer to action of this structure as sinful.

2. A social situation which promotes and facilitates individual acts of selfishness is a sinful situation. For example, zoning and tax systems which allow individual citizens to preserve their privileges at the expense of the poor and powerless provide situations wherein the selfishness of these individuals is made easy. Zoning legislation which makes it impossible for the less economically advantaged to seek more habitable surroundings outside of the central city facilities the selfishness of the more privileged. A tax system which places a disproportionate burden of paying for public goods upon lower- and middle-income people (through numerous loop-holes for higher-income brackets) is clearly a system which promotes the individual selfishness of some citizens in our society.

3. A social structure or situation which is unjust also becomes sinful when one is aware of the injustice but refuses to exert efforts to change it. This is the social sin of complicity. For example, the silent acceptance of an international monetary and trade system which severely injures the legitimate interest

and aspirations of the developing countries in the 1970s is certainly an instance of social sin. With 20 per cent of the world's population controlling 80 per cent of the world's wealth, major decisions are made every day which affect the quality of life of the inhabitants of the Third World without their having the least say in the character of these decisions. A startling instance of this was the decision in the fall of 1971 to devalue the American dollar, a decision costing the voiceless poor nations some $500 million in precious international reserves. Silent complicity as we enjoy the benefits of such a decision constitutes an instance of social sin.

If it is true that it is possible for some of the very structures of our society to constitute in themselves an embodiment of the sin of injustice, then we have the key to discerning a deeply theological reason for the Church's involvement in social action. In the *Constitution on the Church in the Modern World,* Vatican II had clearly stated the single intention of the Church's mission: "that God's kingdom may come, and that the salvation of the whole human race may come to pass" (no. 45). This mission is accomplished in the preaching of the Gospel of Jesus Christ, in fulfillment of the mandate, "Go into the whole world, preach the Gospel to every creature" (Mk 16:15). The Kingdom is established and salvation comes only in the face of a struggle against sin—personal and social.

The theological foundation for *why* the Church is socially involved—not only has the *right* but the *obligation* to be so involved—can be summed up in two propositions: (1) the Gospel that the Church preaches is a Word that frees from sin, and (2) the world is marked by the evil of situations and structures of social sin. This foundation was clearly expressed by the Synod: "Action on behalf of justice and participation in the transformation of the world fully appear to us as a constitutive dimension of the preaching of the Gospel, or, in other words, of the Church's mission for the redemption of the human race and its liberation from every oppressive situation" (Introduction).

II. HOW IS THE CHURCH SOCIALLY INVOLVED?

Sinners are called to *conversion*. Liberation from sin comes in the process of "metanoia." Conversion is the call of the prophets to Israel to return as a people to the worship of the one God, Yahweh; it is the message of John the Baptist, the opening expression of the Good News proclaimed by Jesus: "Repent and believe, the Kingdom of God is at hand" (Mk 1:15) the repeated exhortation of the kerygmatic sermons in *Acts*. A central religious experience, the process of conversion implies a change of heart, a reorientation of life's direction, the acceptance of a new set of values.

I believe it is possible to discuss a theology of *how* the Church is socially involved in terms of conversion, in terms of the actions the Church—as individuals and as community—takes to bring about conversion from social sin. For our purposes here, I suggest three approaches to conversion: prophetic word, symbolic witness, and political action.

A. *Prophetic word.* The Church's primary tool in social involvement is the Word of God. A "two-edged sword," this Word must be spoken fearlessly in situations of social sin and against sinful structures wherever found. According to the Synod document, "Like the Apostle Paul, we insist, welcome or unwelcome, that the Word of God should be present in the center of human situations.... Our mission demands that we should courageously denounce injustice, with charity, prudence and firmness, in sincere dialogue with all parties concerned" (Part III). Thus is the Christian community called to speak the "two-edged sword" of denouncing and encouraging, the prophetic word.

A concrete prophetic word helps to bring about conversion primarily because it challenges our view of "the way things are" and "the way things are done." Certainly the chief obstacle to social change, the main hindrance to remedying conditions of injustice, is our failure to perceive the sinfulness of a situation.

Our perceptions are very contingent upon the prevailing set of images and patterns of perception, the values and behavioral standards, which are inherent in our culture. What the prophetic word does is shatter the images or mindsets by which we are accustomed to perceive reality, especially social reality. As the synthesis of the Synod debates suggests, "We are all to some degree prisoners of the perceptions and visions to which we are educated—by formal schooling, by the pressures of the media, by special propaganda" (no. 19). The Gospel message of liberation frees us from this prison by offering alternate perceptions and visions.

For example, American society places great stress on the ethic of *competitiveness* and exalts being "number one," whether in business, sports, or foreign policy. By and large, this is an accepted value in our society, with children being socialized to it and adults judging events by it. But the Gospel ethic of *sharing*—with consequent emphasis upon moderation, concern for the other, etc.—is in sharp conflict with the ambition of being "number one." Where a prophetic word for sharing is spoken, then, conversion from sinful structures—unjust economic systems, for instance, or unjust foreign policies—based on competitiveness is made both a challenge and possibility for Christians.

B. *Symbolic witness.* Immediately after urging the Church's social involvement by way of prophetic words, the Synod documents notes, "We know that our denunciations of injustice can secure assent to the extent that they are an expression of our lives and are manifested in continuous action" (Part III). This call to witness symbolically—that is, to act out concretely—the values of which the Church speaks is evident in other places in the Synod document and is essentially related to the task of conversion from social sin. The symbolic deed not only manifests our conversion but also in turn deepens our conviction.

The integral link between the prophetic word and the symbolic deed has been cogently explained by Paulo Freire. Designing a "pedagogy of the oppressed," a method of education for liberation, Freire stresses that a word not only conveys information but also effects change. "Within the word we find two dimensions, reflection and action, in such radical interaction that if one is sacrificed—even in part—the other immediately suffers.... An unauthentic word, one which is unable to transform reality, results from the dichotomy imposed upon its constitutive elements. When a word is deprived of its dimension of action, reflection automatically suffers as well; and the word is changed into idle chatter, into *verbalism*, into an alienated and alienating 'blah.' It becomes an empty word, one which cannot denounce the world, for denunciation is impossible without a commitment to transform, and there is no transformation without action" (*Pedagogy of the Oppressed*, New York: Herder and Herder, 1970, pp. 74-75).

Lest Church pronouncements on social matters become an "alienated and alienating 'blah,' " it is crucial that the Christian community witness through symbolic deeds its commitment to transformation through action for justice. Thus the Synod document states: "While the Church is bound to give witness to justice, she recognizes that anyone who ventures to speak to people about justice must first be just in their eyes" (Part III). To achieve a semblance of justice in the eyes of others, the Church is urged by the Synod to an examination of its modes of actions, its possessions, and the life style of all: bishops, priests, religious, and lay people.

Especially noteworthy in this call to symbolic witness is the challenge for a "sparing and sharing" life style. The Bishops at the Synod stressed that the possessions of the Church must never compromise the preaching of the Gospel to the poor, and that "our faith demands of us a certain sparingness in the use" of goods. The theme is taken up with particular relevance to the Catholic Church in the United States—since we Americans are six percent of the world's population but consume forty percent of the world's resources—"Those who are already rich are bound to accept a less material way of life, with less waste, in order to avoid the destruction of the heritage which they are obliged by absolute justice to share with all other members of the human race" (Part III). Studies such as that of the Club of Rome (Dennis Meadows *et al.*, *The Limits of Growth*, New York: Universe Books, 1972) have recently pointed out the *finite* character of our globe and emphasized the limited natural resources and inter-related ecology of our planet. This makes the Synod's call for sparingness all the more urgent and the practice of an austerity of life style all the more dramatic a manifestation of conversion from social sin.

C. *Political action*. Sooner or later in a discussion of *how* the Church is to be socially involved, the issue of the Church and politics must be squarely faced. In the United States this is an especially sticky issue, one which has been clouded emotionally by disputes inside the Church and between the Church and society at large. The reason why political action must be considered in these theological reflections, however, is precisely because social sin is a structural phenomenon. Conversion from social sin is possible only if efforts are made to see that structures are changed—and in the United States, major social structures are changed through the political process. According to the Synod document, "This desire [for justice] however will not satisfy the expectations of our time if it ignores the objective obstacles which social structures place in the way of conversion of hearts" (Part I). Social involvement taken seriously, then, of necessity means that political action is taken seriously.

It is at this point that the true meaning of conversion takes on a special significance. The Christian who pursues just social change through political action must do so because of his or her own justice. The 1968 Medellin documents, statements of renewal by the Second General Conference of Latin American Bishops, make this point lucidly: "The originality of the Christian message does not consist directly in the assertion that it is necessary to change structures, but in the insistence on the conversion of man which in turn calls for this change" (Conclusions, Justice, no. 3).

First personal conversion, then conversion of structures; but no authentic personal conversion without genuine commitment to change structures.

That the Church in the United States is socially involved through political action is a fact which can hardly be denied. Individual Catholic citizens acting on their own do, in the words of the Synod, "involve the responsibility of the Church whose members they are" when they act in the political area "under the influence of the Gospel and the teaching of the Church" (Part II). And certainly the U.S. Catholic hierarchy has been deeply involved in politics in such issues as aid to education and abortion legislation. What is being called for by the Synod, and appears to be supported by our theological discussion of social sin and conversion, is the acceptance of political action as a *religious imperative*, a Christian responsibility. If some social structures in the United States are instances of social sin and are to be remedied, then political action to change them becomes the concrete implementation of that "constitutive dimension of the preaching of the Gospel" identified by the Synod as "action for justice and participation in the transformation of the world" (Introduction).

Conclusion

John Gardner, one of those unique figures who is a public philosopher engaged in practical political action, has noted somewhere that our society continues to be preoccupied with specific evils to be corrected, rather than the development of a society responsive to the need for continuous change. It has been my contention here that for the Church to be socially involved is for it to be concerned about the structures of society—and whether or not those structures are in need of and open to that continuous change which is movement from social sin to conversion to justice. The theological foundation for the Church's social involvement and the theological explanation of its manner of involvement can be found in the 1971 Synod's emphasis on social sin. It should be clear from my discussion that I have been using "Church" in a variety of senses, sometimes referring to the Church as an institutional force, but most of the time meaning simply all the People of God. All of us have the common task of getting the Church socially involved in response to the call to preach the Gospel through "action on behalf of justice and participation in the transformation of the world."

[Major deletions have been made in this edited version.]

ADDITIONAL READINGS

This is not a complete bibliography on conversion, but rather a short list of further readings in English on different aspects of the subject, including a few prominent early psychological investigations, several interesting contemporary inquiries, and a few reminders of classic accounts of the conversion experience (the last important group, deliberately excluded from this collection for reasons of space, are best read in large doses).

EARLY PSYCHOLOGICAL INVESTIGATIONS

Clark, E. T., *The Psychology of Religious Awakening*. New York: Macmillan, 1929.

Coe, G. A., *The Psychology of Religion*. Chicago: University of Chicago Press, 1916.

Hall, G. S., *Adolescence*. 2 Vols. New York: D. Appleton, 1904.

Leuba, J. H. *A Psychological Study of Religion*. New York: Macmillan, 1912.

Pratt, James B. *The Religious Consciousness*. New York: The Macmillan Co., 1924.

Sanctis, Sante de. *Religious Conversion*. New York: Harcourt, Brace and Co., 1927.

Starbuck, E. D. *Psychology of Religion*. New York: Charles Scribner's Sons, 1899.

CONTEMPORARY INQUIRIES

Balducelli, Roger. "A Phenomenology of Conversion" *The Living Light* 10 (Winter, 1973), pp. 545-557.

Congar, Yves M.-J. "The Idea of Conversion." *Thought* 33 (March, 1958), pp. 5-20.

Dunne, John. *The Way of All the Earth.* New York: Macmillan, 1972. Chapter II, Section 2: "The Way of Conscious Individuation."

Fackre, Gabriel. "Conversion." *Andover Newton Quarterly* 14 (January, 1974), pp. 171-189.

Gelpi, Donald. *Charism and Sacrament: A Theology of Christian Conversion.* New York: Paulist Press, 1976.

Gray, Donald, "Was Jesus a Convert?" *Religion in Life* 43 (Winter, 1974) pp. 445-455.

Haughton, Rosemary. *The Liberated Heart.* New York: The Seabury Press, 1974. Chapter 2: "Like Little Children."

Lonergan, Bernard, *Grace and Freedom: Operative Grace in the Thought of St. Thomas Aquinas,* edited by J. Patout Burns. New York: Herder and Herder, 1971.

Soelle, Dorothee. *Political Theology.* Philadelphia: Fortress Press, 1974. Chapter Eight: "Forgiveness, Politically Interpreted."

Tillich, Paul. *Systematic Theology.* Vol. III. Chicago: University of Chicago Press, 1963, pp. 217-220.

Wheelis, Allen. *How People Change.* New York: Harper & Row, 1973.

The Ecumenical Review 19 (July, 1967). Special issue on the ecumenical dimension of conversion:

Paul Löffler, "Conversion in An Ecumenical Context" (252-260).

Nikos A. Nissiotis, "Conversion and the Church" (261-270).

Billy Graham, "Conversion—A Personal Revolution" (271-284).

C. H. Hwang, "Conversion in the Perspective of Three Generations" (285-290).

E. R. Wickham, "Conversion in a Secular Age" (291-296).

Letty M. Russell, "A Case Study from East Harlem" (297-301).

Herbert Jai Singh, "Christian Conversion in a Hindu Context" (302-306).

William Douglas and James R. Scroggs, "Some Social Scientific Perspectives" (307-309).

Christoph Barth, "Notes on 'Return' in the Old Testament" (310-312).

J. W. Heikkinen, "Notes on 'Epistrepho' and 'Metanoeo' " (313-316).

Mid-Stream 8 (Spring, 1969). This special issue on "The Meanings and Practices of Conversion" includes, among other interesting articles, studies of such figures as Clement of Alexandria, Martin Luther, John Wesley, and John Henry Newman.

Pastoral Psychology 16 (September, 1965) and 17 (September, 1966). Special issues on religious conversion:

Earl H. Furgeson, "Editorial: The Renewal of Interest in Religious Conversion" (16:5-7).

Earl H. Furgeson, "The Definition of Religious Conversion" (16:8-16).

Carl W. Christensen, M. D., "Religious Conversion in Adolescence" (16:17-28).

Walter Houston Clark, "William James: Contributions to the Psychology of Religious Conversion" (16:29-36).

John P. Kildahl, "The Personalities of Sudden Religious Converts" (16:37-44).

Robert N. Beck, "Hall's Genetic Psychology and Religious Conversion" (16:45-51).

Earl H. Furgeson, "Editorial: The Mutual Dependence of Psychology and Theology" (17:5-7).

Leon Salzman, M. D., "Types of Religious Conversion" (17:8-20, 66).

Joel Allison, "Recent Empirical Studies of Religious Conversion Experiences" (17:21-34).

Seward Hiltner, "Toward a Theology of Conversion in the Light of Psychology" (17:35-42).

Wayne E. Oates, "Conversion and Mental Health" (17: 43-48).

Charles W. Stewart, "The Religious Experience of Two Adolescent Girls" (17:49-55).

CLASSIC ACCOUNTS OF CONVERSIONS

St. Augustine. *The Confessions, Books I-X.* Translated by F. J. Sheed. New York: Sheed & Ward, 1942.

Bunyan, John. *Grace Abounding.* New York: Oxford University Press, 1962.

Edwards, Jonathan. "Personal Narrative" in *Jonathan Edwards: Representative Selections,* edited by Clarence H. Faust and Thomas H. Johnson. Revised Edition. New York: Hill and Wang American Century Series, 1962.

Merton, Thomas. *The Seven Storey Mountain.* Garden City, N. Y.: Doubleday Image Books, 1970.

Newman, John Henry. *Apologia Pro Vita Sua.* Boston: Houghton Mifflin Co., 1956.

Stanley, David. "Paul's Conversion in Acts: Why the Three Accounts?" *Catholic Biblical Quarterly* 15 (July, 1953), pp. 315-338.

For more extensive references (including French and German) see B. Häring, *The Law of Christ,* Vol. I, pp. 478-481.